THE RESCUE THEY CALLED A RAID

Trooper of the Bechuanaland Border Police at the time of the Jameson Raid. Equipped with the latest Lee Speed .303 calibre rifle and Martini Henry bandoleer, his issue uniform consisted of slouch hat with white puggaree; khaki corduroy tunic with twisted cord shoulder straps that washed "yellowish"; Jodhpur whipcord riding breeches; blue wool puttees and brown ankle boots with spurs. (Painting by Christa Hook © Helion & Company)

The Rescue They Called a Raid

The Jameson Raid
The Failed Attempt to Expand the Empire
at Minimum Cost
1895-96

David Snape

Helion & Company

This book is dedicated to my Mother, Irene Snape, who bought me my first history book when I was seven and has shared with me her love for the past. Thanks Mum!
D.S.

Helion & Company Limited
Unit 8 Amherst Business Centre
Budbrooke Road
Warwick
CV34 5WE
England
Tel. 01926 499 619
Email: info@helion.co.uk
Website: www.helion.co.uk
Twitter: @helionbooks
blog.helion.co.uk

Published by Helion & Company 2021
Designed and typeset by Mach 3 Solutions (www.mach3solutions.co.uk)
Cover designed by Paul Hewitt, Battlefield Design (www.battlefield-design.co.uk)

Text © David Snape 2020
Images © as individually credited
Maps drawn by George Anderson © Helion & Company Limited 2020

ISBN 978-1-913118-77-8

British Library Cataloguing-in-Publication Data.
A catalogue record for this book is available from the British Library.

For details of other military history titles published by Helion & Company Limited contact the above address or visit our website: http://www.helion.co.uk.

We always welcome receipt of book proposals from prospective authors.

Contents

List of Illustrations

List of Maps

Preface

The origins of this book go back many years to when I became fascinated by the Second Boer War and came across Lady Longford's book, *Jameson's Raid*. Here was a 'daring do' story with heroes, villains, conspiracies, and failure. It mixed the world of military adventure, economic expansion and political intrigue; which in many ways epitomised the later years of Queen Victoria's reign.

When I retired from education, I decided to seriously pursue my interest and studied for MA degrees at the University of Wolverhampton in Military History. It was not surprising, therefore, that part of my first dissertation concentrated on the Jameson Raid. This book is an expansion of that work and an attempt to re-examine the background to the Raid, its execution, and the consequences of its failure at national and personal levels.

I would like to acknowledge the support I have received in bringing this book to fruition from my Tutors at Wolverhampton, Dr Spencer Jones, and Professor Gary Sheffield, whose encouragement whilst writing the original dissertations was invaluable. My editor, Dr Christopher Brice, and Helion & Company proprietor Duncan Rogers, without whose advice, guidance, and patience this volume would never have been completed.

David Snape
Wellingborough
December 2020

Introduction

I date the beginning of these violent times in our country from the Jameson Raid.
Winston Churchill, *The World Crisis* (1922)

On a late December evening, Dr Leander Starr Jameson CB, Administrator of Bechuanaland, friend of Cecil Rhodes and conqueror of the AmaNdebele, led a mounted force of police across the Bechuanaland border into the South African Republic. His professed mission was to assist a rebellion in Johannesburg, the centre of the gold mining district of Witwatersrand, against the government of Paul Kruger. Within five days the Raid, as it became known, was over. Jameson's men, armed with cannon and machineguns, had been defeated by a group of amateur soldiers armed mainly with rifles. The uprising in Johannesburg had not happened but its proponents had been taken prisoner and were later tried for their lives. Jameson's leading officers were also tried in British Courts and imprisoned. The real perpetrator of this foolish venture, Cecil Rhodes, was humiliated, and his schemes of imperial expansion exposed and dashed. Chamberlain, the Colonial Secretary, had to fight vigorously to clear any suggestion that he had encouraged the Raid, and the victor, Paul Kruger, President of the South African Republic, received international praise for defeating the Raiders and for his benevolence in the way they were subsequently treated.

These four protagonists, an entrepreneur imperialist, an adventurous, impetuous medical man, a nonconformist millionaire autocrat, and an uneducated, cunning patriot had similar and yet different motives. Each did what they did to improve their country. Three used their position to make themselves richer and all four used their subordinates to bring about their own ends in the face of considerable opposition.

The Raid was not just a military disaster; it was also a threat to the British Government and made it a laughingstock in the capitals of Europe. Yet its effects were to be felt in South Africa for some years and its aim to improve the rights of the immigrants to the South African Republic and to increase the British influence was finally achieved by a much larger military venture; the Second Boer War.

The Jameson Raid is still worth examination because of its links with the Second Boer War and because of the struggles of the major individuals involved to control South Africa in the last decade of the nineteenth century. Its position between the Boer victory at Majuba Hill in 1881 and the defeat of the Boer Republics in the Second Boer War was crucial to subsequent South African history and those who, in their different ways, were involved played an important part in increasing the size and power of the British Empire.

1

The Colossus, Doctor Jim, Uncle Paul and the Master

Cecil John Rhodes, later known as the 'Colossus' because of his ambitions for the British dominance of Africa, was born on 5 July 1853 at Bishops Stortford, Hertfordshire where his father was the Vicar. Cecil was educated at the local grammar school from 1861 until 1869.[1] In the following year, because of failing health, he was sent to Natal in southern Africa to assist his brother, Herbert, in growing cotton. Herbert became increasingly more interested in the seemingly glamorous and lucrative activity of diamond prospecting and he left Cecil to run the plantation in his absence. This proved an educational experience for the young Cecil who learned skills in controlling the indigenous people which were to stand him in good stead in later life.

After the discovery of diamonds in Griqualand, both brothers became diamond prospectors based in Kimberley, a town which was soon to become the centre of the South African diamond trade. In 1871 Herbert, who seemed incapable of staying in one place and doing the same thing for long, handed over his diamond claim to Cecil in order to become a gold prospector at Pilgrim's Rest in the Lydenburg Goldfields.[2] This wander lust eventually claimed Herbert's life for, during a heavy drinking session near Lake Nyasa in 1879, he knocked over a paraffin lamp igniting a barrel of rum which then exploded and set fire to his hut.[3]

Another brother of Cecil, Francis William, known to the family as 'Frank', went to Sandhurst and had a notable military career. In January 1885, at the Battle of Abu Klea during the Sudan Campaign, Frank distinguished himself and, having several horses shot from under him in the course of the engagement, was awarded the Distinguished Service Order. His military career was brought almost to an end, however, because of his involvement with his brother and Leander Starr Jameson.

Diamond prospecting was challenging but Cecil demonstrated his ability to work hard, his sense of purpose, entrepreneurial ability, and the aptitude of adapting to new situations. His health also improved and because of these talents his diamond claim prospered in spite of Kimberley's lawlessness, disease, and the high taxes imposed upon the prospectors. Such was Rhodes' acumen that through an intelligent use of the stock market and successful partnerships with men such as Charles Dunnell Rudd, a fellow prospector and diamond dealer, Rhodes' empire grew. Rudd was later to manage their joint interests whilst Rhodes attended Oxford in order to make up for his earlier break in education. He studied Latin and Ancient History for neither of which he had little aptitude and seemed to be more interested in impressing his fellow students

---

1   *Punch,* 10 December 1892.
2   Sarah Millin, *Rhodes* (London: Chatto and Windus, 1933), p. 25.
3   Chris Ash, *The If Man. Dr Leander Starr Jameson: The Inspiration for Kipling's Masterpiece* (Solihull: Helion & Co. Ltd, 2012), p.37 Thomas Pakenham, *The Scramble for Africa* (London: Abacus, 2011), p.375.

Leander Starr Jameson – 'Dr Jim' and Cecil John Rhodes – 'The Colossus'. (George
Seymour Fort, *Dr Jameson*. London, Hirst & Blackett, 1908)

by playing polo and riding with the Drag hounds than by working to satisfy his tutors' demands. He also
joined the Apollo University Masonic Lodge, No.357, and although he did not initially approve of Masonry,
he was to remain a Mason all his life and the Order of Freemasons may well have influenced his thoughts
by providing him a blueprint for a future utopian society in which the whole world was under British rule.

Rhodes suffered his first heart attack in 1887, and it was his subsequent Will which demonstrated that
his ambitions were political as well as entrepreneurial. His testimony disposed a fortune, not yet amassed,
to establish a secret society dedicated to the worldwide extension of British rule, and to the perfection of a
system of emigration from the United Kingdom which would result in the colonisation of the entire African
continent as well as other parts of the globe. Ultimately, this would lead to Britain's recovery of the United
States of America.[4] Such was Rhodes' imperial ambition that he once wrote he would annex the planets
(to Great Britain) if they were not so far away.[5] Carroll Quigley argued that this secret society still existed
into the mid twentieth century.[6] Its members were alleged to include Lord Milner, appointed Governor of
the Cape and High Commissioner of South Africa in 1897; Lord Selborne, Under-Secretary of State for
the Colonies in 1895, and Sir Patrick Duncan, who became Colonial Secretary for the Transvaal in 1905.
These men were sometimes known as '*Milner's Kindergarten*' or '*Rhodes Crowd*' and Quigley alleged that its
members 'plotted' not just the Jameson Raid but also the Second Boer War.[7] Quigley also suggested that
Rhodes' activities in the political field were full of conspiracy and clandestine action but, since Rhodes'

---

4   John E. Flint, *Cecil Rhodes* (Boston: Little Brown, 1974), pp. 248-252.
5   William Stead, (ed.), *The Last Will and Testament of Cecil John Rhodes* with elucidatory notes to which are added
     some chapters describing the political and religious ideas of the testator (London: Review of Reviews, 1902), p.190.
6   Carroll Quigley quoted in Robert Irwin. Rotberg, 'Did Cecil Rhodes Really Try to Control the World?', *The
     Journal of Imperial and Commonwealth History* (Vol. 42; Issue 3, June 2014), p. 551.
7   Carroll Quigley, *Anglo-American Establishment: From Rhodes to Cliveden'* (New York; Books in Focus, 1981),
     pp. 4-5.

testimony of faith was written when he was 24 and he had yet to demonstrate either his financial or political abilities, a big leap of faith is required to accept there was such a plan so early in Rhodes' career. Rhodes' views certainly changed over time and his first will was revised seven times and his intentions developed from a desire to expand the Empire to a desire to educate its sons.[8]

In 1880 Rhodes was elected to the Cape Parliament as one of two members to represent Barkly West, a mainly Boer constituency near Kimberley. He took his place in the Cape legislature a year later and occupied the seat until his death in 1902. As an MP, he cultivated and made friends with influential men such as, Sir Hercules Robinson, later High Commissioner for South Africa, and General Gordon, who, in 1884, invited Rhodes to visit him in Khartoum.

Rhodes was keen to establish a locally governed federation of South Africa under British rule but with Cape Dutch assent. He also wanted to expand Cape Colony towards the north beyond the Orange River into Bechuanaland. With the support of the Cape Dutch who formed the majority of the *Afrikaner Bund*, he was elected Treasurer for the Cape Colony in March-May 1884.[9] At the same time, he engi-

Sir Hercules Robinson, High Commissioner for South Africa. (*Illustrated London News,* 1896)

neered the annexation of the territory of the Tswana people (Bechuanaland) who had sought the protection of Britain because they feared that Dutch and German settlers might bring about an annexation of their own. When the Dutch did invade these territories and established the republics of Stellaland and Goshen, the British government was slow to react and it was only in 1884, when Britain's colonial rival, German, annexed South-West Africa which led British troops to oust the Dutch from Bechuanaland and offer a Protectorate to the Tswana people.

In 1888 Rhodes, with the support of the German born financier, Alfred Beit and the Rothschild Bank, established the De Beers Consolidated Mining Company and by 1889 he controlled the South African diamond mining industry which produced 90% of the world's diamonds. Not content with his wealth, and tempted by rumours of gold in the territories of the AmaNdebele and Shona peoples (now Zimbabwe) north of the Transvaal, Rhodes persuaded Sir Hercules Robinson, the High Commissioner, to send John Moffatt and Charles Dunnell Rudd as emissaries to Lobengula, King of the AmaNdebele.[10] Lobengula exercised control over his people with great brutality and has been described as being '…a savage in the fullest sense of the word.'[11] He was intelligent, cunning, a skilled orator and politician.[12] In spite of his apparent barbarity, Stuart Cloete described him as, '…a constitutional monarch, pleasing to his people, except (when) he was too prone to restrain them from war with the white men.'[13] Lobengula's hold on his throne was always tenuous as the usual way of transferring power from one ruler to another involved the assassination and purge of the former ruler's family and supporters. Lobengula was also seriously worried by the attempts of colonists,

8   Rotberg, 'Did Cecil Rhodes Really try to Control the World?', p. 552.

9   The *Afrikaner* Bund or Bond, founded in 1881,claimed to represent all those who regarded Africa rather than Europe as their home. They often held the majority in the Cape Parliament but always worked as part of a coalition.

10   Ndebele, often known as the Matabele.

11   N. Rouillard (ed), *Matabele Thompson – His Autobiography* (Johannesburg: Central News Agency, 1957), p. 59.

12   Ash, *The If Man,* p. 64.

13   Stuart Cloete, *African Portraits* (London: Collins, 1946), p.226.

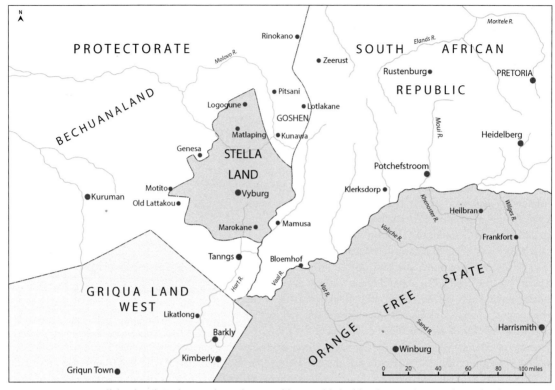

Map 1 Stellaland and Goshen: Independent republics established by the Dutch in Bechuanaland.

particularly British, to interfere with his land.[14] He even complained to Queen Victoria that he was severely troubled by white men who were demanding mining concessions. The Great White Queen's advice was that he should not hastily grant these concessions, but her letter was dated 26th March 1889; five months after Rudd had been granted mining rights

In 1889 two trading companies with similar interests, the Central Search Association and the London-based Exploring Company Ltd combined because of their common economic interests in exploiting the mineral wealth of Africa and a need to secure the backing of the British Government for their expansion. The title of this alliance was the British South Africa Company (BSAC). The Company received a Royal Charter which was modelled upon that given to British East India Company. Amongst its first directors were the Duke of Abercorn who was its Chair, Alfred Beit, and, unsurprisingly, Cecil John Rhodes, who by 1890 was Prime Minister of Cape Colony, an office which he held at the time of the Jameson Raid.

The Charter empowered the Company to treat with African rulers; to own, manage and grant or distribute land and raise a police force; the British South Africa Police (BSAP). In return, 'the Company agreed to develop the territory it controlled; to respect existing African laws; to allow free trade within its territory and respect all religions.'[15] The Charter also authorised the BSAC to create an administration in its own right and required it '...to the best of its ability, to preserve peace and order in such ways and manners as it shall consider necessary and (it) may, with that object, make ordinances (to be approved of by (the) Secretary of

---

14   P.E. Aston (ed.), *The Raid on the Transvaal by Dr. Jameson* (London: Dean, 1897), pp.12-13.

15   BSAC, *Rhodesia: South Africa Company 1892* (London: BSAC, 1909).

First Board of Directors of the British South African Company 1889. Top row: Horace Farquhar, Albert Grey, Alfred Beit, Middle Row: His Grace the Duke of Fife, K.T., P.C. Hon. C.J. Rhodes (Founder and Managing Director in South Africa); His Grace the Duke of Abercorn, K.G., P.C. Bottom Row: Lord Grifford, V.C. Herbert Canning (Secretary), George Cawston. (Anon., *The British South Africa Company Historical Catalogue & Souvenir of Rhodesia: Empire Exhibition.* Johannesburg, 1936-37)

State) ... .'[16] In this way the British Government kept overall control of an area which was defined as the region of South Africa immediately north of Bechuanaland, north and west of the South African Republic (ZAR) and west of the Portuguese Dominions.[17]

By the terms of the Rudd Concession, Lobengula granted Rhodes' representatives 'charge over all metals and minerals' within his kingdom and 'full power to do all things that they may deem necessary to win and procure the same.'[18] In return, Lobengula and his heirs were granted £100 per month, 1000 breech-loading rifles, and an armed steamer on the Zambezi River. The latter was never delivered.

The last ten years of Queen Victoria's reign was a momentous period in the 'Scramble for Africa' during which European powers attempted to grab parts of the continent for their own benefit. At the Berlin Conference of 1884-85 Britain, France, Germany, Portugal and Belgium agreed to divide up the coastal lands of Africa between them. They each proposed to occupy various parts of the 'Dark Continent' but would often pay little attention to the indigenous people over whom they intended to rule. In this respect, the BSAC's Charter was an attempt to show some respect for indigenous people and their customs, as well as acknowledging their existence and having some entitlement to the land in which they lived.

Rhodes was regarded as the 'uncrowned emperor' of South Africa by many of his contemporaries and he lived up to this image by holding 'levies' at the Burlington Hotel when he visited Britain.[19] Politically astute, he cultivated all three political parties in Britain but he was, given his personal ambitions, especially close to the Imperialists in Rosebery's Liberal Party. Rosebery 'liked and admired Cecil Rhodes who was often his guest'.[20] He caused Rhodes to be gazetted as a Privy Councillor and his Ministry promised to transfer large

---

16   *Charter of Incorporation*; 28th October 1889, Para. 10.

17   *Charter of Incorporation*; Para. 2.

18   Charter of Incorporation; Para. 2.

19   J.L. Garvin, The *Life of Joseph Chamberlain, Vol. III 1895-1900* (London: MacMillan, 1934), p. 31. Basil Williams, *Cecil Rhodes* (New York; Henry Holt & Co., 1921), pp. 233, 251.

20   Robert Offley Ashburton Crewe-Milnes, Marquis of Crewe, *Lord Rosebery, Vol. II* (London: John Murray, 1931), p. 563.

areas of Bechuanaland which lay between the Cape Colony and Rhodesia to the BSAC; a promise which Rhodes was keen to extract after the change of Government when Lord Salisbury's Conservatives came to power in 1895.

Eight years earlier, another British ex-patriot suffering from ill health arrived in Kimberley. Leander Starr Jameson, 'Dr Jim' or even 'Jimjams' to his friends, had been born in Edinburgh in 1853, the youngest of 11 children. He obtained a place at London College Hospital in 1870, qualified as a doctor and seemed destined for a distinguished medical career until his health deteriorated, which was probably caused by over work. Consequently, he moved his practice to Kimberley, and it was here that he met and treated the sickly Cecil Rhodes.

Sarah Millin described Jameson as a 'good surgeon, a man of charm, and a gambler' who had made a name for himself as a successful surgeon; a reputation which was to increase when he arrived in Kimberley.[21] Good surgeons were scarce in this developing city and his personal charm endeared him to its rich and adventurous residents. Jameson became the inspiration for Kipling's famous poem *"If"* and Chris Ash, his most recent biographer, claims that the various events of Jameson's life fitted each line of the poem.[22] Wills and Collingridge described him as possessing tact, a sympathetic insight into human nature and above all, 'a charm for which he (had) become so well-known and which (was) so useful in his official career.'[23] Whilst acknowledging that Jameson had character weaknesses, as we shall see, Ash claims these were outweighed by his strengths. Jan Smuts, the Boer commander who later became a British Field Marshall, described Jameson as, '…a great Doer(sic) and one thinks little of the errors that marked the course of his real creative life.'[24] His reputation as a gambler who was prepared to take risks would be clearly demonstrated when he set off on his Raid.

Not every commentator, however, saw Jameson in such a favourable light. Henry de le Prè Labouchère, the MP for Northampton, whose own life and career was full of controversy, was a severe and constant critic of Jameson and was to figure large in the Inquiry which investigated the Jameson Raid. He described Jameson as Rhodes' rapacious henchman. Even Peter Gibbs, an admirer of Jameson, expressed reservations as to his capabilities: 'When Rhodes died, Jameson took on his mantle', but 'the mantle was a little oversized'.[25] 'He was Rhodes' genius and, in the end, his evil genius.'[26] Paulus Kruger, the devout President of the South African Republic (ZAR), who had also been a Jameson's patient, described him, very negatively, has having a nihilistic mind and a believer in nothing.[27]

It was his relationship with Rhodes which gave Jameson his opportunities for success but also led him into folly. George Seymour Fort, a friend of Jameson, distinguished between the 'Colossus' and Dr Jim as follows; Rhodes was an 'initiator, an empire architect,' whilst Jameson was to prove himself 'as great in the sphere of action and executive command.'[28] Although one would suggest that Fort's friendship with Jameson made him play down Rhodes as a man of action when compared with Dr Jim but Jameson's command abilities were clearly shown when he emerged victorious from the First Matabele War in 1893-94 having driven Lobengula into exile and death.

21   Millin, *Rhodes,* p. 115.
22   Ash, *The If Man,* p. 27.
23   A. Wills & L. T. Collingridge (eds.), *The Downfall of Lobengula: The Cause, History and Effect of the Matabele War* (London: Simpkin, Marshall, Hamilton Kent & Co.1894), p. 35.
24   Howard Hensmen, *History of Rhodesia* (London: Blackwood 1900), p. 180.
25   Peter Gibbs, A *Flag for the Matabele* (London: Frederick Muller, 1955), facing p.33.
26   Cloete, African *Portraits* p. 209.
27   Stephanus Johannes Paulus Kruger quoted in Rayne. Kruger, Good-*bye Dolly Gray* (London: Pan Books, 1959), p. 28.
28   George Seymour Fort, *Dr Jameson* (London: Hurst & Blackett Ltd., 1908), p. 8.

In February 1889, Jameson and Dr Frederick Rutherfoord Harris, Secretary of the BSAC in Kimberley, undertook the hazardous and painful two-month journey from Kimberley to Bulawayo arriving on 2 April.[29] There they were joined by James Rochfort Maguire and Francis (Matabele) Thompson.[30] Their objective was to persuade Lobengula not to repudiate the concession of mining rights given to Rudd which were to the advantage of the BSAC. This expedition was the first real test of Jameson both as a negotiator and a military commander and its ultimate outcome was the creation of Rhodesia, the name of which speaks for itself with regard to Rhodes' egotism. Eventually, Jameson felt forced to take military action against the AmaNdebele and this resulted in the end of Lobengula's rule and the BSAC's domination of his country.[31]

Sadly, for the BSAC, the rumours of finding gold in Lobengula's land were ill founded and the Company had to look elsewhere to increase its wealth. Jameson and Rhodes were not ones to miss an opportunity to advance the Company's interests even at the expense of those of the Crown but they were wise enough to know when they needed its support.

Jameson's contribution to the expansion of the British Empire was recognised on his heroic return to England and he was made a Commander of the Order of the Bath by a grateful sovereign. Victoria also sanctioned a medal for all those who had

The Young Kruger. Reportedly the only surviving picture showing his missing thumb. (Paul Kruger, *The Memoirs of Paul Kruger, Four Times President of the South African Republic*. Toronto, George N. Morang & Co., 1902)

taken part in the Matabele War. It bore her image on the obverse and the Company's name on the reverse; an interesting juxtaposition of these two separate interests.

The Company's actions in Matabeleland and the Jameson Raid, one might suggest, could have had differing motives. The two events centred around Jameson, the Company's Administrator in Bechuanaland, as it was he who directed both operations. The Matabele War in 1893 appears to have occurred after extensive provocation by the local native ruler, Lobengula. It had the support, both verbal and physical, of the British Government. The Jameson Raid in 1896 occurred as a result of Jameson's impetuosity, whilst apparently acting outside both the BSAC's and the Government's wishes.

---

29 Jameson suffered from piles.

30 Maguire had become a friend of Rhodes while they were both at Oxford. He was later to become a Parnellite MP but had lost his seat in 1895 after the defeat of the second Home Rule Bill. He was to become Rhodes' 'alternate' or stand in on The BSAC Board. Thompson had acquired this nick name because of his part in the earlier negotiations with Lobengula.

31 For a full account of the First Matabele War and the rebellion which was caused by the Raid see Chris, Ash, *Matabele: The War of 1893 and the 1896 Rebellions* (South Africa: 30° South Publishers, 2016).

One of Jameson's most unlikely patients whilst in South Africa was Stephanus Johannes Paulus Kruger, Oom (Uncle) Paul, President of the ZAR.[32] Kruger was a Boer and, as a nine year old child, had taken part in the *Great Trek* of Boers attempting to escape from British control in the Cape Province to a land beyond the Orange and Vaal rivers where they could live according to their own fundamental Christian beliefs.[33] Kruger's family settled at the foot of the Magaliesberg Mountains in the Transvaal and, in accordance to Boer tradition, when Kruger reached the age of 16, he set up his own farm and subsequently became a successful frontiersman with a penchant for hunting big game.[34] During his hunting excursions, Kruger was nearly killed on several occasions. In 1845, while he was hunting rhinoceros along the Steelpoort River, his four-pounder elephant gun exploded in his hands and blew off most of his left thumb. He treated it with turpentine and cut off its remains with a penknife!

The Boers were constantly at odds with the indigenous tribes and Kruger added to his burgeoning reputation by being elected Field Cornet in command of his fellow Burghers and in 1852 at the age of 27, took part in the Battle of Dimawe against Batswana tribes. As Kruger's military experience grew so did his rank in the loosely linked Boer military organisation and he was appointed *Commandant*.[35] His political influence also grew as his rank increased and as Commandant General, he played a major role in forging the *South African Republic* (ZAR), becoming its Vice President in March 1877; one month before its annexation by the British. Britain's determination to control South Africa was the cause the First Boer War and Britain's 'defeat' resulted in the London Convention of 1884, under the terms of which Britain was forced to recognise the ZAR as a fully independent State. The Convention was signed by Kruger, now President of the Republic. Quite an achievement for a man described by William Morcom, Sir Theophilus Shepstone's legal adviser, as '…an unspeakably vulgar, bigoted backveld peasant', who was 'gigantically horrible'[36]. Shepstone had been responsible for the original annexation which was smashed at the battle of Majuba Hill.

Kruger was certainly uneducated; he had improved his English by comparing passages from a Bible which had parallel texts in English and Dutch, but he was a strong and persuasive orator; a skill which impressed both his friends and opponents alike.[37] He argued that he did not hate the British and only opposed them when they threatened the independence of the South African Republic.[38] Perhaps if Shepstone's promise of Boer self-government, which had been included in the Proclamation of Annexation, been implemented, the First Boer War would not have taken place.

The defeat of the mighty British Empire at Majuba Hill by a handful of farmers enhanced the ZAR's reputation and Kruger was seen as both its embodiment and champion. He believed that Afrikaners had the capacity to extend their influence in the wider southern African sphere and this could replace the British policy of expansion which had faltered after Majuba.[39] On his third trip to Europe which was to result in the London Convention of 1884, Oom Paul met a number of Heads of State which included William III of the Netherlands and his son the Prince of Orange, Leopold II of Belgium, President Jules Grévy of France, Alfonso XII of Spain, Luís I of Portugal, and Kaiser Wilhelm I and his Chancellor, Otto von Bismarck. Such a reception by European royalty must have convinced the man from the veld that the ZAR had a place on the world stage and this would be promoted by Britain's international rivals. In 1885 Kruger

32   Aston, *The Raid*, p. 10.
33   Dutch for 'Farmer.
34   S.J.P. Kruger, *The Memoirs of Paul Kruger, Four times President of the South African Republic. Told by Himself* (Toronto: G.M. Morang & Co. Ltd, 1902), p. 1.
35   Johannes. Meintjes, *President Paul Kruger: A Biography* (London: Cassell. 1974), p. 35.
36   Martin Meredith, *Diamonds, Gold, and War: The British, the Boers, and the Making of South Africa* (New York: Public Affairs; 2007), pp. 76-79.
37   Meintjes, *President Paul Kruger*, pp. 76-79.
38   Kruger quoted Meintjes, *President Paul Kruger*, p. 119.
39   Bill Nasson, *The South African War 1899-1902* (London: Arnold, 1999), p. 23.

met Rhodes during a dispute between Britain and the ZAR over the right of the former to control a corridor through Goshen and Stellaland; two independent Boer republics, which provided access between the Cape Colony and the British Central Africa Protectorate. Rhodes saw Kruger's actions as a threat to British trade interests and attempted to persuade Goshen and Stellaland to agree to free movement between the Colony and the Protectorate. Rhodes received a well-disposed reception in Stellaland but Goshen was much more hostile and demanded British recognition of its independence.[40] Goshen's capital, a farm house called *Rooigrond*, attracted not only independently minded Boers but also a number of freebooters which included wandering hunters, traders, cattle rustlers and illegal diamond buyers who had been run out of the diggings at Kimberley. The two Republics, Goshen and Stellaland merged into the single United States of Stellaland in 1883.

Stephanus Johannes Paulus 'Oom Paul', President of the South African Republic. (Open source)

Kruger attempted to defuse the situation, as well as expanding the ZAR, by annexing Stellaland despite opposition from the *Volksraad*, the Peoples' Council or Parliament of the ZAR, which feared that this step would provoke Britain and put at risk the ZAR's newly won independence. They were correct, as Kruger's annexation was unacceptable to the British who feared that this would increase the ZAR's power in the region and it sent 4,000 men of the Bechuanaland Expeditionary Force, led by General Charles Warren to Stellaland who, meeting little or no resistance, annexed it on behalf of Britain.[41]

Salisbury's Unionist Government, elected in 1895, was keen to establish Britain's superiority over France and Germany who were its rivals in the scramble for Africa. Salisbury, who had been Secretary of State for Foreign Affairs on four separate occasions, was regarded as something of an expert in managing this rivalry by playing off the French against the Germans through cunning diplomacy.[42] By 1890 through Salisbury's skills as a negotiator, Britain, had gained three new protectorates which added at least 100,000 square miles to its empire.[43] It is true that in order to secure this expansion Salisbury had given up land elsewhere but, by doing so, had appeased both France, by giving them a 'sphere of influence' which covered almost a quarter of the dark continent, and the Kaiser, whose interests had now turned to naval expansion.[44]

It was in Salisbury's Third Ministry that 'Pushful Joe' Chamberlain arrived on the Colonial scene. Joseph Chamberlain was appointed Secretary of State for the Colonies, an office which he chose rather than occupying one of the more powerful Ministries for he too was an imperialist. He was a somewhat unusual contender for high political office. Born in 1836, he made his name and his fortune as a Birmingham manufacturer

40   Meredith, *Diamonds, Gold, and War*, p. 148.
41   J.R.H Weaver, *Dictionary of National Biography: [Fourth Supplement] 1922-1930* (London: Oxford University Press, 1937), pp. 889-890.
42   1:2: April 1878; 28 April 1880; 2: 24 June 1885; 6 February 1886; 3: 14 January 1887–11 August 1892; 4: 29 June 1895–12 November 1900.
43   Zanzibar, Uganda and Equatoria.
44   For a full exposition Salisbury's work on foreign affairs during this period, see Thomas Packenham, *The Scramble for Africa* (London: Abacus, 1992), pp. 336-357.

Joseph Chamberlain, Secretary of State for the Colonies.
(Open source)

of screws. Active in local politics he became the city's mayor in 1873 and vowed that Birmingham would be 'parked, paved, assized, marketed, gas & watered and improved'.[45] A self-made businessman, he was a nonconformist and was thus prevented from attending Oxford or Cambridge where many of his political contemporaries had studied. Perhaps because of this discrimination, he was somewhat contemptuous of the aristocracy and used the Liberal grass roots to increase his political influence. He entered Parliament as MP for Birmingham at the age of 39 and, although he was to occupy other positions in Government, his work as Secretary of State for the Colonies was to be his most significant political role.

The Colonial Office was a poor relation of the Foreign Office since the latter was actually responsible for colonial expansion. Until the middle of the nineteenth century colonial affairs had been the responsibility of the War Office, but mounting pressures resulted in the creation of a separate Colonial Office. Chamberlain's appointment, however, was seen as being something of a personal backward step and not commensurate with his abilities. The Colonies themselves were more appreciative of his capacity and potential. On hearing of his appointment, the *Melbourne Argos* trumpeted, 'The Colonies, while Mr. Chamberlain is at the Colonial Office, will find their largest schemes met, not only with practical help but with keen intellectual sympathy'.[46] Chamberlain quickly modernised not only the Colonial Office building but also the way his department worked. 'His staff, from top to bottom, knew that they had "a Chief" who made his predecessors seem shadows.'[47] His management of the colonial empire was described by Henry Massingham, editor of the *Daily Chronicle* and no supporter of Salisbury's government as, 'perhaps the most interesting experiment in administration which has ever been tried in this country'.[48]

Flora Shaw, who was *The Times* Special Correspondent for Southern Africa and the highest paid woman journalist of her day, described the Colonial Office before Chamberlain took over as a 'sleepy leisurely place' but this 'sleeping city' was 'awakened by a touch,' and ruled by *The Master*.[49] Flora Shaw and her dealings with the Colonial Office will appear later in the story of The Raid.

Chamberlain's energy and business experience allowed him to work more efficiently than many others in similar roles. He was able to delegate and relied on his experts, and consequently, the decisions of the Colonial Office were usually the result of his collaboration with them. He often worked late, was tidy with his papers,'

45   Richard N. Kelly & John Cantrell, *Modern British Statesmen, 1867-1945* (Manchester, MUP. 1967), p. 83.
46   *Melbourne Argus*, 28 June 1895.
47   Garvin, The *Life of Joseph Chamberlain*, Vol III, p. 11.
48   H.W. Massingham, *Daily Chronicle, 27* November 1895.
49   Conversation with Garvin recorded in The *Life of Joseph Chamberlain*, Vol III, p. 11.

and 'could get through an immense amount of work in a short time'.[50] Chamberlain, an Imperialist and business man, had a firm desire to ensure that the Colonies relied on British producers and manufacturers but his appointment was not welcomed by Rhodes, who would have preferred a weaker Minister whom he could control.[51] They shared a mutual animosity and, at a meeting between the two, Chamberlain explained that his dislike for Rhodes was based on three main reasons; the Colossus' claim that 'every man has his price', his ideas about illuminating the 'Imperial factor in South Africa', and Rhodes' financial support for Charles Stuart Parnell, the advocate of Irish Home Rule, who had threatened Salisbury's Conservative and Liberal Unionist coalition.[52] One wonders whether Chamberlain screwed in his famous eye-glass during their meeting and Rhodes felt 'sifted to the marrow' during this dressing down.[53] It seems unlikely.

These were the four main players in the drama which was to unfold as the Jameson Raid. It was Rhodes' determination to establish British influence and rule throughout South Africa which was a cause of the Raid. Jameson's devotion to his friend and their joint desire to increase the British control in Africa whilst improving the prospects of the BSAC led to the gamble of attempting to overthrow, or at least diminish, the influence of the ZAR. Against them was the cunning ZAR President, Paulus Kruger, who desired to create an expanding Boer Republic whilst making few concessions to the many foreigners who, drawn by the promise of the fabulous prosperity which the gold and diamond mines offered, provided the ZAR with its wealth. The failure at Majuba Hill had demonstrated that British troops could be defeated by relatively undisciplined farmers and this encouraged the Boers to seek independence and permitted them to take advantage of British and other foreigners, attracted to the ZAR in search of gold or trade. The Boers, called such men *Uitlanders*.[54] Many *Uitlanders* believed that the British defeat at Majuba meant the ZAR could no longer be their home and had left in droves.[55] Those who remained and others who were to join them as the tension within the ZAR eased, were to find that their treatment by Kruger was harsh and unfair and they looked again to Her Majesty's Government for assistance. It was Kruger's desire to prevent British control of the ZAR and Rhodes' dreams of economic and political expansions and the so called 'plight' of the *Uitlanders* in Johannesburg which would lead to the Raid.

The British Government had a somewhat ambiguous attitude to the ZAR. On the one hand, they wanted entrepreneurs to acquire wealth through activities which were lucrative but did not involve Her Majesty's Government. Whilst on the other, they wanted Britain to become *de facto* ruler of the Republic without risking another Majuba. Chamberlain's aspiration to extend Britain's influence and wealth through the Colonies was tempered by his apparent desire to ensure that Rhodes did not get the lion's share of this wealth. He was, however, still prepared to make use of such men as the 'Colossus' and Jameson in order establish British control with minimum risk and little financial expenditure.

---

50   Lord Mount Bretton quoted in Garvin, The *Life of Joseph Chamberlain*, Vol III, p. 14.

51   'Governors of Colonies on the Question of Trade with the United Kingdom', Circular, Downing Street, 28 November 1895.

52   Williams, *Cecil Rhodes*, p. 136; Garvin The *Life of Joseph Chamberlain*, Vol III, pp. 33-34.

53   Conversation with Sir Fredrick (later Lord) Lugard, recorded in Garvin The *Life of Joseph Chamberlain*, Vol III, p. 16. Lugard would later marry Flora Shaw.

54   The term was applied to all foreign workers not just the British immigrants.

55   Henry Rider Haggard, *The Last Boer War* (London: Keegan Paul, Trench, Trubner, 1899), pp. 178-180.

2

'He was not an unreasonable person'[1]

Kruger was worried by the mass of *Uitlanders* who were attracted to the gold and diamond fields in such numbers that, when in 1896 the Johannesburg Sanitary Board, the nearest Johannesburg had to a town council, carried out a census of the inhabitants living within a three-mile radius of the centre of the town, it calculated that of the white population of 50,907, only 6,205 where Transvaalers. Of the 44,702 *Uitlanders* roughly 33,000 were British or from Cape Colony and Natal, the remainder were Irish, Jews, Americans, Hollanders, Germans, Belgians, or Portuguese.[2]

Before the British annexation, the majority of *Uitlanders* came as traders, prospectors or missionaries, but under British rule there was a steady influx of skilled workers and clerks who were needed to carry out those tasks vital to the burgeoning State. Such was *Uitltander* influence that they controlled most of the commercial and mercantile activities but they had little political power. The rural, fundamentalist Boers viewed them with dislike and distrust. In addition, the large number of 'foreign adventurers' were belittled by the *Uitlanders* of English stock and described by Sir Henry Bartle Frere, the High Commissioner for South Africa (1877-1880) as men rarely 'of high character and disinterested aims.'[3] After Britain was forced to give up its control of the ZAR under the terms of the Pretoria Convention in August 1881, all these disparate groups were subject to the rules of the Republic's Government no matter what their country of origin. Consequently, despite having few rights, their labour and commerce provided the Boer Republic with much of its wealth but, in return, their activities were heavily taxed.

In evaluating the reasons for *Uitlander* discontent, Arthur Conan Doyle, who served as a medical officer during the Second Boer War, argued that their cause was a genuine one, but he also suggested that there were sinister influences afoot which increased the *Uitlanders'* unrest.[4] One of these 'forces' was Cecil Rhodes, whose motives ranged from his imperialistic ambitions, through his profiteering drive to genuine sympathy for the *Uitlanders'* conditions.

Conan Doyle described how the revenues of the ZAR had risen from just over £150,000 in 1896, the date of opening the gold fields, to £4,000,000 in 1899. The *Uitlanders*, however, in spite of making the ZAR one of the wealthiest countries in the world by head of population, had no say as to how the taxes were spent nor in the choice of officials who spent them. In addition, they had no control of the quality of the schools set up

---

1   Arthur Conan Doyle, *The Great Boer War* (London: Nelson, 1903), p. 30. Unless otherwise indicated much of this chapter is based upon M. Meredith, *Diamonds, Gold and War, The Making of South Africa* (London: Simon Schuster, 2008).

2   A.H. Bleksley, *Johannesburg Gezondheids Comite, Sanitary Department* (Johannesburg; Standard and Diggers New Printing and Publishing Company, 1896).

3   William Garrett Fisher, *The Transvaal and the Boer, A Short History of South African Republic, with a Chapter on the Orange Free State* (London: Chapman & Hall, 1900), p. 179.

4   Conan Doyle, *The Great Boer War*, p. 30.

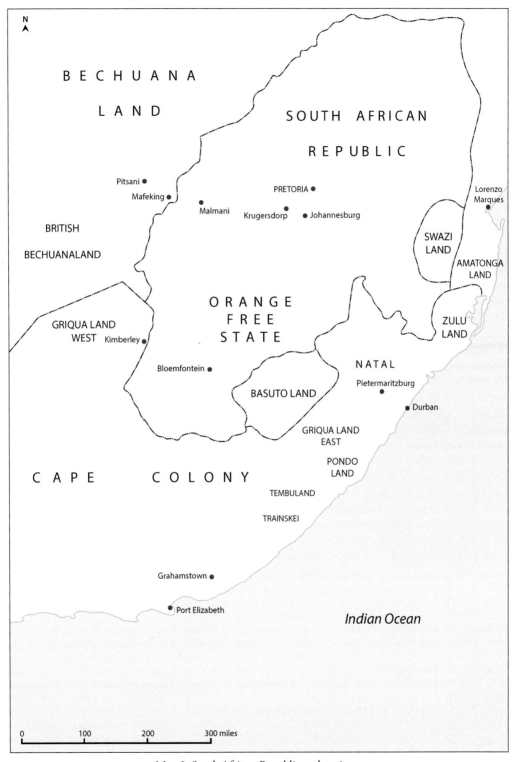

Map 2 South African Republic and environs.

to educate *Uitlander* children even though much larger sums were spent on the education of Boer children.[5] Similarly, the civic amenities in Johannesburg were very basic: buckets instead of drains, waste carts instead of pipes, and a corrupt and violent police force.[6] John Hays Hammond, an American mining engineer working for Rhodes, claimed that Johannesburg suffered from a high death rate and much sickness because of lack of a sewage system and a clean water supply.[7]

However, Byron Farwell, in his account of the Boer War, had less sympathy for the *Uitlanders* and quoted the comments of John Merriman, who was to become the last Prime Minister of Cape Colony in 1908. He described his fellow *Uitlanders* as '…a loafing, scheming, drinking lot who would corrupt an archangel.'[8] Farwell attributed much of the *Uitlanders*' dissatisfaction to their unwillingness to accept Boer ways. Boers were fundamental Calvinists; they led self-sufficient lives often on isolated farms. They were God fearing and maintained a pre-industrial outlook on life which was very different from those who came to their country to find gold.

John Hays Hammond presented a somewhat different view of his fellow *Uitlanders* from that of Merriman. Johannesburg, he argued, was much more like a wealthy manufacturing town than a traditional mining camp as depicted in stories of the 'Wild West'. Life was 'humdrum', and the mines were really 'gold factories'. Life in Johannesburg was similar to that in the settled towns in the eastern states of America and the 'society' consisted of the usual middle-class professionals, their wives and children. Many distinguished visitors came to Johannesburg and the white population was a 'domestic group'.[9] One suspects that Hays Hammond was remembering this life through roseate glasses and the nature of the 'society' in which he moved affected his view. Neither Hays Hammond nor Merriman were much concerned with the great numbers of native Africans who lived in and around Johannesburg and who provided the much-needed hard labour in the mines. These men were not, as was the feeling of the time, considered as being significant in political and social terms as Europeans; a view which was shared almost equally by Boers and *Uitlanders* alike.

Farwell believed that men such as Cecil Rhodes and the Boers were on opposite tracks; the former wanted a united South Africa under the British Flag whereas the latter desired an Afrikaner State independent of Britain and he dismissed Conan Doyle's sympathetic description of the *Uitlanders*' oppression as 'a great exaggeration'.[10]

Rayne Kruger's analysis of the situation in South Africa at the time of the Raid was even more critical of the British. A South African, Kruger researched his nation's records and interviewed survivors of the period and concluded that a major cause of friction between the two factions was Rhodes' imperialist ambition to create a South African Federation under the British Flag in the face of the unswerving opposition of Paulus Kruger. Rayne Kruger concluded that, in order to thwart Rhodes, Oom Paul had to overcome three major problems. First, there was the control which Britain maintained over Boer relations with foreign countries. President Kruger had let it be known that he wished to develop relationships with foreign powers such as Germany, a threat which Britain took very seriously. Germany possessed colonies in East Africa which were described in *The Times* as an attempt to create *mittel-Afrika*[11] but, in 1890, the British Government had thwarted the plans

---

5   Conan Doyle quotes John Robinson, Director General of the Johannesburg Education Council, who calculated that only £650 was spend on *Uitlander* children's education out of the £63,000 allocated. See Conan Doyle, *The Great Boer War*', p. 31.

6   Conan Doyle, *The Great Boer War*, p. 31.

7   John Hays Hammond, *The Truth about the Jameson Raid as related to Alleyne Ireland* (Boston: Marshall Jones, 1898), pp. 18-19.

8   Byron Farwell, *The Great Boer War* (London: Allen Lane, 1977), p. 22.

9   Hays Hammond, *The Truth about the Jameson Raid*, pp. 13-14. One suspects that Hays Hammond was remembering this life through roseate glasses and that the 'Society' he mentions was the elite of Johannesburg.

10   Farwell, *The Great Boer War*, p.15.

11   *The Times* 20 September 1884.

of Carl Peters by exchanging control of Heligoland for that of Zanzibar. Peters was a German adventurer whose ideas for his country's expansion by seizing parts of Africa were similar to those of Rhodes' British imperialism. This exchange defined the areas of influence of the two nations in eastern Africa and brought a temporary end to their colonial rivalries.[12]

Secondly, the *Uitlanders* demanded the vote and the removal of monopolies on materials, such as that placed on dynamite, which were vital for mining operations. In the slump of 1890, many *Uitlanders* lost both their jobs and their money through speculation and so became even more resentful at Kruger's

SLOW AND SURE.

PRESIDENT KRUGER (to British Colonist): "There, see what I am doing for you. Ain't you very grateful. Who is your true friend now?"

'Slow but Sure': Kruger adjusts the Uitlander franchise whilst Chamberlain looks on. Cartoon by J.M. Staniforth. (Open source)

attempts to keep them in their place. Their mood was not improved when it became known that the President had compared their attitudes and behaviour during the slump to that of his angry pet baboon which tended to bite the hand which fed it.[13]

In 1891, Kruger appeared to make a small attempt to satisfy *Uitlander* demands for the vote by establishing a second *Volksraad* or Parliament but, at the same time, he tightened qualification for the franchise. *Uitlanders* initially obtained the vote after one year's residence but by 1892, this had increased to five years' residence and the payment of a £25 fee in order to be naturalised. The Transvaal Government hoped this increase would keep *Uitlanders'* political influence in check, perhaps, believing that many *Uitlanders* would leave South Africa within this time scale. The aim of the fee was to discourage an inrush of new immigrants to the Lydenburg goldfields who might increase the pressure to grant the vote to *Uitlanders* The numbers of *Uitlanders* arriving continued to grow as the goldfields expanded so Kruger proposed that the residence qualification for the full franchise be raised from five years to fourteen years and restricted this to *Uitlanders* who were aged over forty since many of the newcomers were young men keen to make their fortune. Conan Doyle believed that it was the increase in the qualifications for *Uitlanders* to obtain the franchise which was their major grievance and a cause of the Second Boer War.[14] However, in an attempt to remove the restrictions placed upon them by the Boers and their inability to have influence upon not just the political aspects of the country but also the way in which the profits and conditions of industry and commerce was controlled, the *Uitlanders* petitioned the Transvaal government for a shorter residency qualification. Their appeals were ignored.

---

12   Heligoland-Zanzibar Treaty, 1 July 1890. Duane Niler Pyeatt, 'Heligoland and the Making of the Anglo-German Colonial Agreement', Unpublished MA Thesis, Texas Tech University, 1988, p.100.

13   Paul Kruger quoted in Edgar Halt, *The Boer War* (New York: George A. Putnam, 1958), p. 46.

14   Conan Doyle, *The Boer War*, p.35.

In an attempt to sweeten this bitter pill, *Uitlanders* were given the right to take up Transvaal citizenship after only two years' residence for a reduced fee of £5 and to vote in elections for the second *Volksraad*, which had limited functions and whose decisions could be subject to veto by the first *Volksraad* in which the old Burghers remained in control. *Uitlanders* wishing to take advantage of this offer had to renounce all allegiances to their native country and become members of the Dutch Reform Church.[15] Kruger's creation of old and new Burghers meant there were first and second class citizens in the ZAR and the *Uitlanders*, who were firmly of the second class, were unimpressed and unappeased.

They were equally unenthusiastic about Kruger's economic policy which became increasingly corrupt and worked to their disadvantage. Using similar methods to those of Charles I, Kruger granted monopolies to his friends and to companies sympathetic to the Boers and pursued economic policies which might bring new rent-seeking opportunities to those within his patronage.[16] This enabled him to control various manufacturing processes, public utilities such as gas and electricity supplies, the State bank and the municipal services in Johannesburg and Pretoria as well of those other less important towns. This practice of simony provided a significant income for a previously almost insolvent State as well as giving Burghers of both classes the vital goods and services they required. However, rather than guaranteeing the necessities required for life and commerce in the ZAR, these monopolies resulted in high prices through the lack of external competition which was caused by very high tariffs on imported goods. Matters were made worse as many concessionaries failed to provide the services; they had been awarded but held on to them in the hopes of selling at a high profit at a later time so this did not contribute to improved living conditions.

Kruger also indulged in nepotism which added to the corruption. For example, the owner of the concession to supply Johannesburg with water was the President's son-in-law who was also his private secretary. It was claimed that this concessionaire was able to make £20,000 out of the deal 'without so much as digging a spadeful [sic] of earth'. There were many other examples of 'unofficial' monies paid by would be concessionaries to Kruger which he chose to regard as personal gifts. Such behaviour further infuriated the *Uitlanders* as many of the things they required for daily living were in the hands of Kruger's cronies who were determined to keep the prices high.

It was the grant of the dynamite concession which almost certainly annoyed the *Uitlander* miners the most. This concession was sold to Edouard Lippert and a French consortium rather than to its competitor, the Anglo-German Nobel Trust, by the original concessionaire. The Trust was allowed to import dynamite for a period of two years whilst the French consortium built an explosive manufacturing factory. However, the French consortium secretly imported dynamite rather than the raw materials required for its manufacture which proved to be a cheaper way to increase profits. It is said that Lippert was able to make a 200 per cent profit on the explosives he imported and sold to the mines.[17] This fraud caused uproar in the *Volksraad* as well as in the Transvaal press and exposed Kruger to much criticism.[18] In an attempt to appease all sides, the original concession was cancelled and ultimately given to the South African Explosives Company which was to act as agents for the manufacture and sale of dynamite for a period of fifteen years. The Nobel Trust and the French Consortium were allowed to buy shares in this company, and this resulted in all the profits from this essential commodity going abroad rather into the ZAR's coffers. These coffers needed much better controls, since during this period, it officially received over 2.4 million pounds but had no proper accounts to show either its income or expenditure. The need to respond to the corruption resulted in the concessionaires demanding ever higher prices which did little to placate the *Uitlanders*.

---

15   George van Welfling Eybers, *Select Constitutional Documents Illustrating South African History, 1795-1910* (London: Routledge, 1919), pp. 445-463.

16   Jonathan, Hyslop,' Political Corruption in South Africa; before and after apartheid', *Journal of Southern African Studies*, 2005, Vol. 31. Issue 4, p. 779.

17   Phillip Roberts, *Cecil Rhodes: Flawed Colossus* (London: Hamish Hamilton, 2015), pp. 175-76.

18   Meredith, *Diamonds, Gold, and War,* pp. 298–300.

The third problem identified by Rayne Kruger which Oom Paul needed to overcome was the ZAR's international isolation. The Transvaal was almost completely surrounded by British territory and Kruger lacked the control of a port. Both Rhodes and Kruger shared an ambition to gain access to the coast of Mozambique. Kruger apparently had more scruples, however, for he refused to cooperate with Rhodes when the latter suggested that they simply take Delagoa Bay from the Portuguese by force. Oom Paul was prepared, according to his critics, to try to divert the railway line from Pretoria to Delagoa Bay over the farms of his relatives and friends who would be paid large amounts in compensation. Such intentions question whether Kruger's refusal to cooperate with Rhodes was based upon higher moral standards or his desire to increase the wealth of his friends and family.

Kruger's behaviour caused such discontent even amongst the Boers that a genuine opposition arose led by the Commandant General, Piet Joubert, and the 1893 *Volksraad* election was fought with a ferocity not previously seen in the ZAR. Kruger's behaviour was portrayed by his opponents as being characterised by nepotism, mismanagement, and corruption. The President himself was seen as a bad-tempered autocrat who preferred Hollanders to other citizens in the ZAR. Joubert's critics, on the other hand, accused him of being subservient to the *Uitlanders*. One of Paulus Kruger's responses to these difficulties was to place big orders for armaments, especially from Germany. These were not necessarily placed because of *Uitlander* threats but, according to James Fitzpatrick, because both Kruger's supporters and Joubert's Progressive Party openly discussed the use of arms to settle their differences rather than using the ballot box.[19]

Kruger won the election but only by a narrow margin.[20] Many of his voters were worried by the increasing threat posed by the *Uitlanders* whose numbers had continued to grow. *Uitlanders* on the other hand, were further outraged when President Kruger, having obtained his victory, began to repay those who had supported him in the election through his usual method of concessions such as that of cyanide, a chemical which was essential for obtaining gold from ore and of special importance to the mine owners, sometimes known as the *Randlords*, and who included Cecil Rhodes. The name was derived after the Witwatersrand, a 56 kilometre east-west-running scarp which includes Johannesburg and Krugersdorp and contained enormous gold deposits.[21] Kruger was determined to make the trade in cyanide a State monopoly and it was only because of vigorous opposition and a decision by the ZAR High Court that he did not get his way.

The *Uitlander* community, meanwhile, had become increasingly vociferous about their own grievances over political rights. Their first attempt at opposing Kruger was in 1892 when a Transvaal National Union was launched 'to obtain by all constitutional means equal rights for all citizens of this republic, and … the redress of all grievances'. Their leader was Charles Leonard, a Johannesburg solicitor, who reminded the Boer *Burghers* what life, had been like before the coming of the *Uitlanders*:

They had no market; no means; their only means of living was to contract their wants … Who enabled them to live, who made markets for them? We! Yet we are told that we are mere birds of passage, and that, because they were here before us, we have no rights.'

The Union organised petitions in 1893, 1894 and 1895, the latter was signed by a supposed 350,000 but this included some bogus names by which the *Uitlanders* exaggerated their own numbers in an attempt to strengthen their position.

---

19 James Percy Fitzpatrick, *The Transvaal from Within: A Private Record of Public Affairs* (London: Heinemann, 1900, Popular Edition), p. 69.

20 Kruger received 7,854 votes to Joubert's 7,009. Fitzpatrick, who cannot always be relied upon, reported the figures as Kruger 7881 votes and Joubert 7009 votes. See Fitzpatrick. *The Transvaal from Within*, p. 71.

21 *Randlords*: Entrepreneurs such as Rhodes and Beit who controlled the gold fields.

They were particularly outraged when Kruger ordered a mobilisation to deal with Chief Malebogo of the Bagananwa, who had refused to accept Boer authority. The ZAR was determined to demonstrate its power over native rulers and, in response to Bagananwa threats, organised the largest fighting force in its history up to that date.[22] When such danger threatened, it was the custom for men in a District to form a militia which was organised into military units called *Commandos*. Each *Commando* would elect is own officers and, since this was essentially a civilian militia, there were no uniforms; each man wore what they wished which was usually their everyday khaki farming clothes and normally a jacket, trousers and a slouch hat. When joining his *Commando* every man also brought his own weapon, usually a hunting rifle, and provided his own horse and ammunition. The average Boer Burgher was a farmer who spent almost all his working life in the saddle. Since the rifle was essential to his everyday existence, the Boer became a skilled hunter and an expert marksman. A fact which had been noted after the First Boer War when *The Times*, wrote that British soldiers '…were literally over powered and their courage quelled solely by the superior shooting of the Boers.'[23] The Pretoria *Commando*, made up of about 600 Boer fighters and Europeans of diverse origins, was commanded by Commandant Erasmus and later Commandant Uys. It included 85 men of the *Staatsartillerie van de Zuid-Afrikaansche Republiek* (State Artillery of the South African Republic) who were under the command of Captains Schiel and H. Pretorius.[24] In addition more than 800 Rustenburg Burghers were called up for service under Commandant H.P. Malan together with some 200 from the Marico *Commando*, under Commandant Botha. As was the usual practice, each *Commando* either conscripted or kidnapped Africans to carry out menial tasks on its way to the area of battle.[25]

British subjects and the *Randlords*, protested at their compulsory conscription by a Government which denied them the franchise. The Transvaal National Union argued that it is difficult to perform military service as a duty to a State when that State denied them …the rights of citizenship.'[26]

The methods used to defeat the Bagananwa, who were a determined enemy and not easily quelled, were brutal even by the standards of the day. One such strategy used by the Boers was to throw dynamite into the caves in which the Bagananwa lived. This proved ineffective and the use of this precious material in such an indiscriminate way caused further dissatisfaction amongst the miners who were, as has already been explained, forced to pay high prices for this essential resource of their trade. They especially resented the fact that, although it was used in great quantities, this did not result in the surrender of the Bagananwa. One suspects that the humanitarian sympathies which the *Uitlanders* might have had for the Bagananwa were partly motivated by their feeling that the use of dynamite in this way was a waste. The Bagananwa only surrendered after they had been almost starved out of existence. Mahukura has suggested that the barbaric and costly methods used to prosecute the war created a situation where both mutiny at the front and rebellion in Johannesburg and Pretoria seemed imminent.[27]

Amongst those conscripted to the Pretoria *Commando* were 23 British *Uitlanders*, five of whom refused to obey the call up and were subsequently arrested. The Supreme Court found in favour of the State and the dissidents were sent, under escort, to join the other conscripts in the Zoutpansberg, the north east division of the Transvaal. This treatment, though permitted according to ZAR law, caused even greater discontent amongst *Uitlanders*. The cost of the war and claims for compensation by those involved added to Kruger's

---

22   Tlou John Makhura, 'Another Road to the Raid', *Journal of Southern African Studies,* Vol. 21, No. 2, June 1995. p. 259.

23   *The Times*, 19 April 1881.

24   State Artillery of the South African Republic was the one professional military body in the ZAR.

25   P.L. Breutz, *History of Botswana* (Ramsgate: Breutz, 1989), p. 342. C. Sonntag, *My friend Maleboch, Chief of the Blue Mountains* (Pretoria, Sonntag, 1983), pp. 10-13, 19, 53-74.

26   *The Cape Times,* 16 July 1894, Report of a mass meeting of the Transvaal National Union held on the 14 July 1894 at Johannesburg to consider the political situation, p. 45.

27   Makhura, 'Another Road to the Raid', p. 267.

financial problems and resulted in even higher taxes being levied. Similarly, the prosecution of the war caused a significant fall on the stock market, a factor which some commentators such as Geoffrey Blainey, saw as one of the factors which sparked off the Raid.[28]

The British Government ordered Sir Henry Loch, High Commissioner for Southern Africa, to travel to Pretoria to sort out the differences between Kruger and the *Uitlanders*. Loch's reception in the Transvaal capital by pro-British *Uitlanders* was overwhelming and a source of annoyance for Kruger who had gone to the railway station to receive him. He was especially affronted when, during a carriage ride with Loch from the station to the Commissioner's hotel, he somehow managed to get entangled with the British Flag whilst Pro-British demonstrators, singing 'Rule Britannia', unharnessed Kruger's carriage horses and dragged the coach to Loch's hotel. The Boers, unsurprisingly, saw this behaviour as an insult to their President.

Henry Brougham Loch, 1st Baron Loch GCB, GCMG, High Commissioner for South Africa and Governor of Cape Town. (*The Review of Reviews*, 1891)

Loch became increasingly worried by the developing belligerence of the *Uitlanders* and its possible consequences but also felt it might present an opportunity for Britain to increase her influence in The Transvaal. Sir Henry received a deputation from *Uitlander* representatives, who pressed their case for support from the British Government with the promise that, should Britain decide to intervene militarily, there would be 10,000 *Uitlanders*, armed with 7,000 rifles, ready to greet them. The representatives also assured him that there would be a unanimous demand for annexation.[29] Consequently, Loch arranged for a number of rifles to be sent to Mafeking and informed the Colonial Office that he proposed to prepare the Bechuanaland Border Police (B.B.P.) in readiness to advance on Johannesburg if trouble did break out.

Sir Graham Bower, the Imperial Secretary, was more cautious and feared that Loch's presence in Johannesburg might result in a riot for which the High Commissioner and consequently Britain would be blamed. Loch's response to this note of caution was to describe the Imperial Secretary as no Englishman which greatly angered Bower who resigned in disgust.[30] Loch seems to have been a plotter in the ensuing "uprising" and was accused of actively encouraging the *Uitlanders* to act. Jean Van der Poel quotes two examples of Loch attempting to bring about annexation of the Transvaal by force. The first was a letter to the Permanent Secretary of the Colonial Office, Sir Robert Meade, in which Loch had expressed himself in favour of a military solution to the annexation. The second example was a secret dispatch from Loch which set out his belief that the *Uitlanders* would probably win their struggle against the Boers and, if they did, would probably wish to maintain their independence from Britain. The implication was that Britain ought

---

28   Geoffrey Blainey, 'Lost Causes of the Jameson Raid', *The Economic History Review*, Vol. 18, Issue 2, August 1965, pp. 350-66.

29   Jean Van der Poel, *The Jameson Raid* (London: OUP, 1951), p. 15.

30   Van der Poel, *The Jameson Raid*, p.15.

to support the *Uitlander*s in their armed struggle or risk losing its influence.[31] There is some evidence that Loch, as early as 1894, had enquired how long Johannesburg *Uitlanders* could hold out in an armed struggle and if they were prepared to do so, he would come with armed troops to support them.[32] There is no doubt that Loch, who denied these accusations, ardently desired to bring the Transvaal under British rule and he was prepared to take steps to make this happen but was later one of the many important political figures of the time who denied knowledge or involvement in the Raid. However, his ideas would sound very similar to the circumstances of the Raid.

In response to Loch's apparent support of a rebellion by the *Uitlander*s, Rhodes, who also desired this outcome, feared he might not be able to control the High Commissioner. The 'Colossus' was able to display his influence on the Westminster Government by persuading his friend and admirer, the Liberal Prime Minister, Lord Rosebery, to appoint Sir Hercules Robinson as Loch's replacement in 1895. Rhodes' task in reducing Loch's influence was made significantly easier because Sir Henry had been rebuked for his 'extraordinary injudicious manner in coquetting with the would be rebels.'[33] Sir Robert Meade believed that there was a danger that Britain would lose the whole of South Africa if an armed conflict resulted in another defeat such as that at Majuba Hill in the First Boer War.

Rhodes had already shown his flair for the dramatic by his annexation of Pondoland which was on the coastal belt between the Eastern Cape and Natal. This was the only independent native State in the region but it was also a British Protectorate. In 1894, Loch, on a tour of the country had been insulted by Sigcau, the paramount chief, who had kept him waiting for three days before granting him an audience. Rhodes, rather than the British Government, decided to do something about this insult to the High Commissioner and travelled to Pondoland in style with machine guns amongst his luggage. Summoning Sigcau to a meeting, he kept the chief waiting for three days and then informed the him that it was his intention to annex the country. Taking Sigcau to a mealie field where the machine guns had been set up, Rhodes ordered them to fire at the mealies. So powerful was this demonstration that Sigcau immediately agreed to the annexation. Two Germans, who had permission from Sigcau to prospect for precious metals, were deported, and Rhodes took over their concessions. Rhodes had succeeded in taking over a country of 200,000 people without firing a shot in anger at the cost of £7,000 and a £500 a year pension for Sigcau.[34] Rhodes was clearly not averse to strong-arm intervention when the circumstances were right. However, Rhodes later acted beyond his legal authority when, in the following year, he arrested Sigcau and imprisoned him without trial. Sigcau, now a citizen of the Crown, took Rhodes to Court and was released by order of the Chief Justice. In this case *habeas corpus* proved supreme and even the 'Colossus', as will be demonstrated later, could not entirely ignore the rules.

Unsurprisingly, when Rhodes heard of *Uitlander* unrest, he sent Jameson, his right-hand man in such situations, to assess the state of affairs in Johannesburg, where the *Uitlander*s petition of 350,000 signatures had just been rejected by Kruger. This rejection was described by a particularly outraged *Uitlander* as 'a declaration of war to the knife'.[35] Rhodes' view was that typical of an imperialist: 'I do not like the idea of British subjects (the *Uitlanders*) becoming Burghers, that is why I prefer that the Burghers should become British subjects.'[36] The 'Loch Plan' seemed to be an ideal way to bring this about and was adopted by Rhodes who, with similar ambitions, hoped to foster an uprising which would be supported by an armed force assembled on the Bechuanaland –Transvaal border. Hercules Robinson, a man who knew his own limitations and

31   Van der Poel, *The Jameson Raid*, pp. 16-17.
32   Van der Poel, *The Jameson Raid*, p.18.
33   Meredith, *Diamonds, Gold and War*, p. 30.
34   Millin, *Rhodes*, pp. 228-30; Cloete, *African Portraits*, pp. 279-80.
35   Percy Fitzpatrick quoted in Ian Colvin, *The Life of Jameson*, Vol. II (London: Edward Arnold, 1922), p. 12.
36   John Fisher, *Paul Kruger: His Life and Time* (London: Secker & Warburg, 1974) p. 178.

was in ill health, persuaded Bower to return to South Africa as Imperial Secretary and Bower was to play a significant part in the Raid and the Inquiries.

Kruger realised that, should the British intervene in support of the *Uitlanders* his fledgling Republic's survival would be severely threatened. He needed a powerful European ally and the obvious choice was Germany which, Kruger believed, would be strong enough to help him withstand British pressure. In return for this support, Kruger's Government encouraged German companies to invest in the Transvaal and German citizens to emigrate to it. He was impressed by the way in which he had been received by Frederick III, the Kaiser's father, who had treated him as an important Head of State rather than that of a small, insignificant Republic. Kruger claimed that the Germans in the Transvaal, unlike their British counterparts, obeyed the law and did not turn for help to their native country when things got tough.

With German support and the increasing wealth from the mines, Kruger believed that the ZAR was strong enough to withstand British pressure, but this alliance with Germany made the British even more determined to dominate the Transvaal. The British protagonists, who included Rhodes and Jameson, began to actively encourage the *Uitlanders'* discontent and planned to provide them with tangible support.

3

Preparing the Ground and the Drifts Crisis

Chamberlain bitterly opposed Robinson's appointment as High Commissioner, believing, with some justification, that he was Rhodes' puppet. On the other hand, Chamberlain's strong imperialist attitudes were just what Rhodes required to further his own plans. John Merriman remarked, with a certain foresight, that Chamberlain would have this country (South Africa) in a blaze before the year was out.[1] At roughly the same time as Chamberlain's appointment as Colonial Secretary, Jameson, having returned to Matabeleland, was in discussion with Rhodes about the South African situation. Rhodes' motives with regards to intervention in the ZAR and its fellow Boer Republic, the Orange Free State, ranged from pragmatism through patriotism to that of simple profiteering. The only real gold reserves in Africa were to be found in the Rand and the Rand belonged to the Boers. Rhodes argued that, 'If one had Johannesburg, one could unite the whole country tomorrow.'[2]

On 1 August 1895, Frederick Rutherfoord Harris, the BSAC Secretary, and Earl Henry Grey, the Administrator in Rhodesia, both of whom were in Rhodes' thrall, met with Chamberlain but he supposedly refused to discuss any confidential reasons for the transfer of the Bechuanaland Protectorate to the BSAC.[3] Although it seems that Rutherfoord Harris, after the formal meeting, was able tell Chamberlain something of Rhodes' plan to support an *Uitlander* uprising with armed police.[4] Rutherfoord Harris was to refer to what he told Chamberlain as a 'guarded illusion'. Kenneth Wilburn suggests that Rutherfoord Harris' inference was that, if the plan was successful, Chamberlain and Robinson would intervene by replacing the BSAC police with Imperial troops and bring the Transvaal under the British Flag again.[5] All the Company wanted, Rutherfoord Harris is said to have told Chamberlain, was a strip just six miles wide, to use as a jumping off point.[6] The BSAC would become Britain's inexpensive agent in extending the Empire whilst Chamberlain and the Government would be protected if the plan failed as there would be no Imperial troops involved. The content of this conversation was to be a source of considerable controversy and Chamberlain's and Rutherfoord Harris' accounts differ significantly.

---

1   Deryck Schreuder, & Jeffrey Butler, *Sir Graham Bower's Secret History of the Jameson Raid and the South Africa Crisis, 1895-1902* (Cape Town: Van Riebeek Society) 2002, p. 41.

2   Cloete, *African Portraits*, p. 278.

3   Ethel Drus, 'A Report on the Papers of Joseph Chamberlain Relating to the Jameson Raid and the Inquiry', *Bulletin of the Institute of Historical Research, No. XXV 1952*, p. 43.

4   Ethel Drus, 'The Question of Imperial Complicity in the Jameson Raid', *English Historical Review*, No. 68, October 1953, p. 548. Millin, *Rhodes*, p. 221.

5   Kenneth Wilburn, 'The Drift Crisis, and the Missing Telegrams and the Jameson Raid: A Centennial Review'. *The Journal of Imperial and Commonwealth History*, Vol.25, No. 2, May 1997, p. 221.

6   Millin, *Rhodes*, p.266.

The result would all depend upon the *Uitlanders* deciding that their attempts to gain the franchise by persuasion would not succeed and agreeing that some kind of military intervention was the only way to achieve their aims. Jameson, who was a frequent visitor to Johannesburg, where his brother, Sam, was in business, never lost an opportunity to talk with Charles Leonard, Francis Hays Hammond, Lionel Phillips and George Farrar, the principal leaders of the Johannesburg *Uitlanders*. Dr Jim had something of a free hand at this time since his mentor, Rhodes, had only just returned to Cape Colony after a three month visit to England and was engrossed in the Cape's parliamentary business.

Loch, whose plan Rhodes was about to borrow, had declared his intention to retire in the early January and it would take Sir Hercules Robinson, Loch's replacement, until the end of May 1895 to take up his post. Jameson, now Administrator for the newly named Rhodesia, was happy to plot alone. How his meetings with the future Reform Society Members went is uncertain but it must have been encouraging since, on his return to Bulawayo in April 1895, he proposed to the Rhodesian settlers that there was a need for the formation of a new Volunteer Corps.[7] Local Rhodesian newspapers reported that Jameson planned a mounted force equipped with smart uniforms, commercial model Lee Speed military configuration rifles and a brass band. Volunteers would be paid handsomely if they signed up for active service.[8] The force would include engineers and artillery and the BSAC would fund the enterprise.

Lieutenant Colonel (Major) Sir John Willoughby: Commander of the Chartered Company's Forces.
(*Illustrated London News*, 1896)

The unit would be commanded by Lieutenant Colonel (Major) Sir John Willoughby, an officer in the Household Cavalry, who has been described as 'petit, pale and passionless.'[9] He was not the upper-class twit as many described him, having seen action in the Egyptian Campaign of 1882 and on the Nile in 1884-85. Willoughby had been appointed as second in command of the BSAC forces in Rhodesia in 1890 and was Jameson's military adviser during the First Matabele War. He was a skilled soldier with much African experience, some of which had been unconventional which might prove useful in Jameson's coming adventure. He had already demonstrated his willingness to take risks; on an occasion when the pioneers in Rhodesia were short of food, Willoughby crossed into Portuguese territory in order to establish a new supply route by a subterfuge. The plan was that Willoughby would enter Gazaland and the Portuguese would try to stop him by force. Entry into Gazaland was a direct contravention of the orders of High Commissioner Loch and Willoughby was concerned it might damage his career. Seeking Rhodes' advice, Willoughby was told to 'Take all…ask (permission) afterwards.'[10] Willoughby entered Gazaland, was fired on by the Portuguese, Britain protested, and the chastened Portuguese opened the route. Willoughby, it would seem, was just the man to lead the Raid.

7   H. Marshall Hole, *The Jameson Raid* (London: Philip Allan, 1930), p. 44.
8   Reported in the *Bulawayo Chronicle and the Rhodesian Herald*, April 1895.
9   M. Alexander, *The True Blue, The Life and Adventures of Colonel Fred Burnaby, 1842-1885* (London: Rupert Hart Davis, 1957), p. 180. Where appropriate Local ranks are used, and substantive ranks appear in brackets.
10   E. Longford, *Jameson's Raid* (London: Weidenfeld & Nicholson, 1960), p. 62.

The taking over of the Transvaal had been a project of the 'Colossus' for a number of years. In this respect both he and Loch agreed that this might require a *coup de main* assisted by the Johannesburg *Uitlanders* to do so.[11] This idea, expressed too publicly, was the reason for Loch's recall, but Rhodes believed he could adapt the 'Loch Plan' to his own and also to the BSAC's advantage.[12] As has been mentioned, he was able to persuade Loch be replaced by his friend, Sir Hercules Robinson. Rhodes also strongly urged the Government to transfer the Bechuanaland Protectorate to the Company. He needed a base near to the Transvaal Border from which to launch an invasion to support an *Uitlanders*' uprising, restore order and remove Kruger.[13]

Such a base was essential if there was to be a military incursion and Rhodes was determined to acquire one by a stratagem disguised by an apparent legitimate move. In 1892 Lord Ripon, Gladstone's Colonial Secretary, had agreed to transfer a railway strip of 6,000 square miles of Bechuanaland to Rhodes' Bechuanaland Railway Company once it had reached Mafeking. The line had reached Mafeking by 1894 and Gladstone's lethargy in carrying out his Government's promise gave Rhodes a legitimate reason to discuss the Protectorate's future with the Colonial Office.[14] Early in 1895, Rosebery, who had taken over from Gladstone who had resigned over Irish Home Rule, sanctioned the transfer of this railway strip to the BSAC. Since this meant that Imperial control was withdrawn from Bechuanaland, the Bechuanaland Border Police, with a strength of 200, was forced to disband. Rhodes lobbied Chamberlain to agree that these men, who were experienced and useful; be both, allowed, and encouraged to re-enlist in the BSAC police. Chamberlain granted the permission but not the encouragement for them to do so, since, he argued that many would probably re-enlist anyway as otherwise they would be unemployed.[15] Jameson who was appointed Resident Administrator for this border belt, moved his headquarters to Pitsani Potlugo: three miles from the Transvaal border and 173 miles closer to Johannesburg.[16] He quickly set about recruiting since the need for such a police force was obvious to everyone, even Kruger. The Company's railway strip had to be protected and, in spite of Chamberlain's attempts to placate the local chiefs, there was still unrest amongst the tribes.[17] A chief named Linchwe was identified by Rhodes and others as being a major threat to the security of the railways strip and this threat was used to justify the presence of Jameson's force. Linchwe's menace was exaggerated and identified as such by Edward Fairfield, Assistant Under Secretary of State at the Colonial Office, who thought that Jameson's troop numbers should be limited to 350. However, events were to prevent such a reduction from being enforced.

Rhodes having persuaded the Government, perhaps unwittingly, to provide his right-hand man with a launch pad for the possible annexation of the ZAR and Jameson began to make his preparations. Flora Shaw, *The Times*' journalist who was to become heavily involved in the circumstances of the Raid, described Jameson as having two great weaknesses: impatience and overconfidence. His impatience was increased by Kruger who had given the ZAR Railway franchise to the Netherlands-South African Railway Company but by 1891 the company was on the verge of bankruptcy.

The ZAR was forced to rely on British ports and railways for the transportation of imported goods to its borders. Rhodes, seeing a chance to support the people of Johannesburg and to make money, offered Kruger a loan to support the ZAR railways in exchange for permission to build a railway line from Cape Colony to Johannesburg. Having completed this link and knowing that an alternative railway line from Portuguese Delagoa Bay was almost finished, Rhodes reduced the cost of transporting goods from Cape

---

11   Longford, *Jameson's Raid,* p. 142.
12   The National Archives, CO 4851, Loch to Knutsford, 9 August 1892 (Henceforth TNA).
13   Wilburn, 'The Drift Crisis, p. 220.
14   Longford, *Jameson's Raid*, pp. 41-142.
15   Colonial Office to BSAC correspondence quoted in Garvin, The *Life of Joseph Chamberlain*, Vol III, p. 52.
16   TNA CO CP502: G. Fiddes, 'Memorandum on the Concentration of the British South Africa Company's Police on the Frontiers of the South African Republic', 7 January 1896.
17   Longford, *Jameson's Raid*, pp. 41-46.

Colony to a minimum in order to secure as much of the ZAR's traffic as possible. The shrewd Kruger countered by increasing the taxes on goods once they crossed the Vaal River which made the cost of transporting commodities by rail over the fifty miles from the Vaal to Johannesburg exorbitant. In attempt to circumvent this levy, importers unloaded goods at the Vaal and then transferred them to wagons which carried them for the last fifty miles.

In October 1895, Kruger responded by attempting to restrict this method of importing cheaper goods and supplies from the Cape Colony to the ZAR by closing the fords or 'drifts' across the Vaal River through which the wagons, attempting to avoid using the expensive railway, would have to pass. This extreme form of protectionism, known as the 'Drifts Crisis' caused outrage, not just from Rhodes's Cape Colony Government but also from the Orange Free State and many Afrikaners who all benefitted from these less expensive imports. Chamberlain, using High Commissioner Loch, sent an Ultimatum to Kruger accusing him of breaking Article XIII of the London Convention which prevented discrimination against goods coming from any part of the British dominions. Kruger's act was seen as one of serious hostility and could not be ignored by Britain. Rhodes, ever willing to grasp an opportunity, agreed with Chamberlain that the Cape would share the cost of a possible war and troopships, already on their way to India, were instructed to call at the Cape.[18] Faced with these threats, Kruger climbed down and the drifts were quickly reopened. He was not yet prepared to take on the British in an armed struggle.

Jameson made one of his frequent visits to Johannesburg during the Drifts Crisis and found the *Uitlanders* there 'strung up to highest pitch of exasperation' at yet another attempt by Kruger to restrict free access to the essential requirements of their life and work.[19] Realising that the *Uitlanders* were in a receptive mood as far as Rhodes' plans were concerned, Jameson, who had not officially taken up his new post, offered to assist them through military intervention. Initially, the *Uitlander* leaders toyed with the idea of accepting Jameson's offer but his reputation for overconfidence may have cooled their ardour. They needed to be sure that Rhodes was ultimately behind this offer and Leonard and Hays Hammond were sent to Cape Town to confer with the 'Colossus'. They brought with them a manifesto which outlined *Uitlanders'* need for rights.[20] Rhodes is said to have heard them in silence but his interest was stimulated when the manifesto mentioned 'Free trade in South African products'.[21] Rhodes' dual motive in dealing with the ZAR was thus revealed; as an Imperialist he wanted British domination of the Republic but as a man of commerce he wanted to make money.

Shortly after the end of the Drifts Crisis, Jameson, ever conscious of his need to demonstrate that his impending action had a legal basis, journeyed again to Johannesburg and obtained a *Letter of Invitation*, signed by the leading *Uitlanders*, Leonard, Hays Hammond, Phillips and Frank Rhodes, which begged him to intervene to improve their lot.[22] This went some way to satisfy Jameson's sensitivities, since he had made it clear that he did not want to enter the Transvaal as a brigand.[23] The letter, which also became known as the '*Women and children letter*', described the situation for *Uitlanders* in the ZAR and was signed by Leonard, Phillips, Francis Rhodes, Hays-Hammond and Farrar, and is of such significance as being worthy to reproduce in full.

> The position of matters in this State has been so critical of late that at no distant period there will be a conflict between the Government and the *Uitlander* population. It is scarcely necessary for us to recapitulate what is now a matter of history. Suffice it to say that the position of thousands of

---

18   Garvin, The *Life of Joseph Chamberlain*, Vol III, pp. 43-45; Millin, *Rhodes*, pp. 267-68.
19   H. Marshal Hole, *The Jameson Raid* (London: Philip Allan, 1930), p. 75.
20   See Appendix III for Leonard's manifesto demands.
21   Millin, *Rhodes*, p. 111.
22   Ash, *The If Man*, p. 226.
23   Meredith, *Gold Diamonds and War,* p. 324.

Englishmen, and others, is rapidly becoming intolerable. Not satisfied with making the Uitlander population pay, virtually the whole revenue of the country, while denying them representation, the policy of the Government has been steadily to encroach upon the liberty of the subject, and to undermine the security for property to such an extent, as to cause a very deep-seated sense of discontent and anger.

A foreign corporation of Hollanders is, to a considerable extent controlling our destinies, and, in conjunction with the Boer leaders, endeavouring to cast them in a mould which is wholly foreign to the genius of the people. Every public act betrays the most positive hostility, not only to everything English, but to the neighbouring States as well. In short, the internal policy of the Government is such, as to have roused into antagonism to it not only, practically, the whole body of Uitlanders, but a large number of the Boers, while its external policy has exasperated the neighbouring States causing the possibility of great danger to the peace and independence of this Republic.

Public feeling is in a condition of smouldering discontent. All the petitions of the people have been refused with a greater or less degree of contempt, and, in the debate on the franchise petition,[24] signed by nearly 40,000 people, one member challenged the Uitlanders to fight for the rights they asked for and not a single member spoke against him:

Not to go into detail, we may say that the Government has called into existence all the elements necessary for armed conflict. The one desire of the people here is for fair play, the maintenance of their independence, and the preservation of those public liberties without which life is not worth having. The Government denies these things and violates the national sense of the Englishmen at every turn.

What we have to consider is, what will be the condition of things here in the event of conflict? Thousands of unarmed men, women, and children of our race will be at the mercy of well-armed Boers; while property of enormous value will be in the greatest peril. We cannot contemplate the future without the gravest apprehension and feel that we are justified in taking any steps to prevent the shedding of blood, and to ensure the protection of our rights. It is under these circumstances that we feel constrained to call upon you to come to our aid should disturbance arise here.

The circumstances are so extreme, that we cannot avoid this step, and we cannot believe that you, and the men under you, will not fail to come to the rescue of people who would be so situated. We guarantee any expense that may reasonably be incurred by you in helping us and ask you to believe that nothing but the sternest necessity has prompted this appeal.'[25]

It is important to note that the document goes beyond simply complaining about the high taxes which *Uitlanders* were forced to pay without any influence on how the ZAR was run. It mentions a cabal of Dutch and Boers who were extremely anti-British as well as antagonising the neighbouring countries, presumably this included the Cape Colony and, to a lesser extent, the Orange Free State. The mining industry and much valuable property were also at risk and the whole situation was likely to cause conflict between the *Uitlanders* and the State which would put thousands of women and children in danger from the well-armed Boers. For this reason, they appealed to Jameson to come to their aid if disturbances broke out.

The document was cleverly worded and seems to have been for a wider consumption than Jameson alone. It appealed to British patriotism and the country's sense of chivalry and democracy whilst establishing the need to protect the gold mining industry. It also guaranteed the expenses which would be incurred if

---

24   The manifesto was referring to a debate in the *Volksraad*.
25   *The Times*, 1 January 1896. See also C.M Rodney, *Jameson's Ride to Johannesburg* (Johannesburg: Argus Printing and Publishing Co., 1896).

Jameson intervened. Given Rhodes' enormous wealth, this might seem a trifle, but it was another example of an invitation to expand the Empire at minimum cost.

Almost immediately after handing the letter to Jameson the conspirators had a very rapid change of heart and correctly feared that signing such a document, especially as it was undated, might make them very vulnerable. On the following day, they asked Dr Jim to hand it back. 'It's gone to Cape Town on the last train', was Jameson's less than honest response.[26] The Reformers, in an attempt to ease their predicament, made it clear to Jameson that he was not to come to their aid until they sent for him.

Colonel Rhodes, in his evidence to the Inquiry, puts the issue of who should initiate the incursion very clearly. 'Our point is that it was never left to Dr Jameson to choose his own time; that he was absolutely not to use this letter until he heard from us. That is my own conviction, and it is the conviction of the rest of us. I think, Dr Jameson states the other thing, and that is his conviction'.[27] A very gentlemanly response which avoided directly accusing Jameson of lying. Such misunderstandings again suggests the fatal weakness of this complicated plot; it rested not upon the direction of a single mind, but upon the co-ordination of several, each of which had its own hoped-for outcome.

Jameson returned to Bechuanaland to prepare for his rescue mission but the *Uitlander* leaders of the Reform Society were desperately occupied in attempting to find an alternative way of obtaining the improvements they wished without having to recourse to an uprising. Chamberlain and Sir Hercules Robinson were also in communication about the *Uitlanders'* plight and on 6 December 1895, the Colonial Secretary sent the High Commissioner a telegram which stated that, if the *Uitlanders* would accept the British Flag, they could elect their own governor. He also warned Loch of the necessity of avoiding a fiasco.[28] Chamberlain had acquired a reputation of duplicity and unreliability, which on this occasion infuriated Rhodes since the telegram was unclear whether Chamberlain supported or encouraged the Raid or not. Rhodes was very angry and, according to Bower, threatened to ruin Chamberlain if he proved to be deceitful. Rumours and worries that Jameson might do something hot headed began to gather strength. Frank Newton, Commissioner for the Bechuanaland Protectorate, appears to have been persuaded by the charismatic Jameson into agreeing to assist him by accompanying his force when the time arrived. In a telegram to Rhodes, Jameson claimed that Newton had 'expressed a strong wish to go with us … to the Johannesburg races.'[29] However, once away from Jameson's influence, and in the safety of Cape Town, in a discussion with Bower around 18 December the two debated Jameson's potential act of piracy. Newton confided that he was concerned by the bellicose talk amongst Jameson's officers at Pitsani. Bower put this down to the tall talk of young officers and dissuaded Newton from resigning. This buccaneering was likely to be prevented, suggested Bower, as there seemed to be a conspiracy between Chamberlain and Rhodes in which the former was pushing the latter. Hands were being dirtied when they should have been kept clean.[30] Newton was convinced by this argument and took no further part in the Raid. It was becoming apparent, that planning a conspiracy was different from putting one into action. Bower informed Rhodes of Newton's concerns that something unexpected might happen but the 'Colossus' refused to take them seriously. He felt that Jameson would be happy to wait on the border for years which satisfied Bower since they both trusted Jameson to keep a wise head.

---

26   Rodney, *Jameson's Ride to Johannesburg*, p. 325.
27   Colvin, *The Life of Jameson, Vol: II*, p. 38.
28   Schreuder & Butler, *Bower's Secret History* p. 47.
29   South African Republic, *Report of the Select Committee on the Jameson Raid into the Territory of South African Republic* (Cape of Good Hope Parliament House, 1897), Appendix p. 188 (Henceforth Cape Report). 'The Races' was a frequently employed euphemism for a possible incursion into the Transvaal.
30   Cape Report, p. 50.

4

Christmas at Highbury

On 9 December 1895 Chamberlain left Westminster and returned to Highbury Hall in Birmingham, his family home, where he was to remain for three weeks. He maintained connections with the Colonial Office through his Red Boxes and was in constant touch with his staff, working like a Trojan. He continued to receive very contradictory opinions regarding how likely an imminent rising of the *Uitlanders* was. Meade, for example, on 16 December, reported an interview with Flora Shaw of *The Times* which had taken place two days previously during which she had expounded her views about the happenings in the Transvaal. She told Meade about an interview with Dr W.J. Leyds, who was the Secretary of State for the Transvaal, in preparation for an article in *The Times* on the Transvaal situation. Leyds claimed he had come to Europe to seek medical treatment but *The Times* journalist believed, however, that he had really come to seek foreign support with which to thwart Rhodes' and Jameson's plans. During the interview, Leyds had intimated that German public opinion was greatly in favour of teaching Rhodes and Jameson a lesson. Likewise, she informed Meade that the French journal, *Gaulois*, had published a series of articles which were very pro-Boer and which claimed that whatever happened in the Transvaal would not be to Britain's advantage. Even *The Times*, would cast doubt as to whether the *Uitlanders* and their supporters were strong enough to bring Kruger down, since his administration was organised for the exclusive 'advantage of a privileged few' and could 'long resist the force of enlightened public opinion.'[1] This meeting between Meade and Flora Shaw is interesting as Chamberlain's Permanent Secretary felt it worth reporting to his Master which suggests that Flora Shaw's relationship with the Colonial Office staff was of more significance than that of a newspaper reporter simply passing on idle gossip. As will be revealed, Flora Shaw played a significant part in the later events.[2]

On the same day as *The Times'* article appeared, 16 December, Edward Fairfield wrote to Chamberlain predicting that nothing would happen in the Transvaal before the New Year and probably a good deal after the start of 1896. Those *Uitlander* companies not within Rhodes' sphere of influence did not expect an immediate crisis and it was likely that the next move would be that another deputation would approach the Government in Pretoria to demand reform. These demands would, of course, be rejected and only then might action be taken. Thus, Chamberlain was confronted with two conflicting predictions as to whether an uprising by the *Uitlanders* would or would not take place.

On 18 December, events on the other side of the world suddenly affected Rhodes' and Jameson's plans and preoccupied Lord Salisbury's Government, of which Chamberlain was of course, a prominent member. In 1840 the boundary between British Guyana and the newly established Venezuela had been fixed by Britain but the decision had not been confirmed by the Republic of Venezuela which claimed that it had inherited a greater part of the British Guyana's lands from Spain; Venezuela's old imperial ruler. This dispute had rumbled

---

1   *The Times*, 16 December 1895.
2   For further Flora Shaw biographical particulars, see Chapter 19 and *Oxford Dictionary of National Biography* <https://www.oxforddnb.com/view/10.1093/ref:odnb/9780198614128.001.0001/odnb-9780198614128-e-1000898>

on for fifty years, and the United States had suggested that the quarrel go to arbitration. Both Rosebery and Salisbury had strongly argued that the disputed land was an integral part of British Guiana. The situation then took a serious turn when the Venezuelan Government cunningly gave a concession within the disputed lands to an American company and United States President Cleveland, adopting a broad interpretation of the Monroe Doctrine which did not just forbid new European colonies, but declared an American interest in any matter within the hemisphere, decided to intervene. On 18 December, Cleveland issued an ultimatum that the United States would establish a Committee of Arbitration in which Britain must take part or otherwise face the threat of war.[3] Reluctantly Salisbury's government, responding to public opinion which felt that such a trivial matter needed a peaceful settlement rather than a bellicose one, agreed to the arbitration. Ironically, the Committee awarded most of the disputed land to Britain.[4]

Although much of the negotiations over Guyana's future were carried out by Salisbury and the British Ambassador to the United States, Sir Julian Paunceforte, Chamberlain was greatly taxed by the affair as it involved one of Britain's colonies. Whilst the dilemma of a possible incursion into the Transvaal slowly ripened, a distracted Chamberlain '…allowed hardly a day to pass without writing letters and conducting interviews to find a way out of the Guyana dilemma without 'showing a white feather or a provocative red flag'.[5] Even the hard working Chamberlain must have struggled to keep abreast of these two issues as well as his many other concerns. He had to rely on the information and its interpretation provided by his senior subordinates in the Colonial Office to keep him up to date; an issue which was to figure later in the story.

Sir Robert Meade, Chamberlain's Permanent Secretary, galvanised by Cleveland's intervention over the Guyana crisis and the anti-British feelings in Europe, wrote to the Secretary of State that he supposed that Chamberlain would prefer the *Uitlander* uprising to be postponed for at least a year in order to concentrate of the Guyana issue. If this was Chamberlain's wish, the postponement should be agreed immediately to prevent Rhodes rushing into an action which would probably be supported by the Gold Magnates. A delay would cause them to have second thoughts, since an uprising would have a negative effect on the South African mining stock market. Fairfield, the Assistant Under Secretary, and the Colonial Office's expert on South Africa affairs, argued that Meade would be able to arrange the postponement without compromising Chamberlain's position.

Delay and prevarication continued, and it seems that the officials, both in South Africa and London, had begun to accept that an uprising would not happen, at least for the time being. On 18 December, Chamberlain sent a message to Permanent Secretary Meade which became known as the 'Hurry Up' telegram. It suggested that intervention in the Transvaal:

> [S]hould either come *at once* or be postponed for a year or two at least … If not, we had better not interfere … for we may bring about the very thing we want to avoid … then the responsibility must rest with Rhodes and we had better abstain from giving advice.'[6]

Chamberlain's attitude towards the proposed uprising seems ambiguous but there were those, like Flora Shaw, who believed that the Colonial Secretary wanted immediate action in Johannesburg.

The faithful Fairfield tried to persuade James Maguire, Rhodes' go-between when the he was not in England, that the uprising should be postponed but admitted to his Chief that, in spite of all his efforts, his

---

3   C. McKnight Nichols, *Promise and Peril: America at the Dawn of a Global Age* (Cambridge, Massachusetts: Harvard University Press, 2011), p. 39.

4   Venezuela reiterated its claim in 1962 when it proposed that the commission had acted improperly because of a secret deal between Britain and Russia. Britain denied the accusation and the dispute still remains unsettled to this day.

5   Garvin, The *Life of Joseph Chamberlain*, Vol III, p. 67.

6   Garvin, The *Life of Joseph Chamberlain*, Vol. III, p. 72 Chamberlain's emphasis.

arguments for postponement had fallen on deaf ears. However, since the value of South African stocks had already collapsed to a very low level, an uprising would probably not have the negative effect on the value of the market which had been previously predicted. It would be best, Fairfield reasoned, if the uprising occurred as soon as possible. Rochfort Maguire, on 20 December, telegraphed *Groote Schuur* to this effect. However, Fairfield seems not to have told Maguire that Chamberlain had suggested that the decision as to whether an uprising should take place should be left for Rhodes to make.[7]

On 28 December, Fairfield wrote to Chamberlain that he had met Bouchier Hawksley, Rhodes' solicitor, who was annoyed that the revolution in Johannesburg had fizzled out. He was concerned that Rhodes would be so angry that he would order Jameson to 'go in' with the BSAC's police and 'manipulate a revolution' which would breach the Charter.[8] This letter mentions both the uprising in Johannesburg and a possible Jameson incursion. Clear evidence of the Colonial Office's knowledge of Rhodes' plan. On 30 December, Chamberlain sent a confidential message to Robinson saying he believed the uprising would not happen, but that Rhodes and Jameson would try to force matters by an incursion from Bechuanaland using police. Robinson was to remind Rhodes that the Charter would be at risk and he would not be supported by Chamberlain.[9] Chamberlain had clearly absorbed Fairfield's information and correctly linked Jameson and the use of police from Bechuanaland as elements in a possible incursion.

Garvin, Chamberlain's biographer, was keen to portray his subject in a positive light but, as Lady Longford writes, Chamberlain's detailed knowledge could be seen as very compromising when considering whether he and the Colonial Office knew about a potential Raid and how much they were actively involved.[10] Chamberlain's involvement and possible prior knowledge of the Raid became a key issue of investigation for the Select Committee of Inquiry which took place after the Raid's failure.[11]

---

7   E. Reiz (ed.) *Cambridge History of the British Empire*, Vol. III (London: CUP, 1959). p.359.
8   Garvin, *The Life of Joseph Chamberlain*,p,81. Fairfield seemed to think that Jameson was at Gaberones in Botswana not Pitsani.
9   Quoted in Longford, *Jameson's Raid*, p. 228.
10 J. Van der Poel, *The Jameson Raid*. H. Marshall Hole, *The Jameson Raid*, E. Longford, *Jameson's Raid*.
11 HMSO, *Second Report from the Select Committee on British South Africa*. (London: Eyre & Spottiswoode, 1897). (Henceforth Select Committee Report).

5

Christmas at Groote Schuur and Pitsani

There can be no question that Rhodes knew, or at least thought he knew, what was going on at Pitsani and Johannesburg and believed that he was in control. On 20 December he had received Maguire's telegram which suggested that the plan had the full support of Chamberlain who wanted quick action. Telegrams, were busily exchanged between all sides as Rhodes and Jameson became more determined to act and the Reformers increasingly keen to prevent them doing so.[1] However, as Christmas Day arrived, it was clear that the uprising would not take place on the scheduled day; 28 December, as the Uitlanders got colder and colder feet. Even Rhodes' brother, Frank, telegraphed Jameson that, '…the polo tournament was postponed for one week or it would clash with race week.'[2] Dr Jim's frustrated response was particularly scathing. He suggested that Frank was more bothered by such trivia as the Races when others were prepared to take risks and the longer the uprising was delayed, the greater was the risk of discovery.[3] Colonel Rhodes had already shown his indifference to Jameson's plot for when Dr Jim came to visit the Colonel for a previously agreed meeting, Frank had left a note which excused him from the meeting as he had an appointment to teach Mrs X how to ride a bike. As the details for the planning the Raid unfolded, it is difficult to disagree with Lady Longford that Rhodes had made a major error in not giving command at Pitsani to his brother and let Jameson use his dynamic personality to influence the Reformers in Johannesburg.

The reluctant Reformers then came up with another ingenious excuse for a delay. Alfred Beit, who had just landed at Cape Town and was a guest at *Groote Schuur*, had promised to defray half the cost of the uprising. They demanded, through John Hays Hammond, that Beit come to Johannesburg immediately and help the Reformers sort out their difficulties. Beit was in poor health and Rhodes believed that he was more likely to be influenced by the Reformers' timidity than encourage them to revolt. He persuaded Beit to send telegrams on the 19 and 20 December to Lionel Phillips, Chairman of the Johannesburg Chamber of Mines and a prominent *Uitlander*, which stated that 'our foreign supporters urge immediate flotation'; and 'Immediate flotation is the thing most desired, as we never know what may hinder it if it is now delayed.'

Rhodes, through Rutherfoord Harris, also tried to persuade his brother Frank to get on with it. In a telegram of 21 December he urged that Frank should; 'Reply when you can float in your opinion so that I can advise Dr Jameson.' On 23 December the 'Colossus' informed Dr Jim that the '…Company would be floated on 28 December', but he must not start until 2000 hours. A delighted Jameson replied on the following day that he would do all he could to delay until the Saturday but he was finding the Reformers

---

1   The word 'Telegram' is employed throughout this volume, but includes both cablegrams, communications sent by cable from overseas and telegrams – communications by telegraph. Unless otherwise stated, the information regarding the series of telegrams in this section is derived from E.G. Garrett, & F.J. Edwards, *The Story of an African Crisis* (London: Archibald Constable, 1897); Longford Jameson's *Raid;* Colvin, *The Life of Jameson, Vol. II;* Fitzpatrick, *The Transvaal from Within.*

2   Ash, *The If Man,* p. 227.

3   Millin, Rhodes, p. 275.

Cecil Rhodes and Alfred Beit: Brothers in wealth and ambition. (Open source)

shilly-shallying intolerable. Rutherfoord Harris also telegraphed Jameson urging him to respect Rhodes' directive. Dr Henry Wolff, an American doctor in Kimberley and a friend of Rhodes, had set off for Johannesburg and, it was thought, Wolff would be able to galvanise the Reformers into action. Rutherfoord Harris also warned Frank Rhodes that Jameson's mind was made up and he would not allow the delay to go into the New Year.

Dr Wolff had also been responsible for preparing supply depots on Jameson's planned route into the Transvaal and he had set up five sheds at roughly 30 miles apart each of which contained bully beef, biscuits, and forage for the horses. His excuse for such an action was for 'The Rand Produce and Trading Company' which, he informed the Boers, was created in an attempt at ironing out the fluctuating prices of corn and mealies in Johannesburg where these staples were in great demand.[4] Wolff also purchased several hundred horses and established a remount station on the farm of Mr Abraham Malan. Wolff claimed that he was going to set up a new transport service from Johannesburg to the Rand. The total cost of Wolff's preparations was £18,000, roughly £2.3 million at modern prices.

Rather than uniting the Reformers, these telegrams brought their disagreements to a head. They could not decide whether their future State would be an independent republic or a British colony or even remain a part of a reformed ZAR. The new date for the uprising was set as 4 January but, to confuse the Boers, a general meeting was announced for the 6 January. These disagreements, they argued, must be thrashed out personally with Rhodes. Consequently, on Boxing Day, the increasingly frustrated Jameson received a telegram from his brother Sam, who was in Johannesburg, which said that it was absolutely necessary that Dr Jim postpone his action. The Reformers would try to sort things out during the remaining days of December, but no movement should be made until Jameson received the go-ahead from them. Rutherfoord Harris confirmed the content of Sam's message but described the delay as 'too awful'.

By the 27 December, Jameson's frustration now reached its peak and he felt that he could no longer depend on the vacillations of the Reformers. Their hand must be forced, and, to this effect, Jameson telegraphed his brother Sam that his men had already set off to cut the telegraph wires and he expected the 'go ahead' from Hays Hammond. Jameson also telegraphed Rutherfoord Harris that he expected to receive a telegram by 0900 hours on Saturday which authorised the incursion. Later in the day, through a combination of increasing anger and frustration, Jameson informed Rutherfoord Harris that it was too late for him to stop the wire cutting. It was important to stick to the original plan and, unless the *Uitlanders* rose in the next two days, he would act using the *Letter of Invitation,* which he had now dated as 20 December 1895, as his justification. The reply to this ultimatum came from Hays Hammond who absolutely condemned Jameson's intended action. Lionel Phillips added to this censure by predicting complete failure.

On 27 December, Rhodes, in a telegram to Jameson, indicated that he was aware that some might regard the '600' men at Pitsani with suspicion but it couldn't be helped.'[5] In a telegram to his brother on the following day Rhodes urged him to 'keep the market firm'; to stiffen the resolve of the Reformers and to urged Jameson to hold back.[6] Rhodes was clearly having a change of heart. He had been informed by a

---

4   Mealies is South African parlance for maize.
5   *Cape Report*, Appendix QQ, ccxxxvi.
6   *Cape Report.*, Appendix QQ, ccxl.

member of the Cape Legislative Council that rumours were spreading that an invasion was planned. Rhodes' reaction to this was an attempt to allay fears by claiming the police on the Bechuanaland border were simply being gathered together for redistribution and he telegraphed Jameson to this effect.[7] One can detect the basic misunderstanding in Rhodes' response. Jameson wanted to act quickly before the Boers could assemble a force strong enough to prevent his incursion. Rhodes, on the other hand wanted to wait, keeping Jameson in the wings for future use.[8] Rhodes continued discussions with representatives of the Reformers and seems to have acknowledged that, for the moment, the Raid would not take place. He also thought that Jameson was aware of this and had accepted the delay. Rhodes, grasping the seriousness of the situation sent for Sir Hercules Robinson and told him the revolt in Johannesburg had fizzled out.[9] Robinson immediately telegraphed Chamberlain that the revolt had collapsed, and the Reformers would probably try to get the best possible terms from Kruger through negotiation.[10]

Rumours and worries that Jameson might do something hot headed began to gather strength. Bower described a discussion with Rhodes on 28 December 1895 which mentioned that there were a number of Americans amongst the Uitlanders who rejected Chamberlain's offer of the British Flag and hence would not revolt. The real reason, argued Bower, was they were afraid of a fight.[11] Bower may have been correct, but their reluctance may not have been based on a lack of courage but rather on self-interest. Bower went on to point out that 'The bottom is knocked out of the revolution now. 'No one expects Rothschild to die waving a red flag on a barricade and our local Rothschilds are not built that way.'

The question of under which Flag a revolt would take place was considered to be an important one. Hays Hammond claimed that the flag issue was used by Kruger's agents to attempt to convince the American and non-British *Uitlanders* that the revolt was a plan by Rhodes to impose British rule at the expense of American bloodshed and money.[12] Hammond described a meeting of 500 of his fellow Americans in Johannesburg in December 1895 which had begun to get out of hand because Kruger's spies were deliberately disrupting the meeting. Hammond, who was a manager of Rhodes' mines, took the stage and declared that any revolution would be launched under the Boer Flag and would aim to remove Kruger, his cronies and their incipient corruption. "I will shoot any man who hoists a flag but the Boer Flag", was Hammond's declaration. It proved persuasive and only five of the 500 present voted against acting.[13] Hammond's involvement, as we shall see, almost cost him his life. Most of the ordinary miners probably couldn't care less about the flag under which they lived. They were in the Transvaal for the money and, providing they were able to get at the gold, they did not worry too much about the vote. The clear drivers of the unrest were the professionals and the investors in the mines who were keen to be able to influence how the ZAR was run.

To Jameson, the idea of waiting, or that the Reformers had lost heart, seemed to contradict information he had seen from a Reuter's telegram which had been exhibited at Pitsani. It suggested that the Reformers had not lost their determination, and, perhaps more significantly, the Transvaal authorities were aware of the plot.[14] Jameson's response was to send a crucial telegram to Rhodes which declared that, unless he heard to the contrary, he would leave with his men the following evening (Sunday 29 December).

Much has been made as to whether the timing of this telegram was deliberate or not. It was sent on a Saturday and whether Jameson expected Rhodes to monitor the telegraph office at Cape Town at a weekend

7   *Cape Report*, Appendix QQ ccxxxvi.
8   H. Marshall Hole, *The Jameson Raid*, p. 136.
9   Select Committee Report. Evidence Given by Bower, Question 2564: Henceforth Evidence from the Report will be identified with the abbreviation Q followed by the reference number.
10   Colonial Office, Blue *Book*, 7933, No. 3, 1896.
11   Colonial Office, *Blue Book*, 7933, No. 3, pp. 60-61.
12   Hays Hammond, *The Truth about the Jameson Raid*, p. 4.
13   Hays Hammond, *The Truth about the Jameson Raid*, p. 45.
14   *Select Committee Report*, p. ix.

or, knowing that weekends were not proper working days and telegrams would languish until the following Monday, has been frequently discussed. It seems likely that Jameson did not expect a reply until it was too late as was evidenced by a further telegram sent to his brother, Sam, in Johannesburg which stated, 'I shall start without fail tomorrow night.' Finally, Jameson sent his last telegram to Cape Town, addressed to Rutherfoord Harris, Secretary of the BSAC. It indicated that he would leave that night and the purpose of the incursion was to save lives and allow the Reformers to change the 'present dishonest government' so the *Uitlanders* would obtain the vote.[15] It is clear that Jameson thought that his move would force the Reformers into action by either bolstering their courage or increasing their fear of the consequences to them if Jameson and his men failed.

Again, Jameson seems to have taken steps that this message would not reach Rhodes in time for the 'Colossus' to attempt to prevent him moving. It was handed in at 0905 hours at the Mafeking office and arrived in Cape Town at 1030 hours. It was unlikely there would be anyone senior enough on that Sunday morning to react to the news. The Mafeking telegraph office was closed at 1130 hours and the telegraph wire between it and Cape Town was cut as was the line to Pitsani. This isolated Jameson and his men from possible contrary orders from Cape Town. Unfortunately, the wire to Pretoria was not cut and, ironically, Kruger was kept well informed of Jameson's actions. On 29 December, at sunset, Jameson's 500 men mounted and set off towards Johannesburg; the Raid had begun.

Sir William Harcourt, in a speech in the Commons, drew the House's attention to a letter which Sir Graham Bower had sent to Rhodes on the 30 December. Bower claimed to have heard by 2300 hours on 29 December, that Jameson was contemplating an incursion into the Transvaal. In spite of attempts to call upon Rhodes in person on a number of occasions, Bower had failed to find him. He therefore had to recourse to writing to Rhodes to warn him that Sir Hercules Robinson wanted him to know that the Government repudiated the Raid. It was an illegal act which would bring severe punishment on the Raiders and would result in the revocation of the Charter. Harcourt expressed surprised that Rhodes, Managing Director of the BSAC and Prime Minister of Cape Colony, was not present in Cape Town at a moment of crisis for both organisations.[16] He was at *Groot Schuur.*

---

15   *Select Committee Report*, p. 273 Appendix CC, ccxiv.
16   *Hansard*, House of Commons Debate, 8 May 1896, Vol. 40, cols. 893-940.

6

They're off!

Jameson had originally promised the Reformers that he would bring a force of 1,500 men but, in the end, he only had 500 at his back. In the afternoon of 29 December, Jameson had formed his troops in a square and addressed them about the coming action. He read extracts from the Reformers' *Invitation Letter* which spoke of the need to rescue women and children from tyranny and the need to defend *Uitlander* property. The phrase about women and children stuck in every memory and it is possible that Jameson might also have been referring to a very recent report from Reuters which had described women and children fleeing from Johannesburg. He is also reported to have stated that there would be no shot fired and they would get through without any fighting at all. Jameson probably anticipated that this would be the case since his hope of success depended upon the element of surprise. He reassured his more aggressive listeners that, if they had to fight, they were well prepared to do so and the Pitsani men would be joined by the Bechuanaland Border Police stationed at Mafeking.

The *Letter of Invitation* in Jameson's hands became an appeal to the honour of his troops with regard to their duty to defend their British countrymen and women in an hour of need. He also mentioned that the Reformers had agreed to pay any reasonable expenses, which was both a temptation to the troops and an indication of the seriousness of the Reformers' situation. Although the letter had been written in the past, the situation it described was represented as being that of the present. The fact that it had not been dated was, of course, to Jameson's advantage and enabled him to begin the Raid with the necessary justification available whenever he was ready.

The Doctor went on to outline his plan. The BBP would march simultaneously from Mafeking and rendezvous with the Mashonaland Mounted Police (MMP) at Malmani. The Reformers would march out of Johannesburg to join the combined force as they approached the town. Boer lives and property would be respected but Jameson's men would defend themselves if attacked. Although accounts differ it seems that Jameson's usual charismatic oratory did the trick and the men were eager to go. Sir John Willoughby, the military commander, and Major (Captain) Robert White, Willoughby's senior staff officer, were bit part players in this opening act of the drama and it was Jameson alone who influenced the men to agree to join his enterprise. The cheering parade was dismissed singing 'Rule Britannia' and the troops entered into a hive of activity of making final preparations for the ride. The men were given one day's rations, and each received 50lb of feed for their horse. Ammunition for the Lee Speed magazine rifles was also handed out; 120 rounds per man. Six Maxims and one 12½-pdr field gun and their respective ammunition were also made ready for the advance.

Jameson's officers were less enthusiastic than their men since they realised that they had much more to lose. Willoughby was approached by some of his subordinates, who were concerned that Jameson's plan might cost them their commissions. In retrospect one might question why so many serving regular officers were on Jameson's staff rather than with their regiments. Although it was not an uncommon practice at that time for officers to seek service in adventurous activities, they must have been granted leave by their respective commanding officers and knew that by joining the Raid they were putting their future careers at risk if

Women and children fleeing Johannesburg in anticipation of a Boer attack. (*Illustrated London News,* 1896)

Bechuanaland Border Police from which Jameson drew many of his recruits. (*The Graphic,* 1896)

Jameson's plan went awry. Willoughby reassured them that they were not to worry since they were immune from the War Office, the Imperial Authorities, as well as the BSAC and its Directors. Subsequently, when questioned how he knew this, Willoughby, after a lot of obfuscation, said the he had been told this was the case by Jameson.[1] Willoughby subsequently provided a clearer explanation for his actions in a letter written to Redvers Buller, the Adjutant General. He claimed that he had been informed by Jameson that they were acting on the orders of the Imperial authorities and he quoted the names of other officers who would also bear witness to this fact.[2]

The *Uitlander* leaders in Johannesburg were increasingly concerned that the telegrams they had sent to Jameson did not have sufficient potency to dissuade the hot-headed Doctor from carrying out his plan. They sent two messengers, Captain Harry Holden and the American, Major Maurice Heany, both

Jameson calls for volunteers to rescue the people of Johannesburg.
(*Illustrated London News*, 1896)

BSAC Officers, to make completely certain that the Raid would not start without the Reformers' express agreement. Holden rode from Johannesburg and was supposed to change horses at Malan's farm where Wolff's mounts were stabled, but he decided to continue the journey on his own horse and he covered the 170 miles ride in 72 hours. It would later transpire that Wolff had, perhaps been taken in by his own subterfuge of providing horses for a transport system, since many of the horses he had obtained were more suitable to pull coaches than to act as remounts for troopers. Holden's monumental efforts to get to Pitsani, however, seemed to have made Jameson even more determined.

Major Heany also had a difficult journey. He chose to travel by rail and caught the train from Bloemfontein to Kimberley. Rutherfoord Harris had arranged for a 'special' train to link with the mail train from Kimberley to Mafeking. Heany was, perhaps a strange choice for the task of dissuading Jameson, since before he began his mission, he indicated he felt that it would be a waste of time. He was a close friend of Jameson and he would do his best to try to persuade him from taking his peremptory action but he believed that, once the Doctor had made up his mind to do anything, he usually carried it through. It was the American's opinion that Jameson would come to Johannesburg 'as sure as Fate'.[3] Arriving at Mafeking, Heany thought that the town was in a 'queer state' and on alighting at Pitsani from the cart he had hired, he read the message from the Reformers to Jameson from his notebook so there could be no misunderstanding. Both Heany and

---

1   *Select Committee Report*, Willoughby's response. See Q. 5517,5518,5525.
2   Marshall Hole, *The Jameson Raid*, p. 157. The other officers named were Major H. F. White, Captains R Grey and R White. For a complete list of Jameson's Force see Appendix I.
3   Select Committee Report, Q.5484, *et seq.*

Holden claimed that they had carried no personal messages other than instructions not to act. There could be no accusation of duplicity or misunderstanding on the part of the Reformers. Heany, in his evidence before the Select Committee described how Jameson went outside the bell tent in which they were meeting for about 20 minutes to think through his response to the Reformers' message. He then returned with his mind made up to proceed as planned.[4]

The decision to enter the Transvaal on that summer's evening was, in reality, Jameson's alone. It was not authorised by Rhodes and the suggestion that it had been ordered by the Imperial authorities, as Jameson had hinted, was most unlikely. Rhodes had failed to react on the 28 December by not sending Jameson a definitive and direct 'No'. Even the impulsive Dr Jim would have found it hard to disobey a direct order from his superior. Perhaps he thought that Rhodes really wanted his Raid to take place but was being cautious about openly sponsoring it. He may even have thought that the 'Imperial Authorities', perhaps an oblique reference to Chamberlain, were of a similar mind as both Rhodes and the Authorities were familiar with the plan but unaware that Jameson would put it into action on 29 December. Rutherfoord Harris was also in the know as he had received a final telegram from Jameson which stated, *'Shall leave for the Transvaal tonight.'* Wolff was instructed by the Doctor to perform the necessary wire-cutting and meet him on route in order to help the Raiders decide on the best way into Johannesburg.

At Mafeking the situation was somewhat different; the camp of the BBP, unlike the camp at Pitsani Potlugo, was surrounded by a busy township and secrecy was therefore harder to maintain. The bustle of preparation could not but suggest to these experienced troops and, perhaps, the townsfolk, that there was something afoot. A rumour was circulating that the BBP were preparing to fight Linchwe, the Chief identified as a threat to Rhodes' proposed railway line. It was Major (Captain) Charles Coventry who was to reveal the truth; that Johannesburg was the real destination. Someone asked him the key question which had troubled Jameson's officers at Pitsani; were they going under the Queen's or the BSAC's orders? Lieutenant Colonel (Captain) Raleigh Grey, the BBP commander, appears to have been less reluctant than Jameson in stating the truth about the Raid's purpose, and told these doubters that they were not going to fight for the Queen; but for the supremacy of the British Flag in South Africa. The Raiders were left to work out what this actually meant. Most, but not all of the BBP, had accepted the offer to transfer to the BSAC force and were awaiting their discharge which was being organised by Inspector Fuller (Captain) of the Cape Police. When the ex-BBP was paraded, those who had not agreed to transfer were mustered separately and Grey and Coventry attempted to persuade these men to join the others in entering the Transvaal. It was not an easy task but twelve of the reluctant ex-BBP troops changed their minds and joined their less hesitant comrades. One of those who resisted the officers' blandishments, Sergeant James White, would figure later in the story. He was to claim, at the trial of the Raiders at the Bow Street Magistrates' court, that he refused to join because he was a married man and could not afford to 'knock about ' in an irregular corps.

Major White, Willoughby's Chief Staff Officer, who had come to Mafeking to see Grey's preparations, tried to persuade Fuller to assist in putting pressure on the remaining dissenters but he refused arguing that he was in the Cape Government's service not the BSAC. Having failed to obtain information as to where the column was going, Fuller threatened to report Grey's activities to the authorities. Those authorities were locally represented by the Resident Magistrate at Mafeking, the thirty-three-year-old, George Boyes, who, having heard cheering from the BBP's camp realised that something unusual was taking place. His curiosity was further raised when, his neighbour, Colonel Grey, rode past Boyes' house and mundanely called out, 'I have left my gauntlets under the chair on the veranda' and – having picked them up – rode off, shouting out in the dusk to another neighbour, 'Good-bye, Sam.' His curiosity further aroused, Boyes went to his Club and found it in a buzz of speculation and excitement. It would seem that Jameson's fears that the locals in

---

4   *Select Committee Report*, Q.5449.

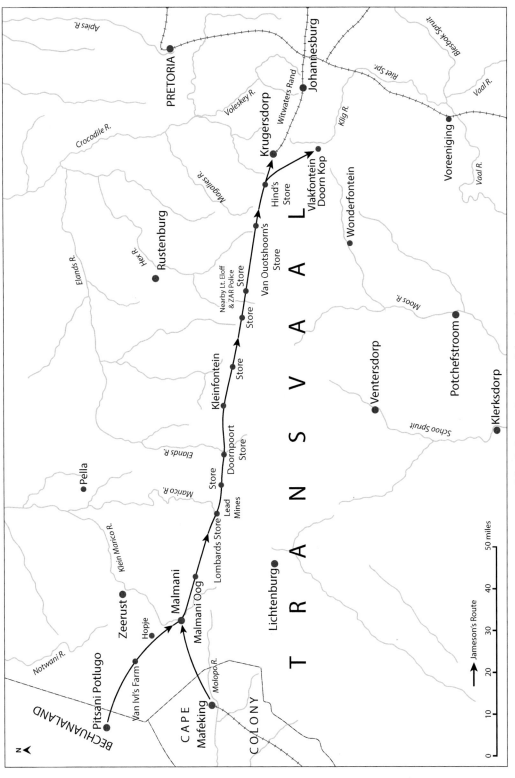

Map 3 Jameson's route to Johannesburg.

Mafeking would guess his plan were ill founded for, in spite of his key position in the town, Boyes seems to have been completely unaware of the real reason for the BBP's preparations.

Two of Jameson's troopers were sent out to cut the telegraph lines in order to maintain the element of surprise which was an essential part of the plan. However, the Boers subsequently claimed that these men were both careless and drunk! What other explanation, they argued, could there be for the fact that although the line to the Cape was cut and both Mafeking and Pitsani were also cut off, the indirect line to Pretoria via Zeerust and Rustenburg was not cut. Consequently, Kruger knew of Jameson's progress by 1400 hours on Monday 30 December. Jameson claimed that the Reformers had failed to keep a promise made before the Raid began to cut the line nearer Johannesburg. Once the Raid was over the Boers made much of the errors made by the Raiders and the accusation of drunkenness figure frequently in the Boers' account of the event.

The BBP left Mafeking at around 0900 hours and began the 26-mile journey to Malmani (Ottoshoop), which was the place chosen for the two columns to meet.[5] The early part of its journey had been observed by Sub-Inspector Brown, who, on Fuller's instructions had trailed the column in order to determine its destination; further evidence that Inspector Fuller was in ignorance of the plan. Once he was sure of the BBP's intentions, Brown returned to Mafeking and reported to Fuller who felt it necessary to acquaint Magistrate Boyes with this information. Boyes was angry and could not understand why Fuller had delayed for so long in passing on his suspicions. It is possible that Fuller wanted to be sure of the ex-BBP men's intentions rather than look foolish in front of his superiors. However, by withholding his suspicions, he was made to look even more foolish.

The union of the two forces occurred at around 0500 hours on the morning of 30 December. The now united force consisted of 512 troopers, roughly 30 pack horses led by 75 native Africans, 8 'Scotch carts', 9 two wheeled carts with a detachable rear panel, and 3 larger Cape Carts, all drawn by horses or mules. These transports were loaded with ammunition and supplies. Heavier fire power was provided by the eight Maxim Machine guns, at one time described as, 'the weapon most associated with British imperial conquest' and their 45,000 rounds together with one 12½ pounder and two 7 pounders each with 120 rounds.[6] The column advanced to Malmani Oog, 'the eye of the Malmani', a somewhat desolate place roughly seven miles from Malmani, where the first of Wolff's stores had been deposited. The food for the men consisted of tinned meat and biscuits but it seems that few took advantage of these delicacies as they were so weary from their ride.

The column's order of march was well suited to the work in hand. Captain Lindsell of the Royal Scots Fusiliers rode first with a guide and a patrol of picked men and they were instructed to start half an hour earlier than the main column by day and a quarter of an hour earlier by night. They were followed by the advance guard, consisting of a troop with a Maxim gun, a squadron marching at the head of the main body, followed by four Maxims and the 12½-pdr, the mounted gun detachments, the Cape and Scotch carts under Lieutenant Jesser-Coojie, the Transport Officer. Next came a further squadron and all the led horses, and finally, a rear guard of one troop accompanied by a Maxim. The column arrived at the stores at 0645 hours and rested for around two hours before they proceeded to Nordin Store, a distance of sixteen miles, where they arrived at roughly 1300 hours. Shortly before arriving, the column was overtaken by a rider from Zeerust, roughly 150 miles North West of Johannesburg who carried a message from J.D.L. Botha, Commandant of the Marico District, who wrote in the name of the Commandant General of the Republic, P. J. Joubert. The message warned Jameson that his invasion was against the law of the land and in contravention to international agreements and he should return to Pitsani.[7] Jameson's reply was forthright but polite:

---

5   Malmani was approximately 39 miles from Pitsani.
6   G. Martin, *A History of the Twentieth Century, Vol. I 1900-1933* (New York; William Morrow & Co., 1997), p. 11, Garrett & Edwards, *The Story of an African Crisis*, p. 90.
7   *Cape Report*, pp. 199-200, Appendix A. lxviii.

Jameson and some of his staff on the way to Johannesburg.
(*Illustrated London News*, 1896)

Sir
I am in receipt of your protest … and have to inform you that I intend proceeding with my original plans, which have no hostile intention against the people of the Transvaal; but we are here in reply to an invitation from the principal residents of the Rand in their demand for justice and the ordinary rights of every citizen of a civilised State.
Yours faithfully
L.S. Jameson[8]

It is interesting that Jameson used the *Letter of Invitation* as his rather flimsy excuse for entering the Transvaal rather than the 'so-called' plight of the *Uitlanders* and their women and children. It is also interesting that the news of Jameson's invasion had already reached the ears of Boer officialdom. Kruger was well informed

---

8   *Cape Report*, p. 200, Appendix A. lxix.

Colonel Francis (Frank) William Rhodes CB, DSO. H. Hensman. (*Cecil Rhodes: A Study of a Career.* London; Blackwood & Sons, 1911)

both of Jameson's plans and his presence in the Vaal. The telegraph line was still extant, in spite of Jameson's orders for it to be cut, and this enabled Pretoria to closely monitor the Raid and Kruger was provided with up-to-date details of Jameson's progress. Oom Paul had been warned as early as 22 December by Joubert that the English *Uitlanders* intended to rise on 31 December in an attempt to overthrow his government. It was Rhodes who was behind the scheme and Frank Rhodes, his brother, was in Johannesburg in order to encourage and superintend the uprising there. Commandant General Joubert was also told that there were a number of troops on the Bechuanaland border ready to support the revolt on the pretence that men and women were being killed.[9]

Oom Paul had a favourite saying which was that it was necessary to wait for a tortoise to stick its head out of his shell before it could be killed.[10] The tortoise had finally stuck its head out and Kruger was not slow to prepare to chop it off. It has already been noted that Boer forces were really made up of individuals who responded to the call when danger threatened. They usually came from distances across the veld and it often took time for *Commandos* to assemble. It was Jameson's bad luck that many of these rural Boers had come into Pretoria and Krugersdorp in order to celebrate Christmas with friends and family and this made it easier and quicker for Kruger and his officials to collect together these men to join the local *Commandos* and to quickly form a larger than normal force with which to oppose Jameson and his men. Seen as a threat to their Republic, Orange Free State Boers also formed a *Commando* of 1,600 men, which was accompanied by 4 artillery pieces. This moved to join Kruger's men in accordance with the two Republics' mutual support treaty of 1889.[11] The speed with which Jameson's secret became known and the large numbers gathering together to oppose him meant that his chances of getting through to Johannesburg were diminishing by the hour. However, in spite of his apparent strength, Kruger took the opportunity to have a horse saddled ready as a precaution in case Jameson was successful in reaching Johannesburg.[12]

Boer scouts began to trail the column and Jameson's hope for a surprise entry into Johannesburg steadily decreased. His promise that it would not be necessary to fire a shot now seemed impossible to keep and fighting his way through to the town appeared to be the only method by which the Doctor could achieve his goal. Aware of this and the fear of being attacked by a much larger force ensured that the column continued to advance at a steady pace with little rest through Monday 30 December.

9   J. Meinjies, *The Commandant General* (Cape Town, Tflelber and Uitgewers, 1971), p. 139.
10   Fitzpatrick, *The Transvaal from Within*, p.106.
11   Meinijes, *The Commandant General*, p. 142; Van der Poel, *The Jameson Raid*, p. 115.
12   Van der Poel, *The Jameson Raid*, p. 142.

7

The Reform Committee's Dilemma

Whilst Jameson and his column were advancing as quickly as the tired men and horses could manage, the *Uitlanders* in Johannesburg, especially the Reform leaders, were beginning to panic. Wild rumours began to spread that Jameson had done something idiotic. Sam Jameson had received a coded telegram addressed to Dr Wolff and when Sam translated the message, he realised that it had been sent by his brother from Pitsani Potlugo on Sunday morning. It was somewhat obscure and read as follows:

> Meet me as arranged before you leave on Tuesday night, which will enable us to decide which best destination is. Make Advocate Leonard speak—make cutting to-night without fail.[1]

Wolff could not be found, and the Reformers fretted that Jameson had acted before he had received their order not to begin the invasion. There was still hope, however, that the earlier telegram they had sent to Jameson had persuaded him to wait and the rumours to the contrary were ill-founded. However, a mysterious telegram, written in the terminology of the racetrack, was received by Abe Bailey, a supporter of the Reformers, which made it even more likely that Jameson had left Pitsani. It was sent from Cape Town by '*Godolphin*', whose identity at the time was unknown

> The veterinary surgeon says the horses are now allright (sic); he started with them last night; will reach you on Wednesday he says he can back himself for seven hundred.

Had the Reformers clearly identified who *Godolphin* was they would have become even more alarmed? It was a pseudonym for Rutherfoord Harris who was trying to tell the Reformers that Jameson was on his way without making it too obvious.[2]

It was not until the afternoon of 30 December that indisputable news that Jameson had, in fact, crossed the border, reached the Reformers when, a meeting to discuss the situation was interrupted by a messenger shouting, 'It is all up, boys. He has started in spite of everything. Read this!' The messenger, showed the Reformers a telegram from Mafeking which stated in the usual obtuse terms of commerce and industry which also acted as a code: 'The contractor has started on the earthworks with seven hundred boys; hopes to reach terminus on Wednesday.'[3]

The Reformers were left in a quandary. They had two options; either to deny Jameson and all his works and show themselves to be loyal supporters of Kruger's government by persuading Jameson to return or throw all

---

1   Fitzpatrick, *The Transvaal from Within*, p. 109.
2   Fitzpatrick, *The Transvaal from Within*, p. 109.
3   Fitzpatrick, *The Transvaal from Within*, p. 109.

Volunteers enlisting at Gold field offices for the defence of Johannesburg. (*Illustrated London News,* 1896)

their efforts behind the Doctor and, as his biographer observed, 'pluck the flower of safety from the nettle of danger.'[4]

Like many committees they were indecisive, and they took neither one of these options but tried to combine both. The most adventurous action which the Reformers had hoped to undertake was to capture the fort and magazine at Pretoria. This might have been easier than it seemed because part of the fort's surrounding wall had been removed and this would provide easy access and the garrison was only 100 men; most of whom retired to bed at around 2100 hours. In the fort were stored some 10,000 rifles, 12,000,000 rounds of ammunition and a number of pieces of field artillery. The plan was to seize the fort and carry off as much of its contents as possible by rail and destroy the rest. As the Reformers dallied unsure what to do this plan was abandoned.[5] They distributed such arms as they had and enrolled every sympathetic citizen into what was now designated the *Reform Committee*. They sent a cordial letter to Jameson whom they assumed had started on his invasion under a misapprehension, having not received their messages, and also opened negotiations with President Kruger. Having originally contributed to the pending danger, the Reformers realised that they had a duty to protect the citizens of Johannesburg and began turning it into an armed camp. They had less than 3,000 rifles at their disposal but, for a short period, the Reformers had control of Johannesburg when the Government withdrew the police and they prepared to defend the city.

---

4   Colvin, *The Life of Jameson*, p. 94.
5   Colvin, *The Life of Jameson*, pp.101-02.

Everyday security was placed in the hand of Andrew Trimble, an Irishman, who had been Chief Detective of the Kimberley Police Force. By the end of Tuesday 31 December Trimble's police had taken complete charge of the town, and, according to a somewhat biased Fitzpatrick, from this time until the Committee surrendered to Kruger, Johannesburg had never before or since been so efficiently controlled as during this period.[6] This seems unlikely since De Wet Trossel, who had earlier replaced Trimble in Johannesburg, estimated that there were at least 2,000 criminals operating in Johannesburg and he was alarmed by the laissez-faire nature of the policing enjoyed by the town's underworld and so he had taken steps to improve the quality of the police force.[7]

Various semi-military bodies of men were formed including 'Bettington's Horse' led by Colonel Rowland Bettington which consisted of a group of men formed into a small, but useful, corps of mounted rifles. However, there seems to have been considerable discontent amongst the *Uitlanders*, who found it hard to believe that the Reformers, themselves, were not the ones responsible for the developing crisis and the threat it posed to life and property. Many mines were closed, and the miners were even more disaffected because the Reform Committee was unable to arm them in face of a possible civil war. Anxious men sent their wives and children on trains to Cape Town.

Some of the gold mines stopped work as a result of the impending threat and, in some cases, the miners offered to help in the defence of the town, but others decided to stay and protect their mines. These closures created a large number of unemployed African workers who roamed around the town which was to prove to be a further distraction for the Reform Committee. They were concerned that devil might make use of these idle hands and so were anxious to control the sale of liquor. They approached the resident Magistrate for permission to close the local canteens which sold liquor and, once this was granted, the liquor sellers were warned that, if they disobeyed the order to close, they faced the confiscation of their entire stock. Again, Fitzpatrick praised the Reform Committee's action which he claimed provided the calmest fortnight than any other 14 days in the town's history.

Perhaps the Reform Committee's most difficult task was to prepare to defend the town against possible Boer attack. Plans were put in place and by the end of Tuesday the rifles which the Committee possessed had been distributed and the Maxims placed on the hills surrounding the town. They even began constructing earthworks

The Reform Committee placed an announcement in the *Johannesburg Star* in order to clarify its position:

> Notice is hereby given that this Committee adheres to the National Union Manifesto and reiterates its desire to maintain the independence of the Republic. The fact that rumours are in course of circulation to the effect that a force has crossed the Bechuanaland border renders it necessary to take active steps for the defence of Johannesburg and the preservation of order. The Committee earnestly desires that the inhabitants should refrain from taking any action which can be considered as an overt act of hostility against the Government.[8]

The Reformers also set up a Relief Fund, the first subscribers of which were amongst the key names in Johannesburg, from which support was to be given to those who suffered from the disruption in the town.[9]

The Americans of Johannesburg met on the afternoon of the 30 December to hear the results of a meeting between President Kruger and a Special Deputation from Johannesburg which included Henry C. Perkins

---

6   Fitzpatrick, *the Transvaal from within*, p. 113.
7   Cornelis Hermanus Muller, 'Policing the Witswaterand, A History of the South African Police, 1886-1899', Unpublished PhD. Thesis, Bloemfontein, University of the Free State, 2016, p. 182.
8   *Johannesburg Star*, 31 December 1895.
9   See Appendix IV.

of Rothschild's London Exploration Company and Hennen Jennings of Hermann Eckstein & Company, which had strong links with Alfred Beit. It seems that Kruger received them with interest and listened to the Americans' view of the potential revolt.[10] Natalie Hays Hammond, the wife of John, records that the delegates argued that, although the Americans recognised the rights of both Boer and *Uitlander*, unless Kruger could positively respond in some way to the latter's demands, support for him by the Americans would not be forthcoming and war was likely. Kruger was no doubt disappointed that Franz Von Herff, German Consul in Pretoria, had told him that, although Germany would insist that things did not change, his country would not make war on behalf of the ZAR.[11]

Kruger both attempted to appease the Reformers and negotiate with them. On 31 December food duties were immediately suspended, and this destroyed the monopolies Kruger had granted to favoured friends. Two 'representatives' of the Government, Eugene Marais, editor of the Boer newspaper, *Land en Volk,* and Abraham Malan, son-in-law of Commandant General Joubert and not to be confused with Commandant H.P. Malan, of the Marico *Commando*, went to Johannesburg to meet the Reform Committee. They were reported to have offered the Committee 'an olive branch'.[12] They attempted to reassure the Reformers that the Government was willing to grant most of their requests as outlined in the Manifesto.[13] The two demands which the Government's 'representatives' felt would not be granted without further discussion were the removal of religious disabilities and the granting of the vote.[14] Marais and Malan on their return seem to have reported to the government's Executive Council that, unless something was done to appease the *Uitlanders,* there would be civil war.

The Reform Committee was anxious to take advantage of the supposed 'olive branch', which some thought meant the Government was feeling vulnerable, and elected the lawyer J.G. Auret, Lionel Phillips and Abe Bailey, a prominent mine owner who was to fight in the Second Boer War, to meet the Executive Council's official representatives: Chief Justice Kotzé, Judge Ameshoff and General Jan Kock, who was a member of the Executive Council.[15] When the two groups met in Pretoria on New Year's Day, Kotzé indicated that they were the Executive Council official representatives. Lionel Phillips expressed surprise since he believed that Marais and Malan had filled that role. Was this an example of Kruger's duplicity or simply a misunderstanding on the Reformers part? Kruger was worried about the threats which Jameson's force seemed to pose and the possibility of an uprising in Johannesburg but did not want to be seen as initiating 'peace' talks. When the Raid had failed and the Reformers had been arrested, a confident Kruger explained that Marais and Malan had made a private visit to the town and had no authority to speak on the Executive Council's behalf. However, this seems unlikely to be true as the two 'emissaries' reported back to a meeting of the whole Executive Council.[16] It is questionable whether two private citizens with no authority at all would be allowed to address such an august audience and it is also possible that the two emissaries were part of a plan to waste time whilst Jameson's failure or success became known.

---

10   Natalie Hays Hammond, *A Woman's Part in a Revolution* (London: Longmans Green & Co., 1897), Chapter 2.
11   Van der Poel, *The Jameson Raid*, p. 115.
12   Fitzpatrick, *The Transvaal from Within*, p. 118.
13   See Appendix III.
14   Fitzpatrick, *The Transvaal from Within*, p. 118.
15   John Gilbert Kotzé, Chief Justice of the High Court of the Transvaal, was no friend of Kruger who had stood against Kruger in 1893 Presidential election. In 1898 he was dismissed by Kruger over a judgment on mining rights. He continued a very successful legal career after the Second Boer War. Herman Arnold Ameshoff was dismissed by Kruger for his support for Kotzé who had argued for the independence of the judiciary. Johannes Hermanus Michiel Kock became a member of the Executive Council in 1889 and died leading the Johannesburg *Commando* at Elandslaage in 1899.
16   General Nicholaas Jacobus Smitt, victorious Boer commander at Majuba Hill in 1881.

In answer to Phillips' query, however, Chief Justice Kotzé confirmed that the Government was prepared to listen to any request which was properly voiced and it was the Reformers who had requested the meeting not the Government.[17] Most Reformers, however, thought they could sense victory in this response and Kruger's Government was about to grant the concessions which the *Uitlanders* were anxious to achieve.

It was during these negotiations that the Reform Committee in Johannesburg received, via the British Agent in Pretoria, Sir Jacob de Wet, a proclamation from the High Commissioner, Sir Hercules Robinson, which repudiated Jameson's incursion in no uncertain terms. It was clear that they would not receive any British Government support.

---

17   Van der Poel, *The Jameson Raid*, p. 117.

8

Triumph?

The anxious members of the Reform Committee were, as we have seen, worried by the possible impending arrival of Jameson's men in Johannesburg and the consequent reaction of the Boers. On the morning of New Year's Eve, the column arrived at Malan's farm where Wolff had stabled the remounts. Abraham Malan, who was a member of the Volksraad and a friend of Commandant Joubert, was less than pleased to see Jameson and to be deceived into in avertedly aiding the Raiders. However, as has already been noted, the mounts available were more suited for pulling Jameson's carts than for his troopers to ride. Consequently, the troopers only took about 40 of the remounts and most of the Raiders continued on their original horses.

Later that day, Sergeant James White, the trooper who had refused to join his fellow BBP colleagues, arrived with a message from Sir Hercules Robinson which had been transmitted to Mafeking on the previous day. White had journeyed for eighty miles with little rest and would have caught up with the column some hours sooner if he had not been stopped at the border by a party of Boers who had been ordered to await an expected invasion which, it was thought, would follow Jameson's incursion. Once the Boer commander read the dispatches which White was carrying and realised their purpose, he released the trooper and White was eventually able to catch up with Jameson. Robinson's message ordered Jameson to return immediately as his violation of a friendly State's territory was repudiated by Her Majesty's Government. In addition, each of Jameson's officers were provided with a copy of the message to ensure they were in no doubt that they were rendering themselves liable to severe penalties.[1]

These officers, no doubt suspecting the letter's contents and given White's past history, were reluctant to open the messages and took them to Willoughby who was equally unwilling to take the responsibility to do so and forwarded them to Jameson. The Doctor, somewhat uncharacteristically, returned them unopened to Willoughby whom he claimed was in military command. Willoughby, who had little sense of responsibility for what had occurred so far or his status in relationship to that of Jameson, ordered the message to be returned to Dr Jim. It must have been with an impending dread that Jameson opened Robinson's message and read its contents. There was a brief pause and then Jameson ordered the column to proceed. He probably had little choice as White would have told him of the Boer patrols which stood between the column and its original base, which meant the Raiders were effectively cut off from behind. The reluctance to open the message was not typical of the impulsive Jameson who had a reputation for taking command over military officials. His personal bravery had already been shown when, before engaging in open warfare with the Matabele in 1893, he had confronted a group of angry and threatening warriors in person.[2]

At 1500 hours the column arrived at the next supply base, the farm of Mrs Boon, where Jameson may have hoped to meet Dr Wolff. Instead they found Lieutenant Saul Johannes Eloff, a grandson of Kruger,

---

1   Garrett & Edwards, *The Story of an African Crisis*, p. 98.
2   For a full account to this confrontation see P. Gibbs *A Flag for the Matebele* (London: Frederick Muller, 1955), pp. 129-30.

who was Inspector of Police at Krugersdorp.[3] Either from bravery or foolhardiness, having left his nine-man escort behind, Eloff approached the column alone to enquire why Jameson had entered the Transvaal with an armed force. Rather than receiving a direct answer, Eloff was arrested and disarmed. According to Willoughby, Eloff told Jameson that Johannesburg was in revolt and it was the Government's fault for not organising a standing army with which to quell it. Although, as we have seen, this description of events was untrue, it must have comforted Jameson since it was apparent that his venture could only succeed with support from Johannesburg. When the column left the farm, Eloff, was released, his weapons restored and, acting as an officer and gentleman, he gave his word that he would give Jameson two hour's start before raising the alarm.[4] When released he passed along the Rustenburg road and met a *Commando* of some 300 Boers, and together they moved round the column and were able to reach Krugersdorp before it arrived. The Boers were beginning to gather in considerable numbers to meet the invading force and were moving with greater speed that Jameson and his tired men on tired horses could achieve.

The Boers shadowed Jameson's column rather than entering into direct conflict because of their fear of the Maxims but, on the evening of New Year's Eve, a small number opened fire on the Doctor's men. The Troopers responded well and used the Maxims to good effect; driving away their attackers. A single Bechuanaland policeman was wounded. Sporadic firing continued throughout the night and the already tired troopers got little sleep. The skills of the small groups of Boers, who were opposing Jameson, should not be underestimated; Churchill regarded the Boers as being the most capable mounted warriors since the Mongols.[5]

In the early morning of New Year's Day, the column arrived at the next supply base, Van Oudshoorn Farm, where Jameson received a fresh despatch from Sir Jacobus de Wet, the British Agent at Pretoria. The despatch was carried by two mounted Boers, one of whom, Daniel Bouwer, was a member of Commandant General Joubert civilian staff. The cooperation between British and Boer officials must have impacted on Jameson as it made it very unlikely that de Wet, who had forwarded the despatch which originated from Robinson, was attempting a double bluff in order to confuse Kruger as to whether Jameson had acted on his own or Rhodes' or even Chamberlain's orders.

The despatch ordered Jameson to return to his base. His actions were totally condemned by the British Government and Jameson would be held personally responsible for his 'unauthorised and improper proceedings.'[6] Bouwer informed Jameson that an immediate response was required, and Fitzpatrick recorded that Jameson's reply only took a few minutes to compose. After acknowledging the receipt of the despatch, Jameson indicated that he would be pleased to comply with Robinson's instructions and retire as ordered. However, he was in command of a large number of mounted men and the supply depots through which he had passed were now empty. His only option was to continue towards Krugersdorp or Johannesburg in order to feed his troops and their horses.[7] One speculates whether Jameson was bending the truth to suit his purpose and it is interesting that he does not mention the large numbers of Boers who had collected in his rear which would also hinder any retreat. Perhaps the fearless Dr Jim was fast realising that the game was up and his only option for both practical and security reasons was to continue towards his original destination. He also added in his reply that he was anxious to fulfil his promise to the Reformers and aid them in their hour of need. He must have been disappointed that there had been so far no sign of a welcoming party from

---

3   Fitzpatrick describes Eloff as Kruger's nephew. and says one hour's stay. *The Transvaal from Within.* p. 70.
4   Garrett & Edwards describe it a one hour start in *The Story of an African Crisis,* p.97.
5   Longford, *Jameson's Raid,* pp. 86-88. Three months Later Eloff was accused of stating that all Englishmen were bastards, and insulting Queen Victoria. Tried and acquitted, he was promoted senior lieutenant.
6   Marshall Hole, *The Jameson Raid,* p. 171.
7   Marshall Hole, *The Jameson Raid,* p. 171.

Johannesburg which had been part of the original plan. Jameson reiterated that he had harmed no one and made it clear that supporting the Reformers was his sole intention.

Later the same day messages were received from the Reformers themselves, prosaically carried by cyclists, Celliers and Rowland; a somewhat Pythonesque occurrence. The positive content of these messages, sent by Lionel Phillips and Frank Rhodes, dated 31 December, was in direct contrasts to the actions of the Reform Committee as described in the previous chapter. They were most encouraging and indicated that although the *Uitlanders* of Johannesburg were well armed and in no danger, they would be glad to see Jameson and his men arrive in the town. Fitzpatrick tried to explain the difference between the content of the letters and the Reformers actual actions as resulting from a time delay between the writing and Jameson receiving them. Additionally, cyclists probably didn't achieve the same speed as horsemen and had taken longer to reach Jameson. The letters also mentioned that Kruger had asked members of the Reform Committee to send representatives to Pretoria to agree a brief armistice. Kruger's request seemed to suggest that it was the Reformers who were in control and not Oom Paul. In addition, Frank Rhodes expressed the opinion that the Reformers were wrong to accede to Kruger's request since this could give him an upper hand.

It seems there was confusion as to some of the content of the letters. Rowland reported that he had told Jameson that there were 2,000 armed men ready to come from Johannesburg and support the column, but Jameson had stated that, although he did not actually need their support, their arrival would probably force the Boers to withdraw. The actual messages had a chequered history after their delivery. Celliers, who was Dutch and had used his supposed loyalty to the Boers in order to pass through their patrols to reach the column, was the man selected by Frank Rhodes to deliver the messages. Rowland seems to have been picked up on the way and was perhaps less well informed as to the real situation in Johannesburg. It was he who reported the number of armed *Uitlanders* ready to join Jameson as 2000. Although the figure had been crossed out in Frank Rhodes' letter it may account for this being the number assumed by Rowlands. There was further disagreement as to what had actually been written about the numbers who would support Jameson by coming out to meet the column. Willoughby, White, Grey and Jameson himself believed that the note promised 300 men, but Frank Rhodes and Phillips said that an imprecise number, *some men*, which was promised. The letter was torn up and scattered upon the veld and it was only by good or even bad fortune that, with the exception of some missing phrases, it could be reconstructed by the Boers. These omissions may account for the discrepancies between the message's author and reader. The letter with the promise of aid was significant for Jameson in a strategic sense, since he had previously stated that he had no wished to enter Johannesburg as a 'pirate'.[8] The invitation by the Reformers would justify Jameson's actions and might prevent punishment if he failed.

In addition to these two messages there was a third from Dr Wolff which advised Jameson that the Boers were likely to defend the Queen's Mine on the road to Krugersdorp since it commanded dominant high ground and it was impossible for the column to skirt around the town as there was no suitable road for Jameson's wagons and artillery.[9] Willoughby later reported that Wolff's message stated that there were only 300 Boers in Krugersdorp.

Jameson's reply to Frank Rhodes' and Lionel Phillips' letters, dictated to Colonel White, was never delivered. It was secreted in the frame of one of the cyclists' bicycles and they were intercepted on the return journey. After their capture, they abandoned their machines with the reply still concealed within the frame where it remained for months and was not discovered until after the excitement of the Raid, and its possible consequences for the Reformers, had passed. It clearly revealed that the Doctor expected a large body of men would meet him at Krugersdorp:

---

8   Marshall Hole, *The Jameson Raid*, p. 179.
9   Marshall Hole, *The Jameson Raid*, p. 174.

As you may imagine, we are well pleased with your letter. We have had some fighting and hope to reach Johannesburg by tonight but of course it will depend on the amount of fighting we have. Of course, we shall be pleased to have two hundred men meet us at Krugersdorp as it will greatly encourage the men who are in great heart, although a bit tired.[10]

Clearly Jameson believed that a body of men from Johannesburg would guarantee his success and wanted to underplay the fatigue from which his men and horses were suffering caused by hard riding, poor food, and sleepless nights, as encouragement for the Reformers to come.

The advice from Wolff to go through Krugersdorp signed Jameson's death warrant, almost literally. Krugersdorp was a ten-year-old mining town with a population of roughly 1,500 situated around 20 miles from Johannesburg at the western end of the gold reef. It was ironic that the Boers decided that this was to be the place to halt Jameson as, in 1880, over 6,000 Boers had gathered there and vowed to fight for the Country's independence, a fact commemorated by a stone obelisk, the Paardekraal, which recorded the Boer victory in the First Boer War of 1881. When, at noon on New Year's Day, the Raiders saw the mines in the distance their spirits must have risen. They were almost within grasp of their goal and had experienced little real resistance having suffered only one casualty. They approached their last supply depot, Hind's Store, which was roughly 7 miles from Krugersdorp, but the food and fodder were equally poor as in the previous stores and neither horse nor man was boosted by the depot's contents. Garvin suggests that it was only this supply depot which proved inadequate, whereas most other commentators indicate that the provisions which Wolff had stored were of poor quality in most if not all the depots.[11] Equally depressing was the information that the opposing Boer forces were nearer to 800 than the 300 which Wolff had suggested.

The cyclists had warned the Raiders that in addition to the few hundred Boers collecting in Krugersdorp, there were other small patrols in the area.[12] Wolff had already described the likelihood that the Boers would occupy the high ground and the difficulties this would pose to the Raiders. In addition, as the Raiders rode towards the supply depot, they found that the track was fenced on both sides which would make their rapid deployment in case of attack very difficult. Willoughby slowed the column's progress by halting every few yards in order to have these wire fences cut. As the column advanced towards the town, it slowly became surrounded. A party of approximately 100 Boers had been resolutely following the column's rear for some miles and Willoughby's scouts had identified another party to the column's left flank as well as the group of Boers in front of Krugersdorp. Finally, the Raiders believed that they had also spotted a group of Boers to the column's right flank. In spite of apparently being surrounded, the Raiders were still able to move forwards.[13] Determined to continue the advance to Krugersdorp, Colonel White, leading the Mashonaland Mounted Police, order up the artillery from the rear, but, by the time it arrived, the Boers to the column's front had ridden off further into the veld. All White's guns could do was fire a few desultory rounds into the empty distance. Garvin indicates that the column's advance guard had surprised the Boers whilst they were watering their horses and the troopers could have done considerable harm to them by using their Maxims. However, Willoughby had previously ordered that the Column should not fire at the enemy unless previously fired upon and the opportunity was lost. Equally, White's use of artillery was a valuable lesson to the Boers, who had not yet received contingents of the States Artillery to assist them.

---

10   Peter Gibbs, *The History of the British South African Police, 1889-1980, Vol. I* (Salisbury: BSAP, 1972) p. 142.
11   *The Story of an African Crisis,* p. 99. Garvin suggests that it was only this supply depot that proved inadequate whereas most other commentators indicate that the provisions which Wolff had stored were inadequate in most if not all depots.
12   Garrett & Edwards, *The Story of an African Crisis,* p. 99.
13   Garvin The *Life of Joseph Chamberlain,* Vol. III, p. 77.

The State Artillery of the ZAR: the only full-time military organisation in the SA Republic.
(*Illustrated London News*, 1896)

The Boer Commander at Krugersdorp was well aware of the importance of artillery and had sent a number of messages to Joubert requesting cannon. There was a delay in the guns arriving, as units of the States Artillery were still at Pietersburg some 200 miles from Johannesburg and were returning from the war against the Bagananwa and could not be brought down in time for the beginning of the engagement.[14] Other artillery units had been retained in Pretoria on Kruger's orders in order to defend his capital against a rumoured attack.

The State Artillery was the only professional military group in the Republic. Originally it also had been recruited under the *Commando* system as were the mounted Boer fighters. In 1874, President Thomas Burgers, the ZAR's fourth President, had purchased some artillery from Europe and also recruited European officers to instruct and organise their use as there were few suitable artillery officers in the ZAR. The new Corps, commanded by Captain Otto Reidell, formerly of the Austrian Artillery Corps, was named the Dingaan Battery after the Zulu chief whose army was defeated at the battle of Blood River on 1 December1838 which is still celebrated as a holiday in South Africa as Dingaan's Day.[15] The first guns President Burgers purchased were four Krupp 65 mm Mountain guns and an obsolete French *Militraileuse* which, having been captured from the French in the War of 1870, had been presented to Burgers during a tour of Europe. The Krupp Mountain gun, although relatively light in weight, could not be dismantled and had to be pulled by horse, ox or mule which slowed them down when moving from one place to another. The *Militraileuse*, which derived its name from the French for grapeshot, was a type of volley gun with multiple barrels of rifle calibre and could either fire single rounds or several rounds in rapid succession and could be described as a forerunner of the Gatling gun. When Britain annexed the ZAR in 1877, the Dingaan Battery was disbanded, its guns taken over by the British and many of its members, who were not Boer, joined the British Volunteer Corps raised to defend Pretoria.

---

14   Garvin, The *Life of Joseph Chamberlain*, Vol. III, pp. 24-27.
15   Batterij Dingaaan.

Following Majuba Hill and the subsequent Pretoria Convention of 1881, which ended the First Boer War, the Executive Council of the ZAR ordered the formation of an Artillery Corps and a Transvaal Mounted Police Corps. Although the numbers of artillery pieces increased, Boer guns were often out of date and even old ships' cannons were still in use.[16] The commander of the State Artillery was the only Lieutenant Colonel in the Boer Forces and second only to the Commandant General. His men were the only Boer unit which donned proper military uniform inspired by those of Austria-Hungary.[17]

---

16 Major D.D. Hall, 'The Artillery of the First Anglo-Boer War 1880 – 1881', *Military History Journal* Vol 5 No 2 (The South African Military History Society, December 1980).
17 D. G Friend, Uniforms of the Staatsartillrie: Influences and Developments. Military History Journal, Vol 9 No 4 (The South African Military History Society, December 1993).

9

Disaster

During the halt at Hind's Stores which occurred at around 1300 hours, Jameson and Willoughby had a difference of opinion as to how next to proceed.[1] Krugersdorp was carefully reconnoitred, and Willoughby's scouts had discovered that the town was built between two ridges, which offered two routes through which Jameson's column could progress. The first and least risky possibility was by skirting to the south of the town in an attempt to avoid the Boers who were known to occupy Krugersdorp. The alternative route was to move directly through the town which would almost certainly involve a fight.

Jameson was guided by Wolff's letter, which he thought had suggested that the Johannesburg Reformers would have occupied the railhead at Krugersdorp, and would, he assumed, attack the rear of the Boers who were defending the town. Willoughby wanted to avoid attacking the town for good tactical reasons; his force was relatively small and becoming outnumbered by the hour and an attack would delay the column's progress. Jameson later claimed that Willoughby's attempts to educate him in military strategy failed and he didn't understand the Colonel's reasoning or the tactics which he advocated.[2] Although Jameson had based his Raid's success on the elements of speed and surprise, his view prevailed, giving proof to the lie that Willoughby was the real military commander. His claims not to understand the niceties of military tactics were somewhat ingenuous for Jameson was no stranger to combat having taken part and, to some degree directed troops, in the First Matabele War with Willoughby as his Military Adviser. However, the enemy in the Matabele War was very different from the Boer forces ranged against Jameson at Krugersdorp. Although their military organisation was somewhat loosely formed, they were expert shots, used concealment well, and were ably led by Piet Cronjé, who made great use of the terrain and was in overall command.[3]

Cronjé, Commandant at Potchefstroom, roughly 90 miles from Krugersdorp, heard about Jameson's incursion on Monday 30 December and ordered his *Commando* to gather, and with his four sons and 250 men, was at Krugersdorp within 24 hours. Such was the speed with which his *Commando* had assembled that some of Cronjé men were still in their 'Sunday best' in preparation for the New Year's celebrations.[4] Making use of the terrain, Commandant Cronjé had placed his troops across a right-angled ridge at the foot of which was a marsh. In order to go through the town, Jameson's troops had to cross the marsh and climb the ridge and, whilst doing so, they would be exposed to Boer fire from the front and the flank. Worse still, their advance was to be across open ground which would provide them with little cover. Perhaps these points were the tactics which Willoughby failed to impress upon the Doctor.

---

1   Garvin's names it as *Hand's Store. The Life of Joseph Chamberlain, Vol III,* p. 77.
2   Colvin, *The Life of Jameson,* p. 79.
3   In 1900 Cronjé's military skills were discovered to be limited and his luck ran out when during the battle of he surrendered to Lord Roberts and over 4,000 Boers went into captivity.
4   Van der Poel, *The Jameson Raid,* p. 125.

Willoughby acquiesced to the more forceful Jameson, and accordingly sent a message to Krugersdorp's Commandant, F.J. Potgieter, that the column was a friendly force and would only take belligerent action if they were prevented from moving through the town. If they were so obstructed, Willoughby declared, he would be forced to shell the town. Accordingly, Sir John, with great chivalry warned, the Boers to evacuate their women and children before the shelling began. One wonders why Willoughby might think that the Boers would be taken in by his so-called reluctance to attack for, as already indicated, he had previously used his artillery against them. However, his was a chivalrous gesture towards the Boer non-combatants and was to his credit.

Willoughby received no response and shelling commenced around 1600 hours at a range of 1,900 yards. As was to happen on a number of occasions in World War One, the effects of the shelling were overestimated but it was to the Boer's credit, though unused to receiving artillery fire, they kept their positions. Willoughby's guns had some success as the 12 ½ pounder practically demolished a disused battery-house which the Boers had fortified as a defensive position. It is unlikely that its occupants escaped entirely unhurt but they later claimed that there were no casualties and, even though they had a tendency to play down the number hurt, it is clear that the shrapnel shells of Willoughby's artillery either burst above the snugly ensconced Boers or buried themselves in the ground in front of Boer positions. Having no artillery, the Boers could not reply in kind and did not respond to the bombardment. Cronjé displayed considerable courage or perhaps foolhardiness during the shelling as he refused to take cover saying that if it was God's wish that he was killed he could do little to prevent it.[5]

Underestimating the Boer tenacity and because there had been little response to the barrage, Willoughby mistakenly believed that the enemy must have retired and ordered an advance by charging the Boer defences. Colonel Harry White led 100 men towards the Boer positions and, as they moved towards the ridge, his men's progress was covered by two of the Maxims. Two other troops attempted to threaten the Boer's flank.

The Boers did not react until White's force, having deployed into extended line, reached the marsh which was around 700 yards from the ridge and occupied by their silent enemy. White's troops were essentially mounted infantry and carried neither sword nor lance and relied entirely on the hope that the weight of their charge would dislodge the Boers from their positions.[6] The Boers opened fire from both the front and the flanks and stopped White's advance in its tracks. Thirty men were killed or wounded and thirty more, who in an attempt to save themselves from the Boer fire, hid in the reeds of the marsh. Not unexpectedly, the remainder retreated out of rifle range. Ash is correct when he describes a hundred-man cavalry charge against what amounted to 300 snipers was 'a truly lunatic endeavour'.[7] Later, during the night the Boers captured the fugitives in the reeds and took the wounded directly to hospital; an early demonstration of the Boers' magnanimity which was to follow.

Cronjé's position was proving impregnable even to the non-military minded Jameson. This one attack had cost around 12 percent of his force. He finally agreed to Willoughby's original plan which was to skirt the town and it was to the Colonel's credit that he was able to extract his force in the growing dusk and move southwards of the Boer defences for a mile without them being aware of his actions. Two of Willoughby's officers; Sub-Inspector Harry Scott (MMP) and Surgeon Captain Farmer, (BSAC), fearing for the fate of the wounded, chose to remain with them and were captured. Their concerns were subsequently proved to be groundless.

Willoughby and Jameson's plight seemed to improve when their force encountered a 'friendly' guide who offered to lead them directly towards Johannesburg by-passing Krugersdorp. Appearing from nowhere, the guide soon disappeared into the veld. Was this guide an agent of the Boers or was Willoughby right to

5   Garrett, & Edwards, *The Story of an African Crisis,* p. 117.
6   Gibbs, *The History of the British South African Police, Vol 1.* p. 143.
7   Ash, p. 243.

blame the Reformers for his predicament after the Raid had failed? Clearly, he put considerable trust in this 'helpful' stranger at a time when it was hard to distinguish friend from foe amongst the populace.

However, having formed the men into the night order of march and almost within sight of Johannesburg, Willoughby made the second and most significant mistake; he turned back toward Krugersdorp! Such was the strength of Jameson's and Willoughby's conviction that the Reformers would send out men to support their advanced that, when tremendous salvos, which included Maxim fire, were heard from the town, they believe that it was the sound of the Reformers attacking the Boers' rear. Knowing that the Reform Committee had Maxims and believing the *Staats Artillerie* would not arrive until the next morning, Willoughby, refused to leave what he supposed were friends in the lurch, and ordered his men to turn around and proceed back towards Krugersdorp.[8] The noise was actually the Boers of Krugersdorp celebrating the arrival of a large force of reinforcements from Potchefstroom.

The Raiders advanced rapidly towards Krugersdorp and the firing, leaving one troop and the transport, on the road. They had only gone a mile when the firing stopped, and Willoughby saw a large party of Boers advancing towards him. He also became aware of another force on his right flank and he feared that these Boers were attempting to cut him off from the ammunition carts he had left behind, so he ordered his men to retreat towards them. As darkness fell the Raiders realised that they had been cut off from Johannesburg and decided that the only thing to do was '…to bivouac in the best position available'.[9] Willoughby blamed the firing on his predicament but it was actually his and Jameson's unshakable belief that the Reformers would come from Johannesburg in order to support them which had caused their indecision: a belief which was founded on the confusing letter brought by the cyclists.

Van der Poel is extremely critical of a report by Willoughby of the events, which was written whilst he was in captivity.[10] The blame for the Raid's failure was placed firmly on the heads of the Reformers, and Willoughby placed great emphasis on the need to support them in their dire needs which, as we have seen, was not the case. This reason, and this reason alone, might have been seen as a rational justification for the invasion. However, the contribution of the mysterious guide should not be entirely ignored. Willoughby reluctantly admits that, had he not been fooled by the firing at Krugersdorp, the advance on Johannesburg would have been well on its way. They bivouacked two miles from their original attack. Rather than the gods conspiring against Willoughby and Jameson, it was their refusal to understand that the Reformers were only lukewarm supporters of their direct intervention and were either not courageous or foolish enough to overtly challenge Kruger.[11]

During the night, the Boers did not attack them but were content to take pot shots at the ambulance tent which bore the only permitted light. Jameson ordered Bugler Vallé to take a verbal message to the Reformers in Johannesburg. The bugler, avoiding the Boers in the darkness, arrived at the Reform Committee's Headquarters at about 0700 and delivered the message to Frank Rhodes whom, as we know, had not received Jameson's message entrusted to the cyclists. The message which Vallé delivered appeared to be less than urgent, however, stating; 'The Doctor is all right, but he says now he would like some men sent out to meet him.'[12]

If Van der Poel's version is accurate, Vallé's message does not sound that its sender was in desperate straits but rather could be interpreted as that Jameson was asking for an escort for his entry into the town. Colvin elaborates on Vallé's message by explaining that the Bugler indicated where Jameson had camped and recounted the details of the battle of Krugersdorp and the subsequent attempted return because of the

---

8   Garrett, & Edwards, *The Story of an African Crisis,* p. 104.
9   Garrett & Edwards, *The Story of an African Crisis,* p. 105.
10   Van der Poel, *The Jameson Raid*, p. 127.
11   Colvin, *The Life of Jameson*, Vol 1, p. 83.
12   Van der Poel, *The Jameson Raid*, p. 128.

Bettington's Horse leaving Johannesburg. (*The Graphic,* 1896)

false assumption that, because of the overheard firing, the Reform Committee had sent support. It seems that Vallé at first delivered Jameson's message with slightly greater emphasis on the need for support; '…they must send out to meet me.'[13] However, when pressed by what '…must send support actually meant', he seems to have replied, that the Reformers must '…send out to meet him.' Omitting the term support.[14] Believing that Jameson wanted a welcome rather than reinforcements and struggling with the ambiguity of the message, Colonel Rhodes, believing that Jameson really needed help but was reluctant to say so, acting on his own authority, collected a hundred Bettington's Horse to provide this escort or perhaps to offer even more positive assistance if it was required.

---

13   My emphasis.
14   Again, my emphasis. See Fitzpatrick, *The Transvaal from Within*, p. 134.

Johannesburg residents awaiting the arrival of Jameson's column. (*Illustrated London News*, 1896)

Having sent men off towards the sound of the firing, Rhodes then woke up Lionel Phillips and told him what had transpired. Phillips and the other Reform Committee members were angered at Frank Rhodes' decision; they were terrified of being accused of jeopardising the agreement with Kruger and this might result in Johannesburg being attacked. If the lack of a substantial defence and the limited number of rifles were discovered by Oom Paul, he would be unlikely to grant any concessions. How could a man who had been proclaimed an outlaw by Sir Hercules Robinson be escorted as a hero into the town they asked? Such a small number of men as that under Bettington's command, the Reformers argued, were insufficient to materially contribute to Jameson's Raiders' battle. Their presence would also reveal the lie that there were 2,000 armed men ready to defend the town. Bettington's men were contacted and told not to go further than 10 miles from Johannesburg and limit their activities to reconnoitring Jameson's position. Assistance should only be given if absolutely necessary. Jameson did not get that close and Bettington's men, finally returned frustrated to the town and left the Raiders to their fate.[15]

At daybreak on 2 January, Jameson's force moved off southwards; the only direction from which they were not directly opposed by Boer forces. The column's guns were used to protect its rear and flanks. The Boers followed doggedly at a distance but there were occasions when fire was exchanged between the two forces. The Raiders were becoming somewhat directionless as, perhaps surprisingly, they did not know the whereabouts of the Johannesburg road. The fiasco was rapidly turning into a farce when another guide was found whose directions also proved to be unreliable.

At roughly this time, J.J. Lace, a Reform Committee member, arrived at Jameson's force with a message from Robinson, which informed the Doctor that he was now an outlaw, and British subjects were forbidden

---

15   Colvin, *Life of Jameson,* Vol. 2, p. 103.

to offer him assistance. The Reform Committee had agreed to obey Robinson's instructions, and this finally ended Jameson's hope of support from Johannesburg. Colvin records that there was a little black humour before this meeting as Lace had been announced as Leyds by an uninformed trooper; which, for a moment only, caused Jameson to think that Pretoria was in a panic and had sent Willem Leyds, the Secretary of State, to negotiate.[16]

What was not in the strictest sense a retreat but rather a diversion continued for a number of miles as the Raiders attempted to find a route eastward. The Boers followed at a safe distance whilst continually attempting to find a good defensive position from which to block the Raiders' way. The Raiders spent an uneasy and disturbed night with two relatively brief bouts of firing. Given the lack of a commissariat, the Boers who provided their own horse, rifle, and ammunition, were running short of the latter. Jameson, Willoughby, Grey, and the two Whites held an impromptu council of war in an attempt to decide the next day's action. They planned to leave at first light in a southerly direction hoping the road was still open. The Raiders were on the long ridge known as the Rand and to proceed along it would mean threading through numbers of mine workings, refuse dumps, and trenches dug by prospectors; all providing good defensive positions for the Boers. They chose a somewhat circuitous route south through the Handfontein Estate by a road which led to the plain below and circumvented a deep little valley in the hills in front of them. It was hoped that the way to the south remained open and the officers anticipated that on open ground they could break through any Boer direct opposition since their real skill was in holding defensive positions.

All was prepared and at 0400 hours Jameson's men set off with defensive patrols being deployed on their left and right flanks as well as in their rear. The Boers quickly responded with fire from every direction but the south and the outlying patrols were driven back to the main body of troopers. With troopers from the BBP and two Maxims on the left flank and the MMP troopers, also with Maxims, on the right, the main body began to descend into the valley. Their progress continued and the rear guard safely followed behind; Willoughby again showing his skills as a commander, but Colvin suggests that Willoughby had expected this ground to be held by the Reformers and had therefore paid insufficient attention to its topography.[17]

A running fight took place over a distance of ten miles during which Grey was wounded in the foot, ignoring the pain he rode at the front with Jameson. Willoughby remained at the column's rear from where, he had decided, would come the biggest threat. This was true as both the rear and the left flank of the column were under constant fire. The Boers did not press any advantage and allowed the column to proceed fairly quickly giving Jameson's men some hope that they might escape the enemy but they were also conscious that the wagons at the rear were filled with wounded and could not easily be abandoned. Where the terrain permitted, small groups of the Raiders made a stand against the pursuing Boers who were never closer than 500 yards away. Having crossed a stream, the road began to climb again and turn eastwards, seemingly towards Johannesburg. They reached a farm known as Vlakfontein and, inevitably, ran into a prepared Boer defensive position.

It is easy to see that the column was gradually being pushed by the various Boer *Commandos* towards this location and is further proof that Cronjé well understood the art of using the defensive position as a method of attack. The Boers also occupied a *kopje* named Doornkop to the column's right which was to give its name to Jameson's final battle.[18] It was impossible to bypass the *kopje* and retreat was out of the question because the Boers in the rear had begun to move closer. Jameson's men were faced with two alternatives; fight their way through or surrender. Initially, they chose to fight in spite of being exhausted and heavily outnumbered. The column's guns attempted to clear the enemy from the *kopje* whilst Willoughby, having ridden the one and half miles from the rear to the column front, consulted Grey.

---

16 Colvin *The Life of Jameson*, Vol. 2, p. 104.
17 Colvin *The Life of Jameson*, Vol. 2, p. 107.
18 Afrikaans for a small hill rising from a flat plane.

The Raiders under fire at Doornkop. (*Illustrated London News*, 1896)

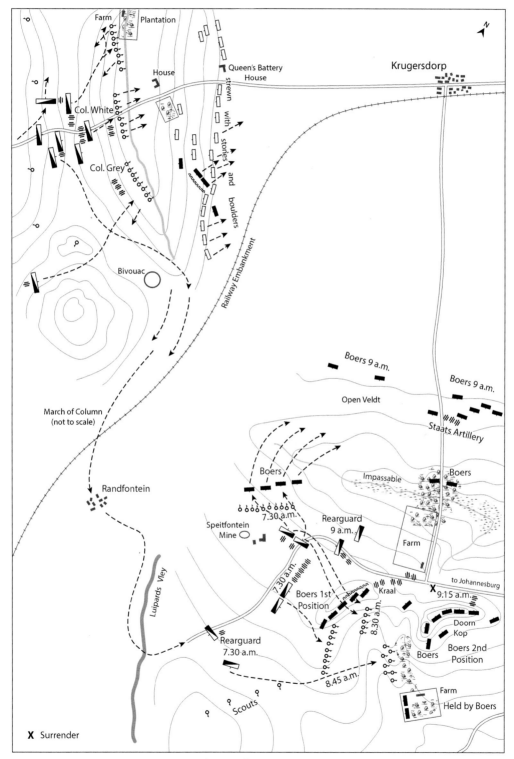

Map 4 Doornkop, 2 January 1896.

Jameson directing fire at Doornkop. (*Penny Illustrated,* 1896)

The column made two thrust against the Boers; one towards the *kopje* led by Major Coventry and one against those Boers on the left flank led by Inspector Bodle. Although Coventry's men appeared to be successful, Coventry himself was badly injured in the process and Inspector Barry of the MMP was killed. Casualties amongst the Raiders grew steadily and, when the column reached Doornkop, their hopes of escape must have disappeared. They were faced with a semi-circular marshy valley. The *spruit* or brook which ran along it could only be crossed at a point towards the right of the column and this *drift* or ford was domi-nated by a rocky *kopje* which rose steeply from the other side of the *spruit*. Beyond the stream the road wound up a gently sloping valley, the sides of which were entrenched and manned by Boers. At the valley's centre, towards its rear, the Boers had placed their guns as the *Staatsartillerie* had finally arrived.

The entrenched Boers employed their rifle skills to shoot down troopers as they attempted to attack their positions. Five of the vital Maxims jammed because there was insufficient water with which to cool them and the artillery ammunition began to run low with only half an hour's supply remaining. Once the *Staatsartillerie* began to fire on the column its situation became impossible. It is said that the white flag which was raised as a sign of surrender was, in fact, the apron of a woman from a nearby farm. It seems that it was not raised by a substantive officer of the column and certainly not on Jameson's orders.[19] Marshall Hole

---

19   Colvin, *The Life of Jameson,* Vol. 2, p. 110.

Boers confronting the raiders at the Battle of Doornkop (*Illustrated London News,* 1896)

suggests that the flag was raised by Major Crosse, the convalescing officer late of the 5th Dragoon Guards, who had accompanied the Raiders in a spirit of adventure.[20] The Raid was over. The casualty rate was 82 killed and wounded and Willoughby was correct in deciding that further fighting would only have increased this number. In addition, roughly 55 Troopers were missing; probably captives of the Boers. Whilst the men from the BBP were seasoned veterans with combat experience, the majority of Jameson's men from the MMP were aged between 18 and 20 and were very lacking in basic skills such as the use of firearms and horsemanship.[21] Cronjé reported his casualties as four killed, one of whom was accidently shot by his own side and one, named Yakoby, killed by a wounded raider whom he had tried to help.[22] In addition, only three men had been wounded. Whilst the Boers had avoided a head on battle with the Raiders, given the prolonged skirmishing and the Raiders' use of artillery, such a small number of killed and injured seems to be an underestimation

20 Marshall Hole, *The Jameson Raid,* p. 188.
21 Van der Poel, *The Jameson Raid*, p. 292.
22 Rev. J King, *Dr. Jamson's Raid. Its causes and consequences* (London: George Routledge & Sons Ltd, 1896), p. 68.

which may be confirmed by the fact that one Boer commander acknowledged that the Raiders' artillery had done great damage.[23] A less gallant member of the Reform Committee was keen to point out that the nobility of the Raider's efforts was somewhat brought into question when one considered the risk to life and limb their actions posed to the citizens of Johannesburg.[24]

There only remained to agree surrender terms. Cronjé, in the security of Doornkop, saw the column's white flag when it was raised at about 0915 hours and took the initiative to dispatch a messenger to Jameson in order to find out what the Doctor intended. Willoughby had pre-empted Cronje's inquiry by sending a message to Potgieter, Commandant of the Krugersdorp *Commando*, and in charge of the Vlakfontein position, offering to surrender providing Cronjé would guarantee a safe conduct out of the country for all those involved. Potgieter, conscious of protocol, replied that he would confer with the other two Commandants and forwarded the note to Cronjé. Cronjé was less sensitive and, without conferring with Potgieter or Malan, sent a message to Willoughby which, having acknowledged the Colonel's letter, demanded that he pay the expenses which the Raid had cost the Republic and that Willoughby surrender both his flag and his weapons. Lives would then be spared but Willoughby was only given thirty minutes to decide.[25] A grateful Willoughby accepted the terms but reiterated, no doubt with an element of responsibility and self-interest as the column's military commander, that his surrender was on condition that the lives of the whole force were spared. Having received the reply, Cronjé set off on horseback, accompanied by his men, and was soon joined by Potgieter and they arrived with around 500 Burghers at the farm which was acting as Willoughby's headquarters. The officers, according to Cronjé, looked dirty and miserable and Jameson was clearly shocked at the enormity and possible consequences of the defeat. Cronjé asked Jameson for the flag under which he had fought but the Doctor replied that he had not fought under any flag, a subtle admission perhaps that the enterprise did not actually have the support of the British Government but also an attempt to avoid possible international controversy.

It was at this point that the proposed surrender took a more sinister turn. Commandant Malan finally arrived and questioned Cronjé about the discussion which had taken place with Willoughby. This was the first that Potgieter had heard of Cronjé's offer of terms and both he and, especially Malan, who may have been the senior Commandant, reminded Cronjé of his actual position; he was neither Commandant General nor President of the Republic. They could accept the Raiders' surrender but could not offer terms. They could only guarantee the safety of Willoughby, Jameson and the others until they were handed over to the Authorities in Pretoria. In this argument, Malan was strongly supported by Potgieter and Cronjé was reluctantly forced to agree. His agreement was preceded by an acrimonious argument with Malan of such intensity that it became known to Joubert and published in the press. During the First Boer War, Assistant Commandant Cronjé had proved himself a ruthless opponent of the British. He had shot a number of Englishmen as spies on very flimsy evidence and he had placed prisoners in positions of risk during the siege of Potchefstroom.[26]

Jameson was informed by an interpreter of the change of terms and bowing, bareheaded and defeated, he agreed that his men would lay down their weapons. Fitzpatrick is keen to suggest some skulduggery on behalf of the Boers as he states that the change in the surrender terms was not communicated to Jameson until after his men had actually stacked their arms. Fitzpatrick also makes much about this duplicity on the part of the Boers, by suggesting that it was 'not by any means unusual for the Boers to seek to stretch to their advantage terms which they have previously agreed upon.'[27] This may have been the case but it should be noted that

23   J. Crwys-Williams, *South African Despatches, two centuries of the best in South African Journalism* (Johannesburg: Ashanti Publishing, 1989), p. 97.
24   Longford, *Jameson's Raid,* p. 98.
25   Van der Poel, *The Jameson Raid*, p. 129.
26   Fitzpatrick, *The Transvaal from Within*, fn., pp.147-148.
27   Fitzpatrick, *The Transvaal from Within*, p. 147.

A somewhat glamorised version of Jameson's white flag surrender.
(*Illustrated London News*, 1896)

some of the Boers, appreciating the plight of the raiders who had been without food for some time, gave them strips of *biltong* to ease their hunger.[28]

At this point, a fourth Commandant, S. Trichardt of the *Staatsartillerie*, a professional soldier, having telegraphed to Commandant General Joubert once he had seen the white flag, arrived with a message from the General. This demanded that the Raiders should surrender unconditionally. In addition, all their possessions should be confiscated, and the rank and file should be taken to Krugersdorp but the officers brought to Pretoria. In the meantime, all of the Raiders should be properly cared for and, it is to the Boers' credit, that they treated the Raiders with the utmost courtesy. Surgeon Captain Garraway was full of praise for the Boers' care for their prisoners especially the wounded who were provided with milk, brandy, meat, and bread and transported on ambulance carts to Krugersdorp where a temporary hospital had been set up with volunteer nurses.[29]

The Hospital was visited by a number of people including a Reuter's correspondent and a representative of the High Commissioner who found the men well cared for in a clean environment.[30] Captain Sir Francis Younghusband, the special correspondent of *The Times*, was allowed to visit the Raiders and described them as being exhausted but hard and determined men whose courage was much admired by their Boer captors.[31] There was a report, however, of a Trooper named Black, who had been taken prisoner during a scouting mission being shot by his captors with little concern.[32] Given the men's experiences of the past few days, one

28 Akrikaans for dried cured meat.
29 Garraway's journal quote by Marshall Hole, *The Jameson Raid*, p. 191.
30 Rev. J. King, *Dr. Jameson's Raid. Its causes and consequences*, p. 69.
31 J. Crwys-Williams, *South African Despatches*, p. 96.
32 Fitzpatrick, *The Transvaal from Within*, p. 50.

Jameson and his men marched into captivity by triumphant Boers. (*Petit Parisien,* 1896)

Captured Maxims being inspected by *Staatsartillerie* personnel. (*The Graphic,* 1896)

suspects that Younghusband's report contained an element of British phlegm and stiff upper lip. The men as they marched away, after a very hearty breakfast, were reported to have joined in the chorus of a popular appropriate song; 'After the ball was over'.[33] Jameson's Maxims and artillery were taken by the Boers to be used against the British in the Second Boer War. They also discovered evidence in Bobby White's despatch case, left in the field, which was very damming for the Reformers. This include a copy of the '*Invitation Letter*' and other documents which would be used against the Reformers in Johannesburg.[34]

---

33   Crwys-Williams, *South African Despatches*, p. .96.
34   See Appendix II for Boer *Commandos* involved in defeating Jameson's raiders.

10

Reaction

It is easy to forget that in the late Victorian Age international communications were well advanced. Chamberlain, still at Highbury, on the evening of New Year's Eve was about to dress to attend the annual Servants' Ball, when he received a messenger from the Colonial Office, sent to Birmingham by fast train, which contained the news that the Raid had gone ahead. Earlier in the day, Chamberlain had been reassured by Hercules Robinson that the Reformers rebellion had collapsed. Somewhat suspicious, in reply the Colonial Secretary telegraphed Robinson to make sure that Jameson had not started his Raid in spite of this collapse. On hearing the news that Jameson had launched the Raid, Chamberlain's reaction, as reported by his biographer, Garvin, is interesting in light of the future official Inquiries; 'If this succeeds, it will ruin me. I am going up to London to crush it.'[1] Good as his word, Chamberlain, having telegraphed Robinson to '… leave no stone unturned to prevent mischief,'[2] arrived at the Colonial Office at 0400 hours New Year's Day and took instant charge. He was unsure at that point whether Rhodes had authorised Jameson's incursion or whether Jameson had acted alone. There is some suggestion that the 'Colossus' still entertained a hope that the impulsive Jameson might succeed and that South Africa would soon belong to England.[3] If Dr Jim was successful he would be a hero as he had been on his return after his victory in the First Matabele War and would, no doubt, receive a reward more significant than his CB. In addition, Rhodes not only would improve his own standing but the BSAC would move forward as an increasingly influential and profitable company whilst Britain's Empire would have been enlarged at a minimum cost. Chamberlain's dilemma was further increased when on January 1, *The Times*, published the *Invitation Letter* at the request of Sir Hercules. The populace now saw Jameson as a crusading hero and not, as he had feared, a buccaneer. Chamberlain was not one to underestimate the power of the press and instructed Robinson to ensure that the editors of newspapers in Pretoria, Johannesburg and Bloemfontein were sent a copy of his proclamation which denounced Jameson as a law breaker. This was insufficient to appease Chamberlain's most vehement critics and on 2 January, feeling the pressure around him and, feeling unwell, he left the Colonial Office and returned home. It was there, in the early evening, that Robert Meade and some Colonial Office colleagues arrived and told Chamberlain of the Raid's failure. No doubt Chamberlain breathed a sigh of relief and his headache began to dissipate. What now would the 'jingo' papers, which had previously accused him of leaving unarmed English men and women at the mercy of the Boers, say?[4] Chamberlain, on the other hand, felt he was in the clear of being complicit in the Raid; his messengers had ordered Jameson to turn back and it was Jameson who had refused to do so. Chamberlain had, however, relaxed too soon.

---

1   Garvin. *The Life of Joseph Chamberlain*, Vol III, p. 89. My emphasis.
2   Garvin, *The Life of Joseph Chamberlain*, Vol III, p. 89.
3   Telegraph to Fiona Shae, *Select Committee Report*, Appendix. p. 599.
4   Garvin, *The Life of Joseph Chamberlain*, Vol III, p. 192. Newspapers which were favourable to an aggressive foreign policy.

A messenger carrying news of Jameson's defeat rests at Chapman's Store on the way to Johannesburg.
(*Illustrated London News*, 1896)

Cecil Rhodes, the 'Colossus', was also considerably challenged by Jameson's unexpected action. In Rhodes' own words uttered in a conversation with W.P. Schreiner, the Cape's Attorney General, Jameson had been his friend for 20 years and 'now he has ruined me.'[5]

Kaiser Wilhelm II, always happy to see his grandmother's country humiliated on the world stage, took it upon himself to send a telegram of congratulation to Kruger. Dated 3 January 1896, the telegram praised Kruger for defeating the Jameson Raiders without having to call upon foreign assistance. Peace had been restored and a threat against Kruger's Republic defeated. This unexpected intervention by the impetuous monarch immediately changed public opinion which was beginning to see Jameson as an avaricious brigand. The change would have been even greater had Wilhelm sent his originally drafted telegram which offered to intervene to protect the Transvaal by sending troops to support the Republic. He was persuaded not to send this message through the combined efforts of his Foreign Minister, Baron von Marschall and the Chancellor, Prince Hohenlohe, who feared a direct confrontation with England. There had been sketchy plans to send a fifty strong German marine detachment to support Kruger on the pretext of defending the German Embassy in Pretoria, but this was thwarted by the Portuguese who refused permission for it to land at Delagoa Bay. Kruger, perhaps not relishing the thought of another foreign 'invasion', reassured the Kaiser that if he really was concerned about the security of the Embassy, Kruger would arrange for 50 of his Burghers to do the

---

5   E.A. Walker *W.P. Schreiner: A South African* (London: OUP, 1969), p. 91.

job.[6] Paul Von Hatzfeldt, the German Ambassador to London, had been told to enquire whether the British Government supported the Raid and, if so, to request his passport as a sign that diplomatic relations between Germany and Britain had reached a crisis point.

Bismarck, the onetime Chancellor of Germany, felt there was nothing wrong with the Kaiser's original telegram which, he argued, could have equally been sent by the British Government itself.[7] Wilhelm, in one of his 'Dear Nicky' telegrams also canvassed the support of his cousin, the Tsar. However, the actual telegram which the three men agreed to send was even more offensive to Britain since its draft had merely congratulated Kruger for defending the Republic's dignity.[8] It was clearly in accord with both the Transvaal's wish to ally itself with Germany which could act as a buffer to Britain's imperial aims in Africa and satisfy Germany's wish to challenge Britain's dominance on the Dark Continent.

The final telegram proved to be a bombshell and united the British public and Press in anti-German feeling. The Kaiser had insulted Britain and his grandmother, their Queen. Such was the strength of indignation that Ambassador Hatzfeldt, who, on reflection three weeks after the Raid, believed that if Britain declared war on Germany at that moment the population would overwhelmingly support the Government.[9]

The Kaiser's grandmother, Queen Victoria, was also angered by her impetuous grandson. Writing from Osborne House, Victoria reminded the Kaiser of the affection he had shown her over the years but the telegram to Kruger was a unfriendly gesture towards Britain and, although she suggested that this was not Wilhelm's intention, she was grieved that it had made '...a very unfriendly impression'.[10]

Chamberlain's response to the Kaiser's offer of sending a naval detachment to the ZAR was something of a *quid pro quo*. British ships were to be sent to Delagoa Bay and a strong naval flying squadron was ordered.[11] Ever sensitive to popular opinion, Chamberlain was keen to sooth the '...wounded vanity of the nation' by demonstrating her military and naval might.[12]

The Kaiser's Telegram outraged Britons but delighted his own subjects and national rivalries began to increase in intensity. *The Times* published a poem by the Poet Laureate, Alfred Austin, entitled *Jameson's Ride* which questioned whether the Raid was wrong headed or had made 'a gallop for life and death' and 'a ride to their kinsfolk's aid.'[13] Austin echoed Jameson's view that if the Raid succeeded, he would have been famous. It was given a wider circulation by being recited on a nightly basis at the Alhambra Theatre by a performer in the uniform of the BSAC on a stage decorated with tropical plants to represent the Transvaal.[14] The poem has been described as having no equal in the English language for its '...sheer sloppiness and unreal sentiment', but it certainly reflected the mood of the general public.[15]

Chamberlain, although appalled by the Raid, strongly hinted in a telegram sent to Sir Hercules Robinson on 4 January that he had sympathies with the *Uitlanders*' grievances and, although such an incursion into a sovereign country by a group of British subjects could not be ignored and should never happen again, those grievances could not be disregarded indefinitely. He had no intention of allowing Jameson's 'filibustering fiasco' to prejudice the claims of the *Uitlanders* or for it to be seen to undermine his support for them. Events in the next three years were to prove Chamberlain's determination to do so.

---

6   Fisher, *Paul Kruger, His Life and Times*, p. 195.

7   Fisher, *Paul Kruger His Life and Times*, p. 191.

8   E.T.S. Dugdale, *German Diplomatic Documents, Vol. II.* (London: Harper & Brothers, 1929.) p. 387.

9   Dugdale, *German Diplomatic Documents, Vol. II*, pp. 403-04. See Appendix V.

10   Fisher, *Paul Kruger: His Life and Time*, p. 193.

11   Garvin, *The Life of Joseph Chamberlain*, Vol III, p. 96.

12   Van der Poel, *The Jameson Raid*, p. 137.

13   *The Times*, 11 January 1896 Alfred Austin Poet Laureate 1896-1913: considered by some to have been the worst in this office.

14   Fisher, *Paul Kruger: His Life and Time*, p. 193.

15   Marshall Hole, *The Jameson Raid,* p. 239.

Kruger and Joubert were not slow in attempting to gain international support for the ZAR. After the Raiders had surrendered, their ammunition was examined, and similar ammunition was found in Johannesburg. Claiming that it was particularly destructive, Kruger sent samples to every Consul in South Africa to be forwarded to their native countries. Consequently, the Raid saw a surge of support for the ZAR from the Netherlands. Many Boers were of Dutch descent and the links between the two countries were strong. In 1881 the Nederlandsch *Zuid-Afrikaansche Vereeniging* (Dutch South African Society NZAV) was formed to improve the links between the two Boer Republics; the ZAR and the Orange Free State. From an initial membership of 300, it reached its maximum, if temporary pinnacle, of 1,600 in 1896 as a result of the Jameson Raid. The Dutch press gave much coverage to the Raid and the Dutch people condemned the Raiders as 'buccaneers' and celebrated the success of the *Commandos* in defeating and capturing the Raiders.[16] However, the Dutch Government in The Hague resisted an emotional response such as that of the Kaiser's and sent Kruger a carefully worded telegram a week after the Raiders' capture. When Willem Leyds had visited Europe, before the Raid, in 1895, he was astonished to discover the animosity displayed towards the Boers in the French and German Press. He believed that this was because Britain had a much more developed and successful publicity machine. His shock caused him, on his return to the ZAR, to offer to resign as Secretary of State and return to Europe with full powers to promulgate Boer interests. Initially, Leyds' offer was turned down because of the cost and his usefulness to the ZAR Government but shortly afterwards he was sent to Brussels as an ambassador with the responsibility to advance the Boer cause.[17] Most European governments received him well, but British diplomats saw his work in gathering European support for the ZAR as a contravention of the 1884 London Convention under which Britain controlled the ZAR's international relations. Flora Shaw was almost certainly correct when she suspected Leyds' visit to Europe involved more than to receive medical treatment.

However, Leyds returned home disappointed, the German government, which was attempting to repair the damage caused by the Kaiser's Telegram, had advised Kruger not to break off relations with Britain by terminating the London Convention and neither France nor Russia were prepared to act alone in support of the ZAR.

The failure of the Raid and the capture of Jameson and his men now freed Kruger to deal with the Reformers in Johannesburg without fear or favour. As has been shown, the threat of a successful Raid and the possibility of Jameson's entry into Johannesburg had disconcerted Oom Paul but with the Raiders literally in his grasp, he was able to turn his anger onto the Reformers and in particular the members of the Reform Committee. Robinson's declaration on 1 January that Jameson was acting outside the law had not condemned the Reformers. Realising that he could not sit by and leave them to their fate, the High Commissioner, in response to a false report in the *Cape Times* that the Reformers had risen in Johannesburg, offered his services to Kruger to try to resolve the dispute. Kruger accepted but at the time was still unaware of the possible outcome of the Raid. Weeks earlier, it had been proposed that if things in Johannesburg reached a crisis, Robinson accompanied by Rhodes would go there in order to mediate. This was now clearly out of the question. On 1 January Sir Hercules received a telegram from Chamberlain which urged him to 'act with vigour'; to be quick and decisive in sorting things out. For the ailing Robinson this was more easily said than done, and he had already indicated that he would only go to Pretoria if things were in extremis.[18] It was during his journey, accompanied by his nurse, that Robinson heard of the unconditional surrender of Jameson's force and, clearly, his bargaining chips had been considerably diminished. Robinson did not try to

---

16   V.I. Kuitenbrouwer, *War of Words, Dutch Pro-Boer Propaganda and the South African War (1899-1902)* (Amsterdam: Amsterdam University Press, 2012), p. 56.

17   Kuitenbrouwer, *War of Words*, p. 60.

18   He suffered from heart problems and dropsy and conducted his negotiations with Kruger and the Executive whilst lying on a couch. Marshall Hole, *The Jameson Raid*, p. 242.

Crowds await the captured reformers outside the Grand Hotel Pretoria. (*Illustrated London News,* 1896)

clarify the terms of the surrender which, as has been explained, were somewhat dubious. Even on his return from Pretoria, he was still convinced that there had been no conditional terms for Willoughby's surrender and, as late as 20 January, informed Chamberlain that this was the case.[19] He was met on his journey by representatives of the Orange Free State who sought assurances that their Republic would not also be attacked. Robinson was able to deal with this to their satisfaction and assure them that there would be no further invasions. The final development, as Robinson journeyed towards a difficult meeting with Kruger, was the receipt of a second offer of resignation by Rhodes. Rhodes' first offer to resign as Prime Minister of the Cape Colony had been refused, claimed Garret and Edwards, as there was still a possibility of Jameson's Raid being successful and Rhodes would be able to take some credit for this.[20] Perhaps with a sigh of relief, or even an greater apprehension as to the resignation's significance regarding Rhodes' involvement in the Raid, Robinson accepted the 'Colossus' offer, but Rhodes did not formally resign as Prime Minister of the Cape Colony until 7 January.

The only remaining unresolved issue was whether the Reformers had actually taken up arms against the ZAR. As has been explained, they had not, but rather prepared the town against a possible Boer attack. Nor had they, with the recall of Bettington's Horse, offered material assistance to the Raiders. Robinson however, had to meet Oom Paul, who was a more cunning adversary and who held the whip hand. Under such circumstances it was very difficult for the infirm Robinson to 'act with vigour' as Chamberlain had instructed. He faced his meeting with Kruger as a defeated man who needed to apologise for his countrymen's reckless

19   Blue Book, C 8063, Part II, No. 13.
20   Garrett & Edwards, *The Story of an African Crisis,* p. 158.

actions. Completely in Kruger's thrall he foreswore anything which might aggravate the wily Boer. Almost tearfully, he rejected Chamberlain's offer of sending troops to Mafeking in order to bolster his arguments and argued that he must have a free rein, but by doing so dealt himself a losing hand.[21] His only advisers were De Wet, who was in a state of panic, and Sir Sydney Sheppard, previously Commissioner for Bechuanaland, who had resigned the previous year to take up a commercial appointment which, it was rumoured, linked him with Rhodes' business empire. All Sir Hercules could do was to request that Kruger act with humanity and to arrange that hostilities ceased until Robinson could arrive in Pretoria. The weakened High Commissioner's influence was made even weaker.

When the news of Jameson's surrender arrived in Johannesburg on Thursday 2 January there was pandemonium. Some *Uitlanders* were keen to attempt to rescue his force whilst others, including the Reform Committee members, were against such a risky action. It seemed that the likelihood of a Boer attack on Johannesburg was now almost a certainty. The Reform Committee's popularity, according to Garrett and Edwards, fell since they had refused to support Jameson by sending men out to meet him.[22] Sir Hercules' actions in the days preceding Jameson's Raid came in for censure and this criticism was increased when the citizens of Johannesburg learned that he had decided to meet with Kruger before meeting with the Reformers.

On 7 January, Robinson, having met with Kruger and his Executive, issued an order that the *Uitlanders* in Johannesburg should lay down their weapons as a condition for beginning negations with the Boer Government. There were 8,000 Burghers waiting to intervene should the Reformers choose to do otherwise. These Boers could not be kept in check for long and therefore needed the Reformers' agreement within twenty-four hours. There was no mention of the Government acceding to the *Uitlanders'* grievances. Fitzpatrick reports that during Sir Hercules' meeting with the Boer Executive there was a potential offer of considering any *Uitlander* grievances which were properly presented but he must have felt that the Reformers' precarious position made a sympathetic hearing of these grievances very unlikely.[23]

The Reform Committee debated their options. They had, as has been mentioned, only a limited number of weapons and, although they had undertaken considerable preparations to defend the town in case of attack, the forces opposing them were significantly larger than their own. They were also concerned as to what would happen to Jameson's men if Johannesburg did not disarm. Would this give Kruger the excuse to execute those who had attempted to free the town from 'Boer tyranny'? Jameson had become a hero for many in Johannesburg as well as in Britain and the Reformers felt that he could not be abandoned to his fate. However, Robinson's message, delivered by the British Agent, de Wet, warned them that to not to disarm would '…forfeit all claim to the sympathy of Her Majesty's Government'.[24] The Reformers entered into a long discussion with the de Wet. They wanted assurances that the Boers would not take revenge on the *Uitlanders* in Johannesburg and, especially, upon members of the Reform Committee; Sir Jacobus felt able to reassure them on both counts. Thus convinced, in the belief that not to disarm would jeopardise Jameson and that Robinson would insist that their grievances be seriously considered, they agreed to disarm. Both Chamberlain and Kruger were informed of the Committee's decision and Robinson expressed the hope that this would result in Kruger considering the *Uitlanders'* grievances seriously. The *Uitlanders* began to disarm in a state of '…sullenness, doubt and doped with words.'[25]

The Boers began to collect the *Uitlanders'* weapons and were both surprised and incredulous that they gathered less than 2,000 rifle and only three Maxims. Surely, they believed, there had to be more. The failure to give up these supposed weapons was a failure in the Reformer's agreement to surrender. Kruger

---

21   Blue Book, C 7933, Nos. 84 and 93.
22   Garrett and Edwards, *The Story of an African Crisis,* p. 211.
23   Fitzpatrick, *The Transvaal from Within,* p. 151.
24   Fitzpatrick, *The Transvaal from Within,* p. 164.
25   Marshall Hole, *The Jameson Raid,* p. 252.

Jameson inside his heavily-
guarded cell in Pretoria.
(*Illustrated London News,*
1896)

Jameson Raid captives whiling away their time in Boer captivity. (*Illustrated London News,* 1896)

Jameson's men undergo inspection by the Governor of Pretoria Prison. (*Illustrated London News,* 1896)

came under considerable pressure from some quarters to take drastic action. Robinson, whom we have seen, was on the back foot with regard to the negotiations, seemed to have exerted himself at this point however, by threatening British Government intervention if this happened. The Reform Committee realised that they must convince the Boers that there were not large numbers of rifles still in *Uitlanders'* hands. Police Commissioner van Niekerk instructed Detective de Witt Tossel to search the 'English' cemetery 'thoroughly' for any hidden arms.[26] No weapons were found.[27] Eventually, Kruger having extended the deadline, was convinced that all the weapons had been surrendered and called off action against the town. Kruger's proclamation of the extension contained the confirmation that all those who had laid down their arms would not be harmed, with the exception of 'all persons and corporations who will appear to be the chief offenders, ringleaders, leaders, instigators, and those who have caused the rebellion at Johannesburg and (its) suburbs.'[28] Such individuals and organisation would, face the ZAR courts to answer for their actions. Robinson, de Wet, and the Reform Committee had been out manoeuvred by the wily old President. Kruger showed even more skill when, in an attempt to quell any uprising in Johannesburg as a result of his threat to arrest the ringleaders, on the final day designated for them to disarm, he informed the people of the town that it

---

26   National Archives of South Africa (NASA) TAB SP 892, Van Niekerk to Tossel, 27 January 1896.
27   NASA TAB, SP 879, Tossel to van Niekerk, 27 January 1896.
28   Blue Book, C 8063, Appendix p. 290.

was his intention to turn Johannesburg into a municipality with a Mayor who would be responsible for its government and organisation. In this way Kruger attempted to reassure and placate the *Uitlanders* by both forgiving and forgetting their past actions. Fitzpatrick was incredulous that Kruger would attempt to fool the *Uitlanders* in this way, having already threatened to arrest and try their leaders. Warrants were issued and 64 leading Reformers were arrested in two swoops and sent by train to the prison in Pretoria which also housed Jameson. The leading Reformers were not surprised by their arrest and some, such as Phillips, cooperated to the extent of giving themselves up at a prearranged spot.[29] Andrew Trimble, who had become the Reformers Chief of Police, had no such ideas of surrender and armed himself with a letter from Frank Rhodes, which stated that 'Trimble has rendered us all good service during the last month, if you can do anything for him I shall be glad'.[30] Disguised as an elderly Boer, Trimble was able to escape from the police headquarters even though it was surrounded by ZARPS.[31] After a series of adventures worthy of 'Boy's Own' stories, he made his escape to Durban.[32]

Kruger then turned his attention to the fate of Jameson and his men. The Raiders had been in the Pretoria jail and he had a number of options as what to do next. He could have insisted that they were tried before ZAR courts but, instead, he suggested that they be sent to Britain to be punished under British Law. Only those of the Raiders who had Transvaal citizenship would come before its courts. At first Kruger wanted the whole group, including the rank and file to be punished, but when Chamberlain protested that they were only obeying orders, it was agreed that only the leaders should be tried. Relieved, the Colonial Secretary thanked Kruger for his magnanimous act.[33] Jameson and thirteen of his officers, including the American, Major Heany, were sent to Durban and embarked for England on the troopship, *Victoria*, nine days before the majority of his men left Pretoria on the 26 January. The wounded Major Coventry remained in hospital in Krugersdorp and such was the severity of his wounds that his parents heard he had died and a memorial service was planned to be held at Mary Magdalene's Church in the grounds of Croome Court, the residence of his father, the Earl of Coventry. On the evening preceding this service, the error was corrected when it was learned that Major Coventry had been wounded but was still alive and would recover. The memorial was hurriedly altered, and a thanksgiving service was held instead.[34]

29   D. Rhoodie, *Conspirators in Conflict* (Elsies River: Tafeberg-Uitgewers, 1967) p. 18.
30   Killie Campbelll Africana Library (KCAL), Trimble Collection, F. Rhodes to C. Rhodes, 8 January 1896.
31   South African Republic Police.
32   Colvin, *The Life of Jameson*, Vol. 2, pp. 142-43 and Muller, *Policing the Witswaterand,* p. 206.
33   Fisher, *Paul Kruger: His Life and Time,* p. 195.
34   M. Krout, *A Looker on in London* (New York: Dodd, Mead & Co., 1899) p. 212.

11

The Trials

On 25 February, the prisoners were disembarked from the *Victoria* on to a tug at Purfleet and were finally taken by police launch to Gravesend. The War Office was apprehensive that there would be adverse publicity, especially since Jameson and his men were seen as heroes by the general public. The Press speculated that the *Victoria*, might either land at Plymouth or transfer its passengers to disembark at Dartmouth or Falmouth; all far from the clamour of London.[1] There was also a consideration of the cost of bringing the Raiders directly to London for, wherever they disembarked, their fellow passengers would also have to land; these passengers were the 2nd Kings Own Royal Lancaster Regiment who were returning from India.

The captive officers were quickly transported by two private omnibuses to Bow Street Magistrates' Court to be tried before Sir John Bridge, the Chief Metropolitan Magistrate. All but the American Heany were charged under the Foreign Enlistment Act 1870 which made it a crime for any British citizen to enlist in the forces of a foreign power at war with any state with which Great Britain was at peace.[2] The prisoners did not reply to the charge and were released to appear in two weeks on personal bail of £2,000 and £1,000 security.

Mary Krout has provided what seems to be an eyewitness account of the proceedings when Jameson and 'his confederates' reappeared before Bridge on 17 March 1896.[3] The Authorities' attempt to make these early legal proceedings discrete failed as both the Bow Street Magistrates' Court and the surrounding streets were packed with Jameson's supporters who applauded the accused when they entered the court room. The uproar was such that Sir John Bridge threatened to clear the room.[4] Amongst the onlookers were Duke of Abercorn, the Honorary Chairman of the BSAC, Colonel Brocklehurst who commanded the Life Guards, Willoughby's regiment, Captain Charles White the brother of the two Whites who took part in the Raid, Captain Stracey, brother of Major Stracey, Major Kincaid-Smith the brother of Jameson's artillery officer, as well as a few of Jameson's troopers who had arrived in England on the 23 January. All the defendants seemed to be somewhat stoical except for Major Coventry, now recovering from his wounds, who seems to have sometimes found the proceedings amusing.

Krout described the various lawyers who represented both the Defendants and the Crown. The leading counsel for the defence was Sir Edward Clarke QC, previously Solicitor-General, during which appointment he represented the accused in the infamous 'Royal Baccarat Scandal' which involved Edward, the Prince of Wales, and many of the representatives of London high society.[5] Now in private practice, Clarke had recently

---

1   *The Times*, 22 February 1896.
2   It appears that this act was passed at the time of the Franco-Prussian War (1870-71) and this may have been the only successful prosecution under the Act.
3   Krout, *A Looker on in London*.
4   Bridge had, in the previous year, presided over the trial of Oscar Wilde.
5   This notorious court case was concerned with an accusation of cheating at cards against Lieutenant Colonel Sir William Gordon-Cumming. When the accusation became common knowledge, Gordon Cummings proceeded to accuse the other players of slander. Edward Prince of Wales, who was a good friend of the lieutenant colonel,

Raid officers on board the SS *Victoria* reading British newspapers for the first time since their captivity. (*The Graphic,* 1896)

Jameson and some of his officers on board SS *Victoria*. (*Illustrated London News*, 1896)

Jameson's men disembarking from a tender which brought them from Harlech Castle to the military docks at Plymouth. (*Illustrated London News,* 1896)

Raid officers before the bench at Bow Street Magistrates' Court. (*Illustrated London News,* 1896)

represented Oscar Wilde in his notorious attempt to sue the Marquis of Queensberry for libel. Amongst the defence team was Edward Carson who had defended Queensbury against Wilde's accusation and Sir Frank Lockwood who had prosecuted Oscar Wilde for sodomy. A number of the defendants including Jameson had engaged their own defence lawyers. It was a very distinguished and powerful team.

The prosecution line up was equally eminent. It was led by the Attorney-General, Sir Richard Webster, QC, MP, who was later to become Lord Chief Justice, Sir Charles Matthews who was also involved in the Oscar Wilde case and was a friend of royalty, and Horace Avory who had also appeared as a prosecutor of Oscar Wilde and was known as 'The acid drop' in legal circles because of his caustic wit. Together they were truly an 'imposing array of eminent men'.[6] The eminence and number of the lawyers involved indicated both the seriousness with which the Government took the Raiders' offence and the means with which the accused had to defend themselves. In addition to the official legal representatives, Sir George Lewis, was also present in the court. He had a reputation for appearing in *causes célèbres* but when questioned about his attendance he explained he was simply an observer on behalf of the BSAC.

Witnesses for the prosecution arrived from South Africa and these included Sergeant White, who had refused to join the Raid and who had carried the message from Sir Hercules Robinson ordering Jameson to return. As the trial continued, witnesses were called, and documents such as the *Invitation Letter* were produced as well as the instruction from the High Commissioner to call off the Raid. The case was adjourned to the following week when more damning evidence was presented against Jameson and his officers. There was an argument as to how much ammunition the Raiders had left when they surrendered. One witness claimed that they still had a quarter remaining suggesting either defeatism or cowardice, but one of the accused said, loud enough for others to hear, this was untrue. The trial was adjourned on several more occasions and it was not until June 16 that the final arguments were heard during which there was an important development as far as the accused were concerned. Webster, the Attorney General, informed Sir John Bridge that he had decided to separate the accused into two groups. First, those who shared the real responsibility for the organisation and the prosecution of the Raid.[7] Secondly, those who had not been involved in the Raid's preparation but had obeyed orders.[8] This, Webster asserted, did not entirely excuse them as they were officers in Her Majesty's Army but they may have been simply led '...possibly by their folly, want of judgment or impetuosity, to participate in it'.[9] If this distinction were not to be made, argued Webster, then all of those who took place in the Raid should be prosecuted. Clarke expressed his gratitude to the Attorney General for separating the accused in this way. Sir John Bridge agreed that, although the nine whom Webster had identified had committed illegal acts, they had done so under orders and he discharged them. The six who really bore responsibility would have to be committed for trial at the High Court since the case against Jameson and his senior officers was too serious to be dealt with in Magistrates' Court with its limited powers of sentencing. The six were released on bail to await their trial.

Prior to the High Court trial, there was some anticipation amongst the Government officials as to what evidence would be presented by the Raider's defence lawyers but also an acknowledgement that those accused could not be forced to give evidence and this would prevent the prosecution barristers interrogating them. The defendants' solicitor, Bouchier Hawksley, however, instructed their counsel, Sir Edward Clarke

---

appeared as a witness and although he admitted to not seeing anything amiss, such was the strength of the accusers' claims, he felt he had to believe that they were true. Gordon Cummings lost his case and was dismissed from the army. Prince Edward became extremely unpopular since the general public were sympathetic to the defendant...

6   Krout, *A Looker on in London*, p. 213.

7   Leander Starr Jameson, Sir John Willoughby, Frederick White, Raleigh Grey, Robert White and Charles John Coventry.

8   J. B. Stracey, C. H. Villiers, K.J. Kincaid Smith, H. M. Grenfell, C. P. Foley, C.L.D. Monro, C.F. Lindsell, E. C. S. Holden and A. Gosling.

9   Krout, *A Looker on in London*, p. 265.

QC, that he should do nothing which might implicate any Government department or official.[10] Was this because there was an unwritten agreement between Rhodes and Chamberlain that the trial of the Raiders would not delve too deeply as to whether the Raid did have the support of the Government or, at least, that of its Colonial Secretary? As will be discussed later, Willoughby thought that his officers had been thrown to the wolves by Hawksley's instructions.

Whilst the Raiders awaited their High Court appearance, important events were taking place in Matabeleland now known as Rhodesia. Jameson had withdrawn the majority of the BSAC troops from the area in order for them to be part of

Jameson under pressure during the Bow Street trial. (*The Graphic*, 1896)

his Raid and this left the country almost defenceless. The Ndebele believed that settlers were responsible for a number of natural disasters such as drought and Rinderpest which were devastating their cattle. They rose in revolt and many lives were lost on both sides. These events damaged Jameson's standing in the eyes of the public and it is suggested that this changed their perspective about the Raid.[11]

The trial at the High Court opened on 20 July 1896 and was presided over by Lord Chief Justice Russell, an Irishman who was the first Catholic Lord Chief Justice since the Reformation. Russell had previously been the Attorney General, with a reputation for separating vital points from obscuring details. He was accompanied on the Bench by Judge Henry Hawkins and Justice Charles Pollock.[12]

Before the case began and the Jury sworn in, Clarke attempted to have the charges against Jameson and the others dismissed, arguing, as he had done in the Magistrates' Court, that the Foreign Enlistment Act did not apply to Pitsani which was not within the British dominions. His argument was described in the *Yale Law Journal* as an intellectual treat. 'It was a marvel of ingenuity, lucidity and logical strength.'[13] However, the three Judges overruled Clarke's objection which had been based on how British sovereignty had been acquired. The Judges were only interested in whether the sovereignty applied to Pitsani or not and they ruled that it did. Clarke also claimed that Jameson had not prepared a hostile expedition and had not expected to fight; he was only attempting to help those who were striving to be free. None of the Law Officers involved, however, considered the possibility that Jameson had acted with "the licence of her Majesty". The British officers certainly believed this was the case as did Clarke, who in his memoirs, wrote that Jameson had quite

---

10   Edward Clarke, *The Story of my Life* (London: John Murray, 1918), p. 327.
11   See Chapter 12.
12   Sir Henry Hawkins had a reputation as a hanging Judge and was thought by some, including Edward Clarke to lean too far towards the prosecution arguments in cases that he heard.
13   John Wurts.,' Seen at the Jameson Trial', *Yale Law Journal* (1896 Vol. 6 Issue 1), p. 35.

'…honestly and truthfully told his officers and troopers that the advance they were making was in the service of the Queen.'[14] David Saks believed that the Raiders were inspired by 'patriotic, imperial motives.'[15]

In his opening statement, Webster, the Attorney General, went to great lengths to explain the status of Bechuanaland and the position of the BSAC. He made it clear that the Foreign Enlistment Act applied to all the land acquired by the BSAC when it was incorporated in 1885. Since Pitsani and Pitsani Potlugo had been ceded to the BSAC, they were still part of the Queen's Dominions. The fact was confirmed by a junior representative of the Colonial Office.[16] This was also confirmed by Major William Panzera, an expert adviser for the British Treasury, who had served during the first Matabele War, and knew the area well. Britain was on good terms with the ZAR which meant the Raid was in contravention of the Act which '…had been secretly and carefully thought out by men in prominent and reputable positions.'[17]

Krout claims that there was little new evidence presented to the Jury in the High Court. All the participants had been given a printed version of the proceedings in the Magistrates' Court and were familiar with what had transpired there.[18] If this was the case, it is hard to believe that the Jury would not be influenced by the earlier trial, but as will been seen, they had not been entirely convinced by Sir John Bridge's conclusion. A number of witnesses appeared for the prosecution: Henry Flowers, the postmaster of Mafeking, who described the cutting of the wires, and Trooper Lawler of the MMP who confirmed that the wires had been cut, which was a criminal act in itself. Rowland, the cyclist, also appeared to confirm he had delivered the Reform Committee's message to Jameson. It was during Rowland's examination by Clarke that the barrister mentioned the ' very great alarm in Johannesburg about the women and children'. The Lord Chief Justice pointed out that the wording in the original transcript was just 'much alarm' and Clarke withdrew his comment. [19] An example of Russell's attention to detail and an example of Clarke's attempts to mitigate the Raisers' actions.

Chief Detective Fred de Wit Tossel described how policing in Johannesburg was taken over by Trimble's men and, during questioning, it transpired that Tossel was actually an Englishman named May who had changed his name. Lieutenant Eloff, was also called and he recounted his meetings with the Raiders and the subsequent fighting at Doornkop.[20]

Clarke's defence of the accused concentrated on the technicality as to whether the Raid had started from land which was part of the Crown's dominions. It would seem that Sir Edward kept referring to this issue in spite of the Judges' ruling because he was attempting to sow a seed of doubt in the minds of the Jurors. His point was that the BSAC had authority in the area of Pitsani Potlugo but, in fact, the Charter clearly stated that final authority for the area which had been ceded rested with the Secretary of State for the Colonies who was a Minister of the Crown. Clarke was eventually forced to admit this was the case. There could be no possibility of him denying that the Raid had taken place and the idea that it was not an offensive act against a friendly power was hard to excuse since the Raiders had taken rifles, Maxims and cannon with them. They also had up to date and accurate maps of the area which suggested that the Raid had been carefully planned rather than being a response to a sudden emergency. The only possible explanation for this apparent aggression was the dire plight of the people in Johannesburg. The withdrawal of the ZARPs, claimed Clarke, had

14   Wurts, *Seen at the Jameson Trial* quoted by Lord Hoffman of Chedworth *The Third Keating Lecture: 16th October 2004* <www.Keatingchambers.co.uk/ resources/publications/2004/keating_lecture_061004.aspx> (accessed 15 August 2014).

15   David Saks, 'The Jameson Raid; A Failed Dress rehearsal for the Anglo-Boer War', *Military History Journal*, Vol. 12, No. 5, 2003.

16   Krout, *A Looker on in London*, p. 276.

17   Krout, *A Looker on in London*, p. 275.

18   Krout, *A Looker on in London*, p. 276.

19   Krout, *A Looker on in London*, p. 278.

20   Krout, *A Looker on in London*, p. 289.

increased the danger to the peaceful inhabitants as it encouraged lawlessness. What would have been said of Jameson if he had not responded to the situation of the *Uitlanders* if they had risen? Jameson had been surprised when he had learned from cyclist Rowland that there had been no uprising. In continuing with the Raid, Jameson was acting from his heart rather than his from his head and proceeding towards Johannesburg was the only way for him to go because he was surrounded by Boer forces. Sir Edward attempted to cajole the Jury by reminding them that, although they were a body of men acting in concert, they were also individuals and they would not be able to hide behind the fact that they would each individually be responsible for a guilty verdict.

Sir Frank Lockwood, who appeared on behalf of Willoughby and Coventry, took up the theme of the Raiders being driven by their honour and their obligation to defend people who were their friends and kin. A guilty verdict would destroy their reputation and deprive them of their liberty but they would always know that they acted as brave and honourable men.

In reply, the Attorney General's closing summary did not rely on rhetoric or play to the emotions of the Jury. Using the Law, he steadily dismissed the points which Clarke and Lockwood had raised in the Raiders' defence. The Foreign Enlistment Act did apply in this case and this was irrefutable. The argument that the Raid was, in fact a rescue in an emergency situation, could be disproved since the there was considerable evidence that preparations for it had taken place over a period of months. When Jameson had been challenged by the Commandant General as to why the Raiders had entered the ZAR, Jameson's reply was that he was helping the citizens of Johannesburg to obtain their rights but he said nothing about them being in danger. Similarly, before the real fighting began, Jameson had been told by De Wet that there had been no uprising. Jameson, Webster argued, should have called off the Raid at that point but, instead, launched an attack on the Boers who were blocking his way. Webster concluded his speech by pointing out the defendants were men of standing and they could not have been unaware of the possible disastrous outcome of their actions. The Attorney General's final flourish reflected the logical methods he had used throughout his presentation. The Jury should only acquit Jameson and the rest if they believed that they had not broken the law.

At the end of the trial, which had lasted four months because of frequent adjournments and delays, Lord Chief Justice Russell, in his six-hour summing up, reminded the Jury about their duty to consider both the evidence presented and the summaries of law provided by his judicial colleagues and himself. Only if there was a reasonable doubt that the Raiders had actually committed a criminal act should they be found not guilty. The accused were all men who owed their positions either through their military rank or, in Jameson's case, from an appointment under the terms of the Charter, for which the final arbiter was the Colonial Secretary.

The Raid was an expedition of trained troops commanded by officers holding the Queen's commission. Their men were well armed and operated as a military unit. Lord Chief Justice Russell clarified the major points at issue. First, was the Raid an 'armed incursion' into a friendly state no matter whether it intended or not to overthrow that state. Secondly, did it intend to meet any opposition with force?[21] Dramatically, Russell informed the Jury that if the Queen had ordered this expedition it would have been an act of war but, if done by individuals without proper authority, it would be illegal. The Transvaal had the right to expect both protection and friendship from the Queen's subjects. For the Raiders to suggest the motive for their actions was to protect women and children was absurd.

The Lord Chief Justice then began to put to the Jury the questions which he said must inform their verdict. At this point, Sir Edward Clarke attempted to interrupt by making an objection but Russell silenced him. Clarke had had his chance. Judge Russell then put the three questions which were at the heart of the case. First, were all or any of the defendants engaged in the preparation of a military expedition against a friendly

---

21   Krout, *A Looker on in London*, p. 291.

state? Secondly, did any or all of them assist in the preparation of that expedition, and thirdly, did any or all of the defendants take part in the expedition? The Jury were told that they must answer 'Yes' or 'No' to each of these questions. The Foreman ask whether they could answer instead with 'guilty' or 'not guilty', presumably to make sure that his colleagues were aware of the implications of simply 'Yes' or ' No'. With this guidance from the Bench, the Jury withdrew to consider their verdict.

As is customary, when they returned, the Jury was asked if they had agreed on a verdict and the foreman answered in the affirmative. A paper was handed to the Judges with the answer to the three questions which, was in each case, 'Yes'. Russell pronounced that this was the equivalent of a guilty verdict. The Foreman replied that they believed that the events in Johannesburg were a great provocation and explained why the Raiders had acted in the ways they did. Russell would have none of this sophistry and repeated that the Jury's answers meant that they thought the Raiders were guilty. The Foreman again answered that they had simply answered the questions asked which implied that they had not actually said that the accused were guilty or not guilty. Edward Clarke, in an attempt to seize an opportunity to defend his clients, tried to make a point but was firmly dismissed by the Judge who continued to address the Jury and directed them to find the Raiders guilty. The Foreman was not satisfied and, no doubt with some trepidation, emphasised that although they had answered the questions put to them in the affirmative, they did not totally agree with a verdict of ' guilty'. Russell was close to losing his patience and again, more forcibly, directed the Jurors to deliver a guilty verdict. Which, after some further discussion, the Foreman did. The trial has been described, somewhat harshly, as a judicial charade, since the reluctant Jury was directed to deliver a guilty verdict when they were clearly unwilling to do so.[22] It is clear that they were patriotic supporters of the 'heroic' Doctor but the Judges insisted that they should come to their decision on the basis of law. Once the verdict had been given, Clarke requested that the sentences be delayed since he would request a retrial as it was clear that the Jury had been reluctant to deliver the guilty verdict.

According to Muller, the Jury were to be kept '...in a place where they should be locked up without fire, light, food, or drink until they came to a decision.'[23] It was said by one of Lord Russell's friends that the Judge believed he was standing resolutely between public opinion and the Jury to ensure that justice was done since the Law was more important to him than patriotism or sentimentality.[24]

In spite of Clarke's attempts to delay them, the sentences were delivered on 29 July. Jameson was sent to Holloway prison for 15 months but only served four because he was taken ill. Kruger thought this suspicious, but it seems to have been a genuine cause for concern about Jameson's health. Willoughby was sentenced to ten months and Bobby White to seven, and his brother Harry, Grey, and Coventry five months each. All sentences were to be served without hard labour which meant they were not required to clean their cells, or wear prison garb. They were, however, permitted to receive their friends who supplied them with many comforts and luxuries not available to most prisoners.[25]

The verdict was unpopular with the public who, thanks to the Kaiser's intervention, regarded Jameson as a hero. This mood was also reflected in the play *An Artist's Model* by Owen Hall, which was being staged at Daly's Theatre at the time of the Raid. It retained many references to Jameson even though it had suffered from the Lord Chamberlain's attentions at the insistence of the Colonial Office.[26] *The Times* reported that the audience applauded loudly when the Transvaal crisis was touched upon but hissed and hooted when the Kaiser was mentioned.[27]

---

22   Krout, *A Looker on in London*, p. 291.
23   Muller. *Policing the Witswaterand* p. 284.
24   Marshall Hole, *The Jameson Raid*, p. 7.
25   Krout, *A Looker on in London*, p. 294.
26   John Russell Stephens, *The Censorship of English Drama 1824-1901* (London: CUP: (2010) pp. 129-30.
27   *The Times*, 13 January 1896.

Field Marshal Lord Wolseley, the Commander in Chief, felt obliged to draw the Secretary of State for War, the Marquis of Lansdowne's, attention to the sentences which had been placed upon the serving officers. The five convicted would be dismissed from the Army but excuses might be made for the behaviour of the other eight who had not been committed for trial at the High Court who, by joining the Raid, argued Wolseley, were driven by youthful impetuosity. However, he did point out that they had disobeyed orders in not returning to Pitsani when told to do so. The final judgement depended upon who had seen which order and who knew what was really going on.

As has been noted, the thought of being cashiered was too much for Sir John Willoughby, who wrote to the War Office claiming that he had acted in good faith and he believed that the Imperial authorities were in the know and this could be proved by telegrams which Jameson had shown him.[28] Buller, the Adjutant General, initially thought that Willoughby's claims were worth investigation but the Colonial Office stepped in, arguing that Jameson was not an officer and did not outrank Willoughby who should have shown more common sense to act on his say so.[29] Accordingly, Buller, having examined the trial transcript, believed there was no real evidence to indicate whether individuals had volunteered to take part in the Raid or had been under orders to do so. Foley, Holden, and Stracey could be considered to be volunteers whilst Grenfell appeared to have acted under pressure. They had not seen the actual orders which directed them to return to the border. These were seen only by Willoughby, Coventry, and Monro but Grey did know of them. Buller wrote formally to each officer asking them if they had received orders to participate in the Raid.[30] He believed that Villiers, Kincaid-Smith, Grenfell, and Lindsell had followed their superiors' orders and so should not be cashiered but lose their secondments. Buller also wrote to each of them to ascertain whether they had knowingly disobeyed the High Commissioner's order. Given this escape route, five of the eight concerned argued that they had obeyed orders at the start of the Raid and were unaware that contrary orders had been given to retreat. Grenfell, in a spirit of nit picking, stated there had been no reliable order to retire and, even if there was, it was too late to obey since they were being pressed too closely by the Boers. Lansdowne was prepared to accept the explanation that they were obeying the orders of the Administrator of Matabeleland (Jameson) as justification for the officers' actions. Buller, however, taking a more thoughtful view, believed that the excuse of simply obeying orders was insufficient to justify their actions and there must be some form of punishment. Consequently, Villiers, Kincaid-Smith, Grenfell, and Lindsell were summoned to the War Office where they received the appropriate reprimand from Buller which was entered on their records. These officers returned to duty on 8 September 1896.[31]

Buller believed that Stracey, Foley, and Holden knew what was going on and should not have joined the Raid and should resign their commissions. Monro, who had been ordered to retreat and had not done so, should also resign as he had knowingly disobeyed an order. Resignation was something of a consolation, since by giving these officers this opportunity, they would be entitled to receive their retiring allowances which had they been dismissed they would not.[32]

Willoughby's supporters continue to maintain the pressure against him being cashiered and, on 18 September 1896, the convicted men were all allowed to resign and so remain entitled to their pensions; Coventry, who was a militia officer, received no such gratuity. Both Coventry and Jameson were released before they had served their full sentences; the former on the 22 August because of his wounds and the latter

---

28   Van der Poel, *The Jameson Raid*, p. 181.
29   British Library (BL): Landsdowne Mss. 88906/16/9, Lansdowne to Salisbury. Letter from Mead to Bower 19.09.96 reported in Van der Poel, *The Jameson Raid*, p. 182.
30   TNA WO 327485: Buller to Haliburton 1 August 1896, note by Landsdowne.
31   Ian Beckett, 'Daring a Wrong Like This: The War Office and the Jameson Raid', *Soldiers of the Queen: The magazine of the Victorian Military History Society*, Issue 161, September 2015. p. 161.
32   Beckett, 'Daring a Wrong Like This', pp. 181-82.

on 2 December, because of his ill health. When Willoughby was finally release on 30 March 1897, all the convicted officers were at liberty.

Whilst the Raiders were being tried under English Law, the trial of the Reformers was a less straight-forward process. Their arrival as captives at Pretoria Railway Station was particularly unpleasant. They were surrounded by an angry mob which hurled abuse, and sometimes kicks and blows, and the mounted Burghers, who were supposed to protect them from the crowd's anger, often caused them even more discomfort by allowing their horses to get too close to the prisoners. The Reformers were housed in the same prison as Jameson, who was awaiting his return to England, and, although it was situated close to the building where Sir Hercules Robinson was staying during his visit to Kruger and the Executive, the High Commissioner chose not to visit them even on a single occasion. Perhaps he thought that to do so might suggest that he approved of their actions in some way but they must have felt abandoned. Their prison was a far cry from the luxurious homes many had occupied in Johannesburg and must have been a harsh contrast. On entering the jail they were searched and confined in cells which had mud floors on which dirty straw mattresses were placed upon which the prisoners slept. Conditions were unsanitary and, in many cases, four or five men were confined in a cell 9 feet long by 5 feet 6 inches wide, with one small grating for ventilation. The stench, particularly as this was summer in South Africa, was unbearable, and the heat made blankets unnecessary.[33] There might have been some justification for this overcrowding since Jameson's men were confined in the same prison and space must have been very limited. However, there were examples of unnecessary hardship, such as when a prisoner suffering from dysentery was locked in a cell with four others for twelve hours without any sanitary arrangements; not even a bucket. It is true that these were probably the standard conditions in the prison, but the numbers involved exacerbated the situation.

After a fortnight, all the prisoners except Hays Hammond, Farrar, Fitzpatrick and Frank Rhodes were released on bail of between £2,000-£4,000; these four were deemed to be the ring leaders of the Reformers and were to remain in the jail for a further four weeks. After protests from within the ZAR itself and from the British Government, the Boers were persuaded to house them in better conditions in a cottage in Pretoria under armed guard. This change to a form of house arrest came with conditions. Each man was required to deposit £10,000 in gold sovereigns as a surety that they would not break the terms of their bail. In addition, they had to agree to pay the cost of their confinement which would include the wages and expenses of their guards, which Fitzpatrick calculated was around £1,000 a month.[34]

The preliminary hearing of the case began on 8 February 1896 and Dr Herman Coster, the State Attorney, was the chief prosecutor. This initial hearing was something of a 'fishing' expedition from which to formulate charges.[35] It also appeared that Kruger's Government was prepared to use the fact that the Reformers entered into open discussion with them as part of the indictment since evidence from Judge Kotzé about the Reformers' identity was based upon a list provided by them to the Boer Government rather than only those he had actually met during his previous negotiations. The Reformers were accused on four counts. First, and most serious, was the accusation that they had conspired to endanger the safety of the ZAR; which was an act of treason. Secondly, that they had prepared to assist Jameson in his illegal invasion. Thirdly, they had illegally distributed arms. Finally, it was charged that the Reform Committee had usurped the authority of the State by, for example, appointing their own police force. After some negotiations, the prosecution agreed to drop the first two charges against those men who were deemed less prominent amongst the Reformers. Similarly, it was agreed that the second, third and fourth charges against the ring leaders would be dropped on condition they pleaded guilty to the charge of treason. Since the prosecution had in its possession a copy of the *Invitation Letter,* retrieved from the battlefield of Doornkop, the leaders had little option.

---

33 Fitzpatrick, *The Transvaal from Within*, p. 175.
34 Fitzpatrick *The Transvaal from Within*, p. 176.
35 Fitzpatrick, *The Transvaal from Within*, p. 179.

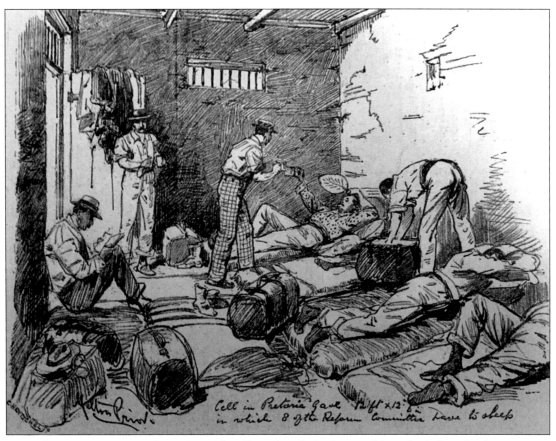

Reformers in captivity at Johannesburg. The cell was described as being 12ft by 12ft which made it luxurious compared with most others. (*Illustrated London News*, 1896)

There was also the question of who would be presiding Judge in the trial proper. Judge Reinhold Gregorowski, who had been a Judge in the Orange Free State and was its current Attorney General, was chosen since so many ZAR Judges had already been involved with the Reformers in one way or another and it was suggested Gregorowski would be able to judge the case dispassionately.[36] However, Fitzpatrick claimed that Gregorowski was notorious for the harshness of his sentences on non-Boers, and, in addition, the Judge had technically no legal standing in the ZAR since he was from the Orange Free State.[37] On the opening day of the formal trial, the Courtroom in Pretoria was surrounded by mounted Burghers, members of the State Artillery and the police. There was a great deal of interest in the Reformers coupled with considerable animosity amongst the population of Pretoria. Gregorowski stated that the trial would be conducted under Roman-Dutch Law which meant that a guilty verdict would result in the death penalty. The likelihood of such a verdict had been greatly enhanced by the discovery of the 'Trommel van Bobby White' a despatch case belonging to Major Robert White which had been discarded at Doornkop and contained many incriminating documents. These included correspondence between Jameson and the Reformers, cyphers, code books such as MacNeil's *General and Telegraphic Mining Code* in which was a copy of the code used

36   Kruger, *The Memoirs of Paul Kruger*, p. 238.
37   Kruger, *The Memoirs of Paul Kruger*, p. 182.

Leaders of the Reform Committee being escorted to jail after a hearing at the Government Building, Pretoria hearing.
(*Illustrated London News,* 1896)

for all the incriminating telegrams and, to the detriment of the Reformers, the *Letter of Invitation.* The Boers alleged that White, in return for certain favours, agreed to sign an affidavit in which he declared that these documents were genuine. White confirmed that he had signed a document to say as much but there had been no such favours involved. Rather lamely he also claimed that he could not remember doing it.[38]

---

38   Kruger, *The Memoirs of Paul Kruger,* p. 188.

The Reformers on trial in the Market Hall, Pretoria. (L & F Philipps, *Some South African Recollections.* London: Longmans, Green & Co. 1900)

All the prisoners were found guilty and the Reformers were split into two groups with regards to sentencing; those who had been merely members of the Committee and those who were deemed to be ring leaders and conspirators with Jameson.[39] George Farrar, Lionel Phillips, Frank Rhodes, and John Hays Hammond were sentenced to death. It is said that as he pronounced this sentence, Gregorowski smiled. There was further speculation as to the four men's fate when it was discovered that a part of the gallows from Slachter's Nek, where in 1831, five Boers had been hanged by the British for rebellion, had been brought to Pretoria. The lesser offenders were fined £2,000 each, sentenced to two years in prison and banishment for three years. However, before this sentence was announced, one of the prisoners, Fred Gray, the father of six children, found the confinement and the threats made to the prisoners intolerable. He borrowed a cut throat razor and committed suicide in the prison lavatory.[40] The Executive began to realise that their propaganda triumph in seizing the Reformers and ending the Raid was beginning to slip away and they were in danger of losing international support if they treated their prisoners too harshly. There then began what Lady Longford described as Kruger's 'cat and mouse' tactics which were designed to damage the prisoners' morale.[41] The death sentence on the leaders was commuted to a heavy fine and lengthy imprisonment. Kruger required the Reformers to petition for mercy, express regret and also promise impeccable behaviour in the future. After

39 See Appendix VI.
40 Fisher, *Paul Kruger: His Life and Time,* p. 198; Longford, *Jameson's Raid,* p. 114; Edwards & Garrett, *The Story of an African Crisis,* p. 263.
41 Longford, *Jameson's Raid*, p. 114.

delivering their petitions, the four ring leaders were sentence to 15 years imprisonment. Ten less incrimi-nated Reformers were released immediately after paying their fines. The remainder of the accused had their sentences reduced to one year and, in a further example of clemency, on 30 May 1896, all but two of the minor prisoners who had refused to petition the Executive, were released. These two most obstinate *Uitlanders*, Aubrey Woolls-Sampson and Walter (Karri) Davies remained in jail for a further year until released by Kruger as a gesture to mark Queen Victoria's Diamond Jubilee. Somewhat ironically after his release, Woolls-Sampson wrote to Kruger for a job which, he asked, must involve 'nothing shady'.[42] During the Second Boer War, he fought and was wounded at Elandslaagte in 1899. Karri Davies became one of the most popular men in Cape Town and, as Colonel Davies, was one of the first to enter Mafeking at the end of its siege during the Second Boer War.[43] The Colonial Office, which was working hard to free the Reformers, did not appreciate the two men's 'headstrong gesture' in not petitioning the ZAR for clemency which, it argued, demonstrated patriotism beyond their country's demands.[44]

There remained the question of the fate of the four ring leaders. Realising that Kruger and his Government were sensitive to public opinion, there were further outpourings of protest from many quarters both in the ZAR and abroad. In addition Kruger did not wish to incur greater British anger and he also feared that the gold magnate Barney Barnato, whose nephew was amongst the Reformers taken prisoner, and who owned the Kimberley Central Diamond Mining Company, might carry out his threat to close the mines which provided the ZAR with so much of its income. On Gregorowski's 'recommendation', 15 years imprisonment was commuted to a payment of £25,000 fine – the equivalent of over £30 million in today's money – and the ring leaders were given the choice of staying out of politics for 15 years or to choose banishment. The fines were promptly paid, and Hays Hammond, Farrar and Phillips agreed not to meddle in politics. Fitzpatrick said that for them banishment was an impossible choice since that they had significant business interests in the ZAR and needed to remain.[45] Frank Rhodes refused the offer and was immediately banished and made his way to Matabeleland to help in the Second Matabele War.

Two of the major players amongst Reformers had not been arrested; Charles Leonard and Dr Wolff. Wolff had avoided the roundup of Reformers in Johannesburg by escaping to Cape Colony under a false name. Leonard was already in Cape Town at the time of the Reformers' arrest suffering from 'nervous prostration' and 'congestion of the brain'. Rather than return to the ZAR to face the music, Leonard claimed it was his duty to return to England to appear at the Committee of Inquiry into the Raid. Edward Fairfield thought 'there was something very mean about (Leonard) running away'.[46]

The War Office was now faced with what to do with the liberated Frank Rhodes, a signatory of the *Invitation Letter* and whose behaviour in plotting and encouraging the Reformers was regarded as more reprehensible that those who had taken part in the actual Raid. He had been one of the leaders of the Reformers and the link between his brother Cecil and Jameson. As such he was thought to have questionable motives for his involvement in a possible uprising and might not as been entirely concerned with improving the *Uitlander* conditions. Having received a private letter from Redvers Buller, Frank resigned from the Army with a pension of £300 a year.[47]

The Raid may have embarrassed the British Government and ruined Cecil Rhodes politically but in the eyes of the general public Jameson remained a heroic figure and manufacturers were not slow to climb upon the Raiders' bandwagon as can be seen from this advertisement for Mazawattee Tea.

---

42   Longford, *Jameson's Raid*, p. 115.
43   *Sydney Morning Herald*, 1 December 1926.
44   Longford, *Jameson's Raid,* p. 115.
45   Fitzpatrick, *The Transvaal from Within*, p. 220.
46   TNA CO 417/181 8401.
47   Beckett, 'Daring a Wrong Like This', p. 7.

Jameson calls a halt for Mazawattee tea on the way to Krugersdorp.
(*Illustrated London News,* 1896)

12

Not consistent with his Duty as Prime Minister

So significant were the international and political implications of the Raid and its failure, that both the Government of Cape Town and the British Government held inquiries in an attempt to discover exactly who was responsible for the fiasco.

The first of these examinations into the Jameson affair to report its findings was that carried out in the Cape Colony which had begun its investigations in May 1896. Its conclusions were set out in the following March in *The Report of the Select Committee of the Cape of Good Hope House of Assembly on the Raid into the Territory of the South African Republic*.[1] The composition of the Committee is worth examining since it would have been impossible to select a group of politicians and influential personalities in Cape Town without them having some connection with Cecil Rhodes. He was Prime Minister of the Cape Colony until the Jameson Raid had forced his resignation. He was extremely influential as Chair of a number of important mining and entrepreneurial companies, which, together with his forceful personality, meant that the threads of his influence extended into almost every aspect of the Colony. In the end, six members were chosen; Sir Thomas Upington, John X Merriman, the Reverend Stephanus Du Toit, William Schreiner, John Rose Innes and Sir Thomas Fuller.

Sir Thomas Upington, the Chair of the Committee, was the Cape Colony's Attorney General, described as a 'crack speaker, brilliant and sarcastic … The clubland (sic) of Cape Town looks to him as its humorous and sententious oracle.'[2] Upington, like Rhodes, emigrated to South Africa because of his fragile health. He had been Prime Minister of Cape Colony for a short period between 1884-86 during which time the troubles with the Boer mini republics of Stellaland and Goshen had occurred. Upington had expressed great sympathy for these republics which had gained him the epithet 'the Afrikaner from Cork'.

Perhaps the most significant Committee member other than Upington was John X Merriman who had been Treasurer General in Rhodes' Government. Merriman resigned over the 'Logan Scandal', in which Sir James Silverwright, a friend and ally of Cecil Rhodes with strong connections to the *Afrikaner Bund*, corruptly offered a 15-year catering contract for the national railway to his friend James Logan. Rhodes was forced to cancel the contract because of the political outcry but compensated Silverwright and Logan with a large amount government funds. The scandal brought about the end of Rhodes' first government.

John Rose Innes had served as Rhodes' Attorney General but had also resigned as a result of the Logan scandal which he had helped to expose. He had become a vehement opponent of the 'Colossus' whom he

---

1   Henceforth, the 'Cape Report'.
2   *Pall Mall Gazette*, 1890.

described as '…the high priest of opportunism'.[3] Rose Innes was later to be appointed Chief Justice of the Transvaal Colony after it came under British control.

Reverend Stephanus du Toit was a founding father of the *Afrikaner Bund* and editor of *Die Afrikaanse Patriot*, a publication which, having started with only 50 subscribers grew into a popular weekly paper because of its supportive Afrikaner stance. Its criticisms of the British Annexation of the Transvaal in 1877, was a major springboard for the First Boer War after *Die Afrikaanse Patriot* called for decisive action against the British.[4] The newspaper's popularity declined, however, when it began to favour Cecil Rhodes against President Kruger. Du Toit was personally bankrupt, having lost money in speculation while in the Transvaal and rumour had it that he was bailed out by Rhodes. This may have been the reason why he had used *Die Afrikaanse Patriot's* influence to support Rhodes over the Jameson Raid.

William Schreiner, the fifth member of the Committee, had been a minister in Rhodes' Government until his resignation after the Raid. Interestingly he was called to give evidence to the Commission of which he was a member which would seem to be a clear conflict of interest. He was to become Prime Minister of the Colony during the Second Boer War.

Sir Thomas Fuller, the Committee's final member had been editor of the *Cape Argos* before becoming a member of the Legislative Assembly of the Cape Colony. Greatly influenced by Rhodes, Fuller became a Director of the De Beers Consolidated Mines Company two years after the Raid.

The Commissioners knew Rhodes well and were very familiar with his imperialistic views. They also were aware that he had numerous business interests in which some of them were involved. Perhaps they suspected that these views and interests were intertwined and at times found it was difficult to separate Rhodes' motives and whether the expansion of the Empire or increasing his wealth, lay at the heart of his actions. What was certain was that Rhodes' involvement with the Raid was a major setback to his political influence and temporarily, his business life. The wealth of documentary evidence reviewed by the Committee included the numerous telegrams which were sent to and from members of the conspiracy and formed the basis of information about the preparation for the Raid and the fluctuating opinions amongst the Reformers in Johannesburg. As will be discussed, the telegrams were both mysterious and yet informative. The Committee had to evaluate 39 such telegrams concerning Cape Town and the Raid, some of which were indecipherable because the code books which had been used to construct them had been lost.[5] Others had been transmitted under pseudonyms meant to disguise the sender and or, the recipient.[6] The Commission called 29 witnesses to give evidence. These witnesses did not include Jameson, who was in custody, nor Cecil Rhodes who was a broken man and had left the Colony for England, nor any the Reformers other than John Hays Hammond, since the rest were languishing in ZAR jails. Rutherfoord Harris, Rhodes right hand man in the Colony, however, was summoned to give evidence before them.

The Committee concluded that there had been no member of the Cape Colony Government, other than Rhodes, who had any knowledge or suspicion of the plan to send an armed body into the ZAR. No officer of the Colonial service other than Arthur Bates, who was Clerk to the Resident Magistrate at Kuruman in the Cape Colony, knew of the Raid.

Bates story is an interesting one. He seems to have taken part in his own 'incursion' into the Transvaal. Leaving his post at Kuruman without permission after having received a letter from F. J. Newton, the Commissioner for Bechuanaland, which promised him a 'very good billet' in the BSAC. He went to Mafeking where he was given a 'secret mission' by Major Grey. Borrowing a horse, he rode to Jacobsdal in

3   J. Gauntlett, *James Rose Innes: The Making of a Constitutionalist*, Vol. I (Cape Town: ConsultusI, 1988) p. 11.
4   H. Giliomee, *The Afrikaners: Biography of a People* (London: C Hurst & Co., 2003), pp. 215–20.
5   Cape Report, p. 282, xxxii.
6   Cactus/Ichabod … Rutherfoord Harris; Zahlbar … Jameson; Giovano,…Gold Fields of South Africa; Toad/Zebrawood … Frank Rhodes.

the ZAR where he hired a cart with money provided by Grey to take him to Rustenberg. Bates was reluctant to answer direct questions about what he was up to, such as why he was at Jacobsdal in the first place, but the Cape Committee were much more successful in overcoming Bates' reluctance to 'criminate' himself or others than the British Select Committee was able to do with many of its witnesses. Bates was, however, just a lowly clerk who did not possess the wiles of the more eminent witnesses who were called to give evidence and explained that his 'secret' mission was to discover whether the Rustenburg Burghers were likely to form a *Commando* in order to oppose Jameson. He was to do 'something else' in certain circumstances but, even after much questioning, he denied either cutting the telegraph wires or knowing who, if not he, might have done it. This denial was maintained in the face of an attempt to make him believe that Inspector Fuller had already named him as the culprit.[7] Bates, an ex-policeman from Swaziland, arrived at Krugersdorp before Jameson and his men had reached the town and then drifted into Johannesburg after Jameson's surrender. Although there might be a ring of truth to Bates' evidence, the Committee members were surprised that an ex-policeman would not have been interested to discover who had cut the wires. It is clear, however, that Bates was involved in the preparations for the Raid in some way and, by his own admission, would have liked to have been with the Raiders.[8]

The Commissioners also determined that there was no evidence that any member of the Customs Services connived in assisting the unlawful importation or distribution of arms and ammunition into the ZAR. Nor were members of the Railways Department responsible for this importation. The provisions, weapons, and ammunition necessary for the Raid were stored in the premises of De Beers Consolidated Mines, one of Rhodes' companies. The Cape Report concluded that the local directors of De Beers were negligent in their lack of curiosity about the preparations for the Raid, and 'it was inconceivable' that these preparations could have occurred without the directors being in the know. The situation regarding the knowledge of the BSAC officials was somewhat clearer; not only Rhodes but also Alfred Beit were fully aware of the plan and, together with Rutherford Harris and Jameson, were its active promoters.

The Commissioners also noted that the date for the Raid had been fixed six weeks in advance and the *Letter of Invitation* had been obtained four weeks before the date which Jameson had appended to it. Pressure for the so-called 'flotation' during December 1895 and the finance and development of the Raid's plan had originated from outside Johannesburg and had been actively pursued by 'certain' directors and officers of the BSAC. It was Rhodes who was thoroughly acquainted with the plan and the assets he had from three major companies which made the Jameson Raid possible.[9] However, the Commissioners concluded that there was no evidence that Rhodes wished Jameson to enter the ZAR uninvited. On the contrary, the Raid was intended to support an internal revolt by the *Uitlanders* rather than to be an invasion. The telegrams of late December clearly show that, though preparations for the Raid were complete in the Cape Colony, a hitch had occurred in Johannesburg which centred upon under which flag the *Uitlanders* would rise. Was it to be the British flag which would suggest an extension of the British Empire, or the ZAR flag under which the *Uitlanders* lived and whose government they wished to reform?

The *Uitlanders'* change of mind regarding an uprising was illustrated by the fact that Charles Leonard had been sent by them to Cape Town in an attempt to persuade Rhodes and others to call off the incursion. Jameson was repeatedly advised not to begin his Raid, but Rhodes did not give a direct instruction forbidding Jameson to start nor did he take any action which might have dissuaded Jameson from entering the ZAR. The Committee noted, however, that Rutherford Harris and Rhodes had drafted a telegram to Jameson in the afternoon of the 29 December which included a phrase that Rhodes '…strongly objected to such a course'. The message could not be transmitted because the line had been cut, but after the line

7   Fuller was not called to confirm this as he was in England in order to be a witness to Jameson's trial.
8   Bates' Evidence, Cape Report, Q. 4308-2415, pp. 130-33.
9   BSAC, De Beers Consolidated Mines and Gold Fields of South Africa.

had been repaired on 30 December it was still not sent. In this sense it was clear that Rhodes did not approve of Jameson entering the ZAR when he did, but this disapproval did not exonerate Rhodes from responsibility for the Raid. Although Jameson was directly accountable for the last fatal step, this did not clear Rhodes of responsibility for planning the event which might have still occurred when circumstances in Johannesburg were more favourable. Similarly, Rhodes did not leave *Groote Schuur* for Cape Town on Monday 30 December 1895 and he did not tell his government colleagues that the Raid had begun. The only communications with Jameson from Cape Town had been sent by Sir Hercules Robinson, the High Commissioner, and by the British Agent, Sir Jacobus De Wet from Pretoria, both advising against the Raid; both of which Jameson had chosen to ignore.

In conclusion, the Committee regretted that Rhodes did not appear before them.[10] His behaviour regarding the Raid was not '…consistent with his duty as prime minister of the Colony'.[11] The Report was signed by all the members of the Commission but Upington felt it necessary to include a minority report. This concurred with the findings of the main Report but emphasised that there was no evidence that the British Directors of the BSAC appeared to be implicated in the plot. The chief protagonists were Rutherfoord Harris and, of course Dr Jameson. Upington pointed out that, in spite of sifting through substantial evidence, the Committee could not conclude that Rhodes' involvement in 'Jameson's rash actions' was a deliberate plot to subvert the independence of the ZAR and his writings and telegrams could be given meanings which wholly different from what he actually intended.

Whilst acknowledging that the Committee would not have been justified in examining Rhodes' conduct other than that connected with the Raid, Upington stated that Rhodes did not know that it was Jameson's intention to invade the ZAR on 29 December and, when he did become aware of Jameson's impetuosity, Rhodes did all that he could to stop it and acted in good faith. Rhodes could not be held personally responsible for any improper communications between any official of the BSAC, Jameson, or any of his subordinates. There was also insufficient evidence, concluded Upington, to comment on the financial arrangements between Rhodes and his brother Frank which may or may not have been used to support the *Uitlanders'* uprising.[12]

Although Upington had agreed with the findings of the Committee, one feels that his interpretation of the evidence is less damning towards Rhodes than the views of its other members. As he was the Chair of the Committee it would have been strange if he had adopted a different stance from the outcome of their deliberations but, by being more circumspect about Rhodes' actions and his involvement in the Raid itself, it made the 'Colossus' appear to be slightly less culpable. One must ask whether the communications sent by Rhodes' subordinate's which were considered to be improper, would or could have been sent without Rhodes' knowledge or whether he followed the practice of not actively asking them what they were doing on the principle that ignorance was bliss.

Millin, Rhodes biographer, has little to say about the Cape Inquiry. She suggests that, immediately after the Raid Rhodes was a '…disintegrated man, unable to collect himself or confront the life about him.'[13] Jan Hendrik Hofmyer, a prominent figure in the *Afrikaner Bund* and a long term friend of Rhodes' and who had guided Robinson to repudiate the Raid, visited the 'Colossus' at *Groote Schuur* shortly after the incursion. Rhodes had already decided to resign as Premier of the Cape Colony but Hofmyer argued that this was not enough to save Cecil's reputation. He should condemn Jameson's actions much more strongly, dismiss the Doctor as Administrator of Mashonaland and involve the law. In this way Rhodes would be clearly seen as demonstrating disavowal of the Raid and he might salvage some of his reputation within the Colony as well

---

10   Summoned to Britain by the BSAC board, he subsequently returned to deal with the N'debele rising known as the Second Matabele War.

11   *Cape Report*. pp. 7-9.

12   *Select Committee Report, Minority Report*, p. 12.

13   Millin, *Rhodes*, pp. 90-291.

as the rest of the world. Rhodes refused to do it; Jameson had been an old and close friend for too long. It was the last meeting between the two. Hofmyer claimed to have felt deceived by Rhodes's actions just as a cuck-olded husband would feel. Such was Hofmyer's sense of betrayal, that he attempted to persuade Chamberlain that there must be a change in the way in which the territories ruled by the BSAC were administered. Its actions, he argued, had proved dangerous to the security and peace of South Africa.

Chamberlain seems to have been torn two ways; should BSAC rule be curtailed, or should it be modi-fied in some way so as to prevent future conspiracies. Chamberlain did reassure Rhodes, however, that the 'Colossus' would still retain control over Rhodesia and much of the status quo would be preserved. Chamberlain feared that converting the territories of the BSAC into Crown Colonies would only increase the ZARs influence over the Cape Colony since such a step would prove be very unpopular with the Afrikaners there. He argued that the BSAC had an excellent record of development.[14] It was also empire building on the cheap.

A further inquiry by the British Parliament could not be avoided and even the Directors of the BSAC requested a full investigation into the circumstances of the Jameson Raid since it was obvious that it threat-ened their Company's interests. This may be seen a strange appeal since the BSAC was clearly involved in some way and it might reveal that theirs was the 'smoking gun', but the share price of the BSAC had fallen considerably since the Raid and the Directors were anxious to clear the BSAC of involvement in order to boost their value.[15] Similarly, the Cape Colony Government requested that the British Government hold a full inquiry and even Queen Victoria demanded it. After much manoeuvring, Chamberlain was forced on 30 July 1896, two days after Jameson's trial, to move before Parliament that a Committee of Inquiry be set up. The timing was significant since the Parliamentary session was about to end which meant that a new Committee would not be finalised until a new session of Parliament began. This second Committee would not open until the following year thus providing those likely to appear before it, as well as Chamberlain, time to prepare.

During the interim, Rhodes was not idle and had physically defended his 'empire'. After his meeting which Directors of the BSAC he had travelled to Rhodesia, where there was discontent amongst the local tribe, the Ndebele in order to avoid appearing before the Cape Committee. Jameson had defeated the Ndebele and subdued them as a nation in the First Matabele War. The tribe had now broken out into open revolt for which there were three main causes. First, Jameson's actions of withdrawing the majority of the troops, the presence of which, enabled the white settlers to live in relative security in Rhodesia, encouraged the Ndebele to feel that they could be able to overcome the white settlers and gain revenge for the defeat of Lobengula. Jameson had suggested that after that defeat, the Ndebele ought to have been disarmed as a precaution, but Chamberlain's predecessor, Lord Rippon, had thought that this was too harsh an imposition on the proud Ndebele, who had a military organisation similar to that of the Zulu. This resulted in large numbers of rifles and thousands of rounds of ammunition remaining in their hands. The settlers allowed the Ndebele to remain on the land as labourers, so a once proud military nation was reduced to semi-slavery.

Second, after achieving its victory over the Ndebele, the BSAC had confiscated many of their cattle as punishment and these were given as loot to the settlers who had supported the war. Cattle were not only seen as a sign of wealth but also as essential in ritual observances and in marriage transactions. In theory only the royal herds were to be confiscated but greed and Jameson's tendency of giving cattle as gifts to his friends, meant that those of others were also taken. Such was importance of the herd that the indiscriminate confis-cation of cattle destroyed the Ndebele society To make matters worse, in the early months of 1896, a severe outbreak of Rinderpest occurred, killing many of the few cows which the Ndebele still owned. The BSAC

---

14   Garvin *The Life of Joseph Chamberlain*, Vol. III, pp. 118-19.
15   Falling from £5 5s 6d on 28 December 1895 to £3 2s 6d in mid-January 1896. They had been selling at £9 on 24 September 1895.

added to the problem by killing cattle as a method of preventing the spread of the Rinderpest which added to the uncomprehending Ndebele's resentment.

Third, a spiritual leader, the *Mlimo,* a rather shadowy figure who may have been more than one man, convinced the Ndebele that the settlers were responsible for this disaster and the lack of BSAC troopers provided them with the opportunity to rid themselves of the white invaders. On 22 March 1896 the Ndebele attacked three different groups of settlers, killing and mutilating their victims. The surviving settlers had little option but to congregate in Bulawayo which was the only defensive position open to them. They organised patrols to scour the countryside for any settlers who had not been massacred. Relief columns were organised, one of which was accompanied by Cecil Rhodes, who had a temporary military command. The siege of Bulawayo was ended and shortly afterward, the *Mlimo,* was assassinated.[16] After this assassination Rhodes showed great personal courage in spite of generally reckoned, even by his friends, as not being particular brave, by walking unarmed into an Ndebele stronghold in the Matopos Hills and persuading them to lay down their arms.[17] In doing so, Rhodes put the Colonial Office in his debt which Chamberlain was later to repay.

---

16   There is a dispute as to who the Mlimo actually was or whether the man assassinated was actually the Mlimo. See Terrence, *Ranger: Revolt in Southern Rhodesia, 1896-97: A Study in African Resistance* (London: Heinemann, 1967) for one theory as to his importance and identity.

17   B. Farwell, *The Encyclopaedia of Nineteenth-Century. Land Warfare: An Illustrated World View* (New York: W.W. Norton, 2001), p. 539.

13

Solving the Mystery

The period between July 1896 and February 1897 saw hectic activity during which both sides; those who were part of the Rhodes faction and those who represented the Colonial Office, struggle to decide who would take the blame for the Raid. This conundrum would be resolved to the satisfaction of both parties if the Inquiry was cancelled. Sir Alfred Milner, who as Hercules Robinson's successor, was to become Governor of Cape Colony and High Commissioner in May 1897, had secretly advocated that the Government should support the *Uitlander* helots by helping them to become citizens of the ZAR.[1] Milner expressed the hope that an earthquake would engulf the Select Committee on its opening session, such was his fears as to what it might reveal.[2] Van der Poel suggests that a war with the ZAR was a possible alternative to an Inquiry and this was contemplated by Chamberlain as a way of avoiding the exposure of his involvement in the Raid; which he feared would be revealed by Rhodes and his associates. However, it would have been unwise to simply declare war if the ZAR had not offered a *casus belli* but Chamberlain would not have been sorry if this happened.[3] There was even a detailed paper written by Sir George Fiddes, Bower's successor as Imperial Secretary, which set out reasons why Britain should declare war on the ZAR.[4] Chamberlain made a request to the Cabinet that the British garrisons in South Africa be increased by a force of 10,000, a number which would include a large proportion of cavalry and artillery; units useful for offensive action. He was forced to drop his plan since it was opposed by both the War Office as being too risky and the Treasury as being too expensive.[5] There were also changes in diplomatic personnel in South Africa. De Wet, who believed that he had done his best to keep the peace between the Boers and the Britons, was retired and replaced 'in order to strengthen the British at Pretoria.'[6] Hercules Robinson, now Lord Rosmead, returned to South Africa, but retired to England in January 1897 and was replaced by Milner.[7]

The Select Committee on British South Africa opened its proceedings on 5 February 1897 in Westminster Hall and this inaugural meeting became something of a sensation as it was attended by many of the influential figures in late Victorian society. Its most distinguished spectator was the Prince of Wales, who was on cordial terms with both Rhodes and Jameson. His friendship with the Duke of Abercorn, President of the Company, made him less than an unbiased observer and this led to criticism of his presence. He continued to attend committee meetings whenever possible, however, and such was the speculation as to why the future

---

1   H. Chisholm, (ed.), Viscount. Alfred Milner, *Encyclopaedia Britannica* 18, 11th ed. (London, CUP 1911) pp. 476–48. Helots: Greek for those between slaves and citizens.
2   Frederic Whyte, *Life of W.T. Stead*, Vol. II (London, Johnathan Cape Ltd., 1925), p. 96.
3   Montagu White, Transvaal Consul, quoted in Van der Poel, *The Jameson Raid*, p. 184.
4   TNA Colonial Office, No. 528, July 1896.
5   Garvin, *The Life of Joseph Chamberlain*, Vol III, pp. 139-40.
6   G.E. Buckle (ed.), *The Letters of Queen Victoria, Third Series* (London: John Murray, 1931) Chamberlain to Victoria, 25 August 1896, p. 70.
7   For the sake of clarity, I will continue to refer to address Lord Rosmead as Hercules Robinson.

King Edward VII was so interested in the Committee's proceedings, that according to J.A. Spender, the Editor of the influential Liberal paper, *The Westminster Gazette*, who claimed to have attended every session himself, it was rumoured that Edward had '...rashly committed himself to the Raiders' and it was necessary to conceal his involvement at all costs.[8] Although there was not a word of truth in the rumour, Edward's behaviour in attending the Committee meetings was so uncharacteristic of the playboy prince that it is not surprising there was such speculation. Even Chamberlain's sister-in-law, an ardent admirer of Jameson, was also present on that Friday in February, which was somewhat tactless since her brother-in-law was likely to be given a difficult time.

Fearing that this interest in the Committee's work might be a distracted by the society élite, its Chair, William Jackson MP, soon ordered the room cleared of all but MPs and journalists. The *Saturday Review* reported that because of this decision, the Committee's proceedings had been 'divested of all dignity' and seemed to have been organised 'on the cheap'[9] Its members sat in a horseshoe with the witness chair before it; not in the Great Westminster Hall but in one of the adjacent rooms next to it. Its remit was:

> To inquire into the origin and circumstances of the Incursion into the South African Republic by an Armed Force, and into the Administration of the British South African Company, and to report thereon, and, further, to report what alterations are desirable in the Government of the Territories under the control of the Company'.[10]

Such was the machinations of those involved; its final report did not cover the last section with regard to recommend changes which should be made in the way the BSAC governed its Territories.

The committee consisted of fifteen members with a quorum of seven and its membership deserves examination. Its Chair was William L Jackson, a Conservative MP, who was also Chair of the House of Commons South Africa Committee, and had formerly been Irish Secretary. Jackson was to prove to be an inefficient Chair, but as will be suggested, his key work may have been behind the scenes in editing the crucial telegrams which have already been mentioned and writing the Inquiry's report. Lady Longford believed that Jackson was no match for the cunning witnesses who appeared before the Committee.[11]

Perhaps the most surprising member of the committee was Chamberlain himself. Even to the uncritical observer he was clearly involved in some way in the Raid as Colonial Secretary and was known to have had a number of discussions about events in South Africa with many of his officials and representatives of the BSAC. When the news about the Raid became known, he had at initially offered to resign and one might question whether the motive for this gesture was from a sense of ministerial responsibility or a feeling of personal guilt. It was clear that the Colonial Office's involvement in the Raid and even his own knowledge would be under scrutiny and he may have thought that being part of the investigation was the best way to limit the personal harm which its revelations might bring about. Even more surprising was the fact that he also appeared as a witness before the Committee at his own request which, in itself suggests the Committee's procedure was full of flaws.

Henry Du Pré Labouchère, another Committee member, had motives completely different from those of Chamberlain. Labouchère was the maverick Liberal MP for Northampton, and no supporter of Rhodes, Jameson, or the actions of the BSAC. Between 1893 and 1894, he asked questions and made speeches in the Commons which were critical of the BSAC's involvement in the First Matabele War on no less than

8   J.A. Spender, *Life, Journalism and Politics*, Vol. 1 (London, Cassell & Co. Ltd., 1927), p. 82.
9   *Saturday Review*, 20 February 1897.
10   *Hansard*, HC Deb 28 January 1897, Vol. 45, columns 62-78, *Select Committee Report*, p. iii.
11   Longford, *Jameson's Raid*, p. 255.

twenty-one occasions.[12] Labouchère also censured the apparent weakness of Chamberlain and the British Government for not controlling the actions of representatives of the BSAC and was described as a loathsome and a foul specimen' by a devotee of Jameson.[13]

Although Labouchère had made a name for introducing Section 11 of the 1885 Criminal Law Amendment Act which made all homosexual acts of 'gross indecency' illegal, his own probity was not high in some circles, but one contemporary described him as '…one of the most remarkable characters in contemporary politics who used *The Truth* to hold up a mirror to men who shrank from contemplating their features as Mr Labouchère reveals them.'[14] He was to take every opportunity during the Committee's proceedings, to expose Rhodes and his associates.

The Honourable George Wyndham, late of the Coldstream Guards, was another of the Committee members, who was later to become Secretary of State for War. Van der Poel describes him as 'an imperialist of the crudest sort', and 'wholeheartedly in sympathy with Rhodes'.[15] Wyndham had been sent to South Africa to confer with Rhodes. Bower claimed that Wyndham's mission was to persuade Rhodes not to use the incriminating telegrams in return for the Commission exonerating the BSAC and saving the Charter.[16] Rhodes was being urged by his solicitor, Bouchier Hawksley, to use the telegrams to implicate Chamberlain in the Raid on the basis of 'if I am to be ruined so will he'. Hawksley had informed Chamberlain that he had certain telegrams which would incriminate the Colonial Secretary and had refused to send copies to the Colonial Office when 'Pushful Joe' requested he should do so. These telegrams were gaining wider circulation; Edward Clarke had seen a dossier of telegrams during his preparations to defend Jameson in Court but had been instructed not to use them. Chamberlain was determined to find out what was in them so he ordered Fairfield to insist that Hawksley produce them. The astute Hawksley compiled a selection of the telegrams which he sent for the Colonial Office's perusal and return.[17] It is unlikely; however, that Hawksley did not expect that Chamberlain would have the telegrams copied for future reference. A panicked Chamberlain, having seen the telegrams thought of resigning as already described but, regaining his courage, decided to fight to the death. He had little respect for his accusers; he told Fairfield, that if '…they wanted him with his back to the wall, they would see some splinters'.[18] The BSAC could potentially have lost its Charter if Chamberlain recommended that it should do so and this prevented Rhodes from using the telegrams either during Jameson's trial or during the Select Committee Inquiry in spite of Hawksley urging him to do so. Chamberlain returned the original telegrams to Hawksley with the veiled threat that it they were made public they would be dealt with in detail and …as they deserve[d]'.[19] It appears however, George Wyndham's visit was sufficient to dissuade Rhodes from using these documents to his advantage and to the disadvantage of the Colonial Secretary.

Another significant Committee member was Henry Campbell-Bannerman, a future prime minister and an influential member of the Liberal party. He was known by his friends as CB because he disliked his hyphenated name which he had been forced to adopt as a beneficiary of his uncle, Henry Bannerman's, will. CB had been Secretary of State for War in Rosebery's Government from 1894-95 and gained his knighthood by joining a group of politicians and influential army officers which persuaded the Duke of Cambridge to resign as Commander in Chief.

12   *Hansard*, 21 July 1893-15 February 1894.
13   Ash, *The If Man*, pp. 76-77.
14   Marshall Hole, *The Jameson Raid*, p. 43. *The Truth* was a crusading newspaper which Labouchère owned.
15   Van der Poel, *The Jameson Raid*, p. 187.
16   Van der Poel, *The Jameson Raid* quoted in Sir Graham Bower's unpublished 'Reminiscences', p. 31.
17   W.T, Stead, *Joseph Chamberlain: Conspirator or Statesman?* (London: Review of Reviews,1900) p. 91.
18   Garvin, *The Life of Joseph Chamberlain*, Vol III, p. 116.
19   Schreuder & Butler, *Bower's Secret History*, p. 305.

The remaining members of the Committee were Sir William Harcourt, Leader of the Opposition in the House of Common, who took a very active part in questioning the witnesses, Edward Blake, an Irish Unionist Member of Parliament who had been first Premier of Ontario, Charles Cripps MP for Wycombe, John Bigham, MP for Liverpool Exchange, Sydney Buxton, MP for Poplar, later to become Governor General of South Africa, Sir William Hart Dyke, Conservative MP for Dartford, John Wharton, Unionist MP for Ripon, Sir Richard Webster, The Attorney General, who participated in the Raiders' trial, Sir Michael Hicks Beech, the Chancellor of the Exchequer and finally, John Ellis MP for Rushcliffe.

The influence of Bouchier Hawksley, Rhodes solicitor, on the Committee's membership should not be underestimated. He seems to have suggested prospective individuals, such as Wyndham, to sit on the Committee and argued that Rhodes would never agree to attend if certain of his enemies, such as Labouchère, were appointed to it. Shortly after Rhodes' arrival in Britain, Hawksley made his final attempt to get the Inquiry stopped. On 26 January he had a meeting with Chamberlain at the Colonial Office. Hawksley's argument was that it would be better for the country if they could avoid a national scandal and the country's reputation was much more important than that of Chamberlain, who was just a transitory figure. Chamberlain's counter argument was that it was too late to stop the Inquiry and, if this could be done, the result would be a greater evil as everyone would assume that things were being covered up. Even the more radical members of the Committee were aware that the national honour was at stake as well as the fate of the Government. Chamberlain was aware that an examination of the circumstances of the Raid by Parliament could not be prevented and to be seen to attempt to do so would appear suspicious. Lord Albert Grey a Director of the BSAC, a confidante of Rhodes, and the main link between Rhodes and Chamberlain, wrote to Chamberlain to say that if he was called before a Commission, he had two options if questioned as to the Colonial Secretary's knowledge of a likely rising in Johannesburg. He could either choose to refuse to answer or to admit that he had told Chamberlain that such an uprising would take place and that it would be desirable if an armed force was stationed on the ZAR's border to be used to support it if necessary. Grey agreed that Chamberlain had officially refused to acknowledge this warning but it seems that the granting of the railway strip to the BSAC indicated that Chamberlain had taken the information on board. Grey agreed, however, that Chamberlain did not, nor could not, know when the Raid would take place.[20]

The lack of rigour shown by the Committee, which met twice a week, was to be evident throughout its proceedings. Strangely, they invited applications from those who wished to appear before them which may have been a catch-all decision meant to make sure that interested parties were not overlooked. It gave the main protagonists, however, the opportunity to demonstrate their willingness to cooperate, perhaps in the hope that this would be taken to mean they had nothing to fear. Bouchier Hawksley wrote on behalf of Rhodes, Jameson, and the BSAC Directors requesting they be allowed to appear. Other letters were received on behalf of Alfred Beit, Lionel Phillips and Rutherford Harris.[21] A number of additional interested parties also asked to attend and they included the Eastern Telegraph Company which wished to give evidence regarding certain telegrams.[22]

The Committee agreed that the principal witnesses would be given permission to be represented by counsel. The Select Committee chose to run their proceedings entirely themselves and only use counsel when they thought it necessary. Although the Committee members were able men and familiar with the law, one wonders whether this was an attempt to make sure that proceedings did not get out of hand and stray into the sensitive areas which might have repercussions for the Government, the Country and, of course, the

20   Grey to Chamberlain 10 December 1896, Grey Papers: University of Durham quoted by J.S. Galbraith, 'The British South Africa Company and the Jameson Raid', *The Journal of British Studies,* Vol. 10, No. 1, November 1970, pp. 148-49.
21   *Select Committee Report*, pp. xix-xxiii.
22   *Select Committee Report*, p. iii.

Colonial Secretary. Each of the Committee members, except perhaps, Labouchère, had a reason to defend one or more of these interests. The BSAC, anxious to demonstrate its probity and show cooperation, offered to submit a number of documents which showed how the cattle seized at the end of the First Matabele War had been allocated and a number of other matters which it believed to be important to its defence.[23] The Committee also had the *Cape Report* and the proceedings of the Bow Street Trial and High Court trial to assist its deliberations.

The Inquiry began by calling the chief witness; Cecil Rhodes. He began with a cleverly worded statement in which he accepted *Cape Report*'s conclusions that he was responsible for the actions of those who had served directly or indirectly under his orders.[24] After a shaky start under interrogation, Rhodes grew in confidence during his six appearances before the Committee and much of his evidence involved hectoring the members for their lack of knowledge about South African politics, the plight of the *Uitlanders*, and the misdeeds of the Transvaal Government which was antagonistic towards the Cape Colony. He also claimed Kruger and the Kaiser's Government were working together to undermine British authority in South Africa. Rhodes denied the suggestion, made by Harcourt, that the unrest of the *Uitlanders* had been manufactured by the gold magnates. He asserted that the *Uitlanders* had risked life and property in contemplating the uprising and, as a result, nearly every leading citizen had been jailed; an exaggeration which was not challenged by the Committee. The *Uitlanders* uprising would have been a defensive rather than an offensive revolt based on the need to establish their common rights.[25] Labouchère attempted to challenge the seriousness of the *Uitlanders'* conditions which allowed Rhodes to enter into a diatribe by suggesting that his imperialistic aims were similar to those of the Government. Wyndham and Chamberlain, amongst others, were keen to support Rhodes' assertions and Wyndham used the Committee to deliver a lengthy, venomous and biased attack against the ZAR which should have been challenged by a more robust Chair.

Even Chamberlain attempted to defend the *Uitlanders'* revolt by proclaiming that the Government of the ZAR was '…a threat to the peace of South Africa' and hostile to the economic development of the Cape Colony: which was a policy statement rather than part of an inquiry into the facts.[26] With this type of support, Rhodes was able to control the information which he gave to the Committee by obfuscation, meandering replies and, on occasion, refusal to answer questions. He was able to clear Sir Hercules Robinson, now Lord Rosmead, but only just; when asked if he had told the High Commissioner of the real reason why the troops were congregated at Pitsani. After some hesitation, Rhodes suggested that the Committee ask his Lordship in person. In an unusual attempt to further press the 'Colossus' to be clearer in absolving Robinson, Harcourt reminded Rhodes that Robinson had already stated that the only reason Rhodes had given for assembling the troops at Pitsani was a cheap way to protect the railway. Rhodes' reply to this rejoinder is worth inspection as an example of his responses when faced with tricky questioning. He regretted that Robinson was not present to answer in person: he was too ill to appear before the Committee. Rhodes then suggested that he thought Robinson was aware of the trouble brewing in Johannesburg and he knew there was a force on the border. However, Rhodes would not like to say anything else (about whether Robinson linked these two facts) but would rather Robinson have answered for himself. Rhodes was personally prepared to accept the former High Commissioner's statement that he knew nothing.[27]

Later in his interrogation Rhodes was challenged on the telegrams printed in the *Cape Report* which referred to the 'Chairman' and was asked whether this was a pseudonym for Robinson. Rhodes asked for time to consider the question and after a delay of three days and probable coaching from Hawksley, he admitted

---

23   The indiscriminate confiscation of cattle was one of the causes of the Second Matabele War.
24   *Select Committee Report*, p. vi.
25   *Select Committee Report*, Q1150-93 and Q. 1553-1930.
26   Van der Poel, *The Jameson Raid*, p. 202.
27   *Select Committee Report*, p. 203.

that this did mean Robinson, but the telegrams did not mean that Sir Hercules knew about the conspiracy even though they seemed to suggest that he did. Although it was obviously untrue, the Committee members were willing to accept Rhode's statement since it suited their own agenda. The ailing Robinson was shocked by Rhodes' evidence and telegraphed Chamberlain in order to unequivocally state that, until he had read Rhodes' evidence, he '...never believed it possible that the code word 'Chairman' referred to (him)'.[28] The telegram was accepted by the Committee without equivocation. Rhodes successfully avoided answering questions about the 'knowledge of third parties' by suggesting as, he had done when questioned about Robinson's knowledge, that they should answer for themselves. When asked whether Chamberlain was aware of the plot, Rhodes answered that so far as he was cognisant, Chamberlain did not know.

The only exception from Rhodes' attempts to absolve the Colonial Office was when he admitted that Sir Graham Bower, the Imperial Secretary, knew of the preparations which had been made. Rhodes was aware that Bower was determined to admit his knowledge of the plot. This intention was also known by some of the Committee members and Rhodes saw no purpose in attempting to defend Bower. It seems that Rhodes hoped that by actually implicating one person might enhance the Committee's acceptance of his own assertion that others were innocent.

Rhodes also shielded *The Times* from accusations of complicity even though Moberley Bell, the Managing Director of *The Times*, had already demonstrated his knowledge of a likely Raid by expressing the hope that any action in the ZAR would not take place on a Saturday as *The Times* did not publish on a Sunday and so would miss a scoop. Rather than implicating the newspaper as a whole, Rhodes said that Flora Shaw, *The Times* African correspondent, had telegraphed that the uprising and Raid should not be delayed on her own authority and not on the instructions of Bell, or her editor, George Buckle.

None of the Committee members seemed willing to really press Rhodes in a determined way and consequently, it was thought by most observers, that the 'Colossus' had won this particular round of the Inquiry. After six appearances before the Committee over a period of three weeks, he had only admitted what he wanted to admit and shrugged off accusations which he did not wish to acknowledge. Even Labouchère grew to like him and his habit of having porter and sandwiches during the Committee's recesses, and he thought Rhodes '...an entirely honest, heavy person.'[29] Praise indeed from a man who had spent years trying to reveal that Rhodes' financial greed was even a greater motive than his imperialism. Rhodes was helped to obscure his questionable dealings with the Colonial Office by the fact that many of the Committee members were biased and could not or would not believe that Chamberlain was involved. Almost immediately after giving his evidence, Rhodes returned to South Africa 'on BSAC business 'and so, unlike a number of other key witnesses, he could not be recalled to give further evidence.

Rhodes' appearance was followed by two Afrikaners, members of the Cape Parliament and also members of the *Afrikaner Bund*. Jackson, the Committee's Chair indicated that they would be able to give the 'Dutch' point of view of the situation in the Southern African region and should be heard early as they had to shortly return to the Cape. This was one of the few examples when the Committee considered the second part of their remit; the administration of the British South Africa Company, and what changes were desirable in the government of the territories it controlled. It also interrupted the order of witnesses which seems to have been carefully chosen in order to apparently pursue the culpable. The two, Thomas Louw and Matthys Venter, both agreed that, in their view, the territories were better administered by the Company than they would be by Colonial officials. Louw went further by suggesting that this was the opinion of '...nearly every Afrikaner in the Colony.'[30] He also argued that the BSAC's treatment of the native African was good, probably better

---

28   *Select Committee Report*, p. 59.
29   Labouchère quoted in John G. Lockhart & Christopher M. Woodhouse, *Rhodes*, London, Hodder & Stoughton, 1963), p. 375.
30   *Select Committee Report*, Q.2157.

than it ought to be but the Company had been correct in attempting to deny arms and ammunition to them.[31] When questioned as to why he thought that the BSAC was better at administering the territories than the Colonial Office would be, Louw pointed out Rhodes' many years of experience in Africa and that he employed men with similar knowledge. The Colonial Office did not select such highly qualified men to administer the country. Even High Commissioners needed years in the job before they were competent.[32] When describing the treatment of native Africans, Louw painted a rosy picture which glossed over the many instances of ill treatment and claimed that he had never heard of natives being flogged for other than serious disobedience.

When Labouchère heard similar stories of the BSAC's competence and benevolence from Venter, he began to smell a rat and embarked upon a series of questions which he hoped would demonstrate that the two Afrikaners had been put up to supporting the BSAC by Hawksley. How was it that the two happened to be in England at such an opportune moment? Why had they applied to be heard before the Committee, and did Hawksley know what their testimony would be? One would suggest that Labouchère was on to something which suggested a conspiracy for the benefit of the BSAC.

The next witness was the unfortunate Sir Graham Bower, the Imperial Secretary at Cape Town. Bower had served in the Royal Navy and began his diplomatic career as Private Secretary to Robinson before being appointed as Colonial Secretary to the High Commissioner to South Africa. He had already demonstrated his particular sense of honour by resigning when Loch had insulted him. Prior to giving evidence he had told Chamberlain that he intended to tell the truth about his own knowledge of the intended Raid and also to reveal that the Colonial Secretary also knew of it. Bower seemed to believe that Chamberlain would inform the Chair of his intentions to do so and Jackson would ensure that the Committee would respond leniently towards him. Unfortunately, Bower had not calculated on the potential ferocity of the Liberal members of the Committee such as Labouchère. By 'confessing' Bower had made himself fair game to their vicious interrogation. Chamberlain attempted to partially protect him but Bower had offered himself up as a sacrificial lamb which was ultimately convenient as it provided someone to blame for the Colonial Secretary's ignorance. In one attempt to ease the pressure on Bower, specifically as to why he had not told Robinson about Jameson's intentions, 'Pushful Joe' suggested that Bower had not been able to do so since Rhodes had given him the information in confidence. Bower agreed that this was true and Rhodes had put him on his honour not to tell Robinson.[33] Sir Graham was faced with a possible threefold defence; maintaining Rhodes' confidence by not revealing the information, defending Robinson by clearly stating that he had not told him about Rhodes' intentions or protecting himself. This was an impossible task for Bower as it involved too many dishonourable contradictions. Finally, in a state of confusion, Bower offered the weak excuse that he believed that Rhodes had never really intended that there should be an uprising, so it was not necessary to inform the High Commissioner about it. This was clearly untrue and brought Bower's reliability as a truthful witness into question.

A furious Labouchère, sensing blood, rounded on Bower and, in unparliamentarily language, accused him of lying. An alarmed Jackson tried to bring the outraged Committee to order but was challenged by Labouchère who saw this as an attempt to prevent him from properly interrogating Bower. The Chair, sensing things were going wrong, reproved Labouchère for insulting the witness. There followed an exchange during which Labouchère strongly suggested that Bower had changed his evidence and if this change was not acknowledged and exposed, it would prove that the Committee was the sham which was being rumoured.[34] Jackson, not wishing to expose himself to such an accusation, allowed Labouchère to continue to grill Bower

---

31   *Select Committee Report,* Q.212, 2204.
32   *Select Committee Report,* Q.2257-2258.
33   *Select Committee Report.* Q.2502. Q. 2524.
34   *Select Committee Report,* Q 2975.

about his knowledge of Rhodes' actions and whether, once the Raid had begun, Bower still felt that Rhodes had not authorised it. In doing so, Rhodes would seem to have broken his own promise to Bower which was that he would tell Robinson that a Raid was proposed before the troops were actually used.[35] Bower did his best both to defend Robinson and not implicate Rhodes, under the probing questioning of Labouchère. He admitted that being trusted with confidential matters was useful to his work but left him bound by a bond of secrecy not to reveal the information or its source. This intellectual fencing match brought Bower's actions under even closer scrutiny and slowly destroyed his reputation both as a witness and as a servant of the Colonial Office. However, he did go some way to exonerate Rhodes by affirming on a number of occasions during his evidence, that he understood that the troops at Pitsani would only cross the border if the rising in Johannesburg occurred. This implied that Jameson had acted without Rhodes' permission, as well as without his knowledge and Rhodes only found out when it was too late.[36] Towards the end of his interrogation a frustrated Bower, feeling that Chamberlain had left him unprotected took a swipe at the Colonial Secretary's reputation for being swift to act, by saying that it was Rhodes' view that the Government, as represented by Chamberlain, was too slow to take action regarding the ZAR and therefore he would act on its behalf.[37] However, Sir Graham did not think that 'we had a very slow Secretary of State'; which was an oblique reference to Chamberlain's clandestine activities surrounding the uprising and the Raid.[38] His evidence lasted one and a half days and because, he had tried to protect Robinson and Rhodes, he exposed himself to severe criticism and an accusation of covering up the truth. Lady Longford believed that, in Bower's eyes, Chamberlain was the prime mover of the catastrophe.[39]

Sir Graham was followed by William Schreiner, the former Attorney General of the Cape Legislature. Schreiner said that he had visited Rhodes at *Groote Schuur* on 29 December and he had no reason to believe from what occurred at this meeting, that the 'Colossus' was aware that Jameson had begun his Raid.[40] Schreiner went even further by claiming that, although he was aware of the *Uitlander* discontent, he did not believe that Rhodes was associated with the unrest in Johannesburg even though Leonard, a signatory of the *Letter of Invitation*, was at *Groote Schuur* at the time of his visit. One might also add that Schreiner must have been at least aware that Rhode's brother, Frank, was in Johannesburg even if he didn't know he was fomenting discontent.[41] Schreiner had been unaware that the Raid had begun until the afternoon of the 30 December and he immediately went to see Rhodes. When questioned as to what passed between the two, Schreiner assured the Committee that he had nothing to hide but couldn't add very much to the evidence which he had given during the Cape Inquiry and he did not feel that the Select Committee would gain much by hearing it from him directly. Harcourt, his questioner, assured Schreiner that he did not want him to say anything he didn't want to say; a good example of the Committee going soft on certain witnesses.

When he arrived at *Groote Schuur,* Schreiner said that the 'Colossus' was very distressed and clearly surprised that Jameson had 'gone in'.[42] To his knowledge, Rhodes had never previously admitted involvement in the Raid or the Johannesburg uprising until he had done so before the Select Committee.[43] The questioning of Schreiner continued over a period of four days and covered many areas of Rhodes' administration in the Cape, his involvement with the *Uitlanders* in Johannesburg, and Rhodes knowledge or responsibility for the Raid. One particular reply from Schreiner must have seemed like Manna from Heaven to Chamberlain.

35   *Select Committee Report,* Q.2985.
36   *Select Committee Report,* Q.3002-3055.
37   *Select Committee Report,* Q.2832 2834.
38   *Select Committee Report,* Q.2834.
39   Longford, *Jameson's Raid,* p. 272.
40   *Select Committee Report,* Q.3239.
41   *Select Committee Report,* Q.3239.
42   *Select Committee Report,* Q.3269-3273.
43   *Select Committee Report,* Q.3275.

When asked what the best way was to administer the Charter territories, Schreiner was very clear that using BSAC employees to act on behalf of the Imperial Government was not the best way. Such men often did not have the right qualities and it created an autocracy with one man at its head. 'There should be no one man in Africa, even with the presence of High Commissioner representing the Imperial Government, who could practically be an autocrat in relation to the Chartered territories.[44] In the final part of his evidence Schreiner, during questioning by Labouchère, indicated that Rhodes' had accepted Chamberlain's idea of a conference to settle the differences between the *Uitlanders* and the ZAR. This, argued Schreiner, was further evidence that the 'Colossus' had not been involved in the conspiracy and equally, since as Chamberlain had made such an offer to Rhodes, it would suggest that the Colonial Secretary had been unaware that Rhodes was involved in the conspiracy. Chamberlain, unsurprisingly, was quick to agree that he did not know and, since Rhodes had already admitted this was his belief his ignorance was bliss.[45] Rhodes and Schreiner had been close colleagues even though they had political differences but, on the voyage home, Schreiner began to believe that Rhodes' actions had been motivated by greed rather than principle, and by the time they arrived at Cape Town they had become bitter enemies.[46]

It was now time for the Committee to examine the main character in the drama; Leander Starr Jameson M.D. C.B., who began his evidence with a prepared statement which described both the Raid and the reasons for his actions. He acknowledged that he had received telegrams or messages which had informed him that the *Uitlanders* had postponed their uprising, but he did not believe this actually meant that they had abandoned their revolt. He had been worried that the British Government might interfere with his ability to act in fulfilling his promise to the *Uitlanders* to come to their aid. It was the Reuter's '…women and children leaving message' he received on 28 December and the fear that both British and Boer authorities already knew about his plans, which had forced him to act.[47] George Wyndham reminded the Doctor that he had said that he did not expect 'a shot to be fired' during the incursion and questioned therefore why had he attacked Krugersdorp rather than going round it?[48] Perhaps Wyndham was unaware of the conversation which Jameson had with Sir Fredrick Hamilton, Editor of the *Johannesburg Star*, and later one of the Reformers tried by the ZAR, about the intended Raid during which Hamilton expressed doubts about the plan. Jameson's reply was that Hamilton did not understand the power of the Maxim gun. 'I shall draw a zone of lead a mile each side of my column and no Boer will be able to live in it.'[49] Hardly confirmation that the Raid was an entirely peaceful venture. Jameson took the opportunity to exonerate Willoughby from the criticism that attacking Krugersdorp was an act of military folly. He (Jameson) had order Willoughby to do so confirming, at this point at least, it was Jameson who was in command even though he was not a commissioned officer. Jameson confirmed, after a little nudging, that he believed if he did not take Krugersdorp there would be no uprising in Johannesburg.[50]

Jameson was much less equivocal about whether he had told his officers that his proposed Raid had the approval of the Imperial Authorities and asked the Committee to permit him not to repeat his 'private' conversations with the officers. Under cross examination by Labouchère, Jameson then shifted his ground a little by stating that there may have been conversations about whether the Authorities had agreed to the incursion but if there had been, they were confidential. He had, Jameson claimed, never directly told his officers that he had the Authorities' approval but may have mentioned something about it but he couldn't remember exactly what or how he had put it. His officers were informed that the High Commissioner would

44   *Select Committee Report*, Q.3883.
45   *Select Committee Report*, Q.4507.
46   Lockhart. & Woodhouse, *Rhodes*, p. 376.
47   *Select Committee Report*, Q.4513. Jameson's Statement'.
48   *Select Committee Report*, Q4515-4516.
49   Jameson quoted in Lockhart & Woodhouse, *Rhodes*, p. 510.
50   *Select Committee Report*, Q.4527-4531.

go to Johannesburg when the uprising occurred, but he had not told Sir Hercules that he and the Raid were involved with the Reformers plan. By doing so, Jameson cleared Robinson of direct knowledge of the Raid.

Labouchère pressed him again as to whether the officers were justified in believing that the Imperial Authorities approved of what they were about to do. Hedging his bets, Jameson replied he could not say one way or the other.[51] Towards the end of his evidence, Jameson acknowledged that Labouchère had forced him to say more than he intended about what he had told his officers. At the time of beginning the Raid, Jameson admitted that he did not accept that approval by the Authorities was important since he believed that he would succeed and his actions, if irregular, would then be forgiven; his ends would justify his means. Jameson got off lightly when compared with the earlier examinations of other witnesses such as Bower. He spent less than a day before the Committee, but one must remember that he had already been convicted by the Courts and was already judged to be guilty. It was the scalps of others that some members such a Labouchère, were really after.

Newton, the Commissioner in Bechuanaland, was quizzed over how much he knew, and his attempt to prevent Jameson from launching the Raid. The Commissioner admitted that as early as December 4, in a conversation with Jameson, the Doctor had explained that the troops at Pitsani were to protect the railway strip but were also there in readiness for an expected uprising by the *Uitlanders* against Kruger's government in Johannesburg. Newton confirmed that Rhodes had a telegram from Johannesburg which confirmed that the Commissioner would assist in the plan since he was keen to 'go to the races'; a euphemism for the Raid. By the middle of December Newton had changed his mind and he had gone to Cape Town to meet Robinson. He confirmed that he had not mentioned to Robinson the secondary reason for the troops being at Pitsani or his own initial desire to help with the plot since Jameson had told him these things in confidence. Newton also denied any knowledge that Rhodes was involved but Bower however, as had been mentioned by Jameson, had discussed with Newton his own reservations about Jameson's plans and the fact that his 'police force' at Pitsani seemed more like an army. Newton also met with Rhodes to discuss the situation at Pitsani as, together with Bower, he was aware of what was going on, but he had not told Robinson what he knew about the plan. It is clear that Newton and Bower had a singular view as to whether they felt obliged to inform Robinson about their knowledge since its source was confidential. Confidentiality it seems had a higher sway than their obligations to the Crown.

It might have seemed to Newton that his 'code of silence' defence was keeping him out of trouble until Henry Campbell-Bannerman asked him to explain his reply to Chamberlain's questions immediately after the Raid when Newton had written, ' Neither I nor any other officer of the Crown, was aware of a probable raid'.[52] Campbell-Bannerman suggested that, given Newton's admission before the Committee that he did know about the incursion, such a reply was not the appropriate language to use to the Colonial Secretary; which was a euphemism for a lie. Newton attempted an extraordinary 'read between the lines' explanation by arguing that, if he really had not known, he would have expressed his ignorance more clearly. Even when Newton knew the Raid had begun, he still did not communicate with Robinson as the Telegraph Office was closed and, even such as he couldn't send a telegram until Monday when it reopened.

Newton was reminded that Chamberlain had defended him in a debate in the Commons on 14 February by confirming that one of the reasons why Newton had not told Robinson what he knew was because he was absent from Bechuanaland for two weeks. Campbell-Bannerman was careful to make sure that the reason for Chamberlain's ignorance was evident to all as his officials had not told him about the Raid since they were kept in the dark themselves. In the final round of questions, Newton was made to clarify that he had not been forbidden by Rhodes to tell Robinson about a likely incursion which assumed that Rhodes was leaving

51   *Select Committee Report*, Q.4546.
52   *Select Committee Report*, Q.4722.

the timing of this disclosure to Newton's own judgement. A judgment which seemed to have failed him even after the Raid had begun.

It was then the turn of Frank Rhodes to face the Committee and he began by stating that he appeared only because his presence had been requested and he 'had no particular evidence he wished to give'.[53] Not satisfied with this attempted brush off, Campbell-Bannerman, sought to establish Frank's unsuitability for the post of Managing Director of Consolidated Goldfields by probing the administration of its New Concessions Account which was used to fund the 'the movement in Johannesburg'. The money came directly from his brother, Cecil, but Frank claimed never to have consulted him about withdrawals from the account, even when they had been as much as £10,000. The account also provided funds for Wolff to use in purchasing horses and supplies for the depots. This admission clearly established that Rhodes had paid much of the finances for the Raid which, though not a revelation, further cemented a cloak of guilt around the 'Colossus'' shoulders. In Frank's estimation, the Concessions Account had been drawn upon for about £250,000 with which to finance the aborted rising in Johannesburg.

When asked about the *Letter of Invitation*, Frank confirmed that Jameson had asked for the letter rather than it being freely offered by the Reformers, and that it was originally undated. Carefully questioned about the events leading up to the Raid, Frank confirmed that the Reformers were surprised when Jameson launched his incursion and did their best to attempt to stop it. They had not invited him to launch the Raid, and so they had actually not left him in the lurch when the support he expected from them did not materialise.[54] This piece of evidence placed the timing of the Raid and its failure squarely on Jameson's shoulders and not the Reformers.

Frank returned to appear before the Committee the following day having reconsidered his testimony regarding the *Letter of Invitation* which had put all the blame on Jameson. He wanted to make it clear that Dr Jim had no trouble in obtaining the letter and Frank had signed it willingly. At least one of the Committee, John Bigham, Liberal Unionist MP for Liverpool Exchange and shortly to be appointed a High Court Judge, showed signs of sympathy for Frank by reminding the Committee of the ways in which the Colonel had already been punished for his involvement in the Raid. Frank said he believed the punishments to which he had been subjected were fair but the one which hurt him most was having to resign his commission. Labouchère, on the other hand had little sympathy; he challenged Frank Rhodes on whether publishing the *Letter of Invitation* placed the populace of Johannesburg in greater danger than they had been in before the Raid. This suggestion brought about a protest from Rhodes' counsel since he claimed that it was asking for Frank's opinion about something (publication of the letter) of which, at the time of its wider dissemination, he was unaware,

Colonel Willoughby, the senior military officer involved in the Raid, was then questioned, and much was made of his financial interests in Rhodesia; presumably to establish another motive than simply to support the Reformers. When asked by Labouchère whether he had told his fellow officers that the proposed Raid had been endorsed by the British Government he declined to answer. Although Willoughby was several times urged to respond to this important question, he was only prepared to admit that he had 'reassured' any officer who had doubts. A frustrated Labouchère reminded Willoughby, and his Committee colleagues, that this was an investigation committee which needed to get to the truth. Finally, after several more attempts and with the assistance of Jackson acting as Chair, Labouchère got Willoughby to admit that he had said that if the Raid was successful, they would not be bothered by anybody. Labouchère took this as an answer to his original question about whether the Colonel had suggested that the Raid was properly authorised by the Imperial Authorities, but it was not.[55] However, Willoughby admitted that he did believe that the authorities

---

53   *Select Committee Report*, Q.4956.
54   *Select Committee Report*, Q.5140.
55   *Select Committee Report*, Q.5499-5551.

had approved of the impending Raid as a result of a conversation he had with Jameson; the contents of which he refused to disclose. Labouchère attempted, but with little success, to get the other Committee members to agree that since Jameson was Willoughby's senior officer, the conversation was at least 'semi-official' and not a confidential one. Even when the Chair drew Willoughby's attention to Jameson's replies about this matter, the Colonel's responses remained vague. The Committee had been, to some extent, hoist by its own petard of allowing witnesses to refuse to answer question properly because these might incriminate third parties.

Colonel Willoughby was further able to cloud his evidence by claiming that the letter which set out his case, sent to Redvers Buller at the War Office, was also confidential and he could not, nor would not, reveal its contents; another case of double bluff since Willoughby had not written the letter himself. Not daunted, and having temporarily discharged the Colonel, the Committee were eventually able to obtain a copy of the letter in which Willoughby (Hawksley), in an attempt to save his commission and those of his fellow officers, stated clearly that he had been told by Jameson that the action was both known and approved of by the Imperial Authorities. The War Office's reply was unequivocal; Willoughby and the rest had been misled by Jameson into committing a serious offence. They had also ignored a direct order from Robinson to return to Pitsani. An officer of Willoughby's experience should have required greater proof of the Imperial Authority's approval than simply the word of Dr Jameson.

Having obtained the letter, the Committee recalled Willoughby who consequently found himself somewhat on the back foot. He was reminded that he was a convicted criminal, guilty of taking part in an attack on a friendly state and had thus forfeited his right to maintain confidentiality. Harcourt continued to probe him and Willoughby continued to prevaricate. Eventually, the Committee went into camera and decided that Willoughby must answer Harcourt's questions. Harcourt pointed out to Willoughby that Jameson had denied telling the officers that their actions had Imperial approval. Since this evidence was on record, as was Willoughby's letter to the War Office, it was no longer a question of keeping a private conversation private. Willoughby's evidence and that of Jameson, were in complete conflict. Hawksley attempted to help his client out but was prevented from doing so by the Chairman who adjourned the Committee and promised to recall Jameson to clarify exactly who '… the Imperial Authorities were'.

It turned out that Jameson was referring, somewhat obscurely, to Sir Hercules Robinson and he said that to suggest that he had meant 'Her Majesty's Government would be idiotic.'[56] He confirmed that Hawksley had written Willoughby's letter to Buller and also agreed that he knew that Willoughby had assured the officers that their commissions were safe. Willoughby had not asked Jameson's authorisation to make such a claim but if Willoughby had asked Jameson permission, he would have agreed.[57] Harcourt pressed Jameson as to whether he was right to assume that the Government would have forgiven him and his officers if the Raid had been successful as this was an attempt to decide or influence the way in which the Government would or should react to the incursion. Jameson had the good grace to admit this may have been true but he had not seen things in this way while he was at Pitsani.

John Ellis, the Liberal MP for Rushcliffe in Nottinghamshire, a wealthy mine owner, began to explore the key question of whether Jameson knew before he left Pitsani that he was no longer welcomed by the Reformers. The important letter brought by the cyclists was seen as less significant evidence for the Reformers' support since Jameson, under questioning, was forced to agree that the letter might actually have said that some men would meet his force at Krugersdorp rather than several hundred. This suggests that they would only be able to act as guides to show the Raiders the best way into Johannesburg and were not an armed force intended to fight alongside Jameson's men on their way into the town.

Willoughby was recalled and began to feel the pressure as member after member pressed him on who had approved of the Raid. He feared they were trying to trip him up and he was not used to battling in this kind

---

56   *Select Committee Report*, Q.5663.
57   The word used by Jameson was 'sanctioned'.

of arena. Willoughby argued that as he had just come out of prison he felt dazed and vulnerable. Sydney Buxton, Member of Parliament for Poplar, who had served as Under Secretary of State for the Colonies from 1892-1895, again took up the question of the meaning of the term' Imperial Authorities'. Willoughby began to struggle and first the Attorney General and then Chamberlain came to his aid. They objected to Buxton asking Willoughby directly whether he alleged knowledge of the identity of 'the Imperial Authorities' and whether they had given assent to the Raid.[58] Buxton, somewhat chastened, backed off and claimed that he only wanted to know whether Willoughby agreed with Jameson's view that the term 'Imperial Authorities' meant Hercules Robinson. Jameson and Willoughby both had agreed in their testimony that the letter to Buller was carelessly worded and could be seen to mean more than they had actually meant it to say. This explanation would seem questionable but both men may have been attempting to retract their testimony since its obvious interpretation was that the 'Imperial Authorities' meant Chamberlain, or, at least, the Colonial Office. Such an interpretation would seem most likely since, rather than a hastily constructed letter by two challenged individuals, the letter to the War Office had been drafted by Bouchier Hawksley, who would have advised them to use the strongest information at their disposal to build up their defence. Hawksley did not approve of Rhodes' instructions that he should not implicate any Government official and might have hoped that using the obscure reference to 'Imperial Authorities' might have persuaded official sympathy for Willoughby *et al*. If so, this would explain why Chamberlain came to Willoughby's defence when the questions became closer to exposing the possible identity of the mysterious Authorities.

Major Heany and Dr Wolff were then examined. Heany described how he was sent by members of the *Reform Committee* to Jameson at Pitsani and fenced with his interrogators when they asked him about the message which Phillips had given him telling Jameson not to come. Heany tried to suggest that the message actually told Jameson to postpone any incursion. He did, however, agree that these were the genuine wishes of the Reformers and not a double bluff in which don't come actually meant come. According to Heany, he and 'everyone' presumably he meant the officers, knew that Robinson's telegram ordered the Raid be stopped and the Raiders should return.

Wolff appeared as a voluntary witness before the Committee and confirmed much of the story which had already been exposed and described how he had arranged the supply points along the Raiders' route. Significantly, he confirmed that there had been a genuine attempt to stop the Raid.

The Committee had now reached the Easter Recess and adjourned until 30 June. They were determined to conclude the first part of their brief; the facts about the Jameson Raid, before the summer and the celebrations for Queen Victoria's Diamond Jubilee which were to take place on 22 June. This meant that they had roughly eight sessions left to conclude their deliberation and then produce a report which would be debated in the House of Commons. The need for haste was apparent to all.

---

58   *Select Committee Report*, Q.5798.

14

Committee of No-Inquiry

Rutherfoord Harris, Secretary of the BSAC, was interrogated about his dealings with the Colonial Office and the proposed railway line through Bechuanaland. His responses seemed harmless but obviously sufficient to discomfort Chamberlain, who then offered himself as a witness to give his version of what had happened.[1] There followed the unusual sight of an interrogator being sworn in as a witness by his own inquiry. Chamberlain explained his initial objections to handing over Bechuanaland to the BSAC. Being new to the Colonial Office, he needed time to review the situation himself and there were the interests of native chiefs in the area to be considered. He agreed in principle that the railway should be built as it was his intentions to improve and extend the communications between Cape Colony and the lands administered by the BSAC. The railway proposed by Rhodes was one such method and he applauded it. Chamberlain had pointed out to Rutherfoord Harris that it was 'not absolutely necessary' to transfer the whole of the Bechuanaland Protectorate to ensure this; a strip of land on which to build the railway line would be sufficient. The three major Twsana chiefs from Bechuanaland, Khama, Sebele, and Bathoen came to see Chamberlain in London, and their arguments against granting British Bechuanaland to the BSAC had finally changed his mind.[2]

The Chiefs' visits to Britain in September 1895 is an interesting story in itself. Sebele had become chief of the BaKwena in 1892 and succeeded his father who had reigned for 60 years and had been a friend of the missionary David Livingstone. In later life, Sebele was prone to compare himself with Edward, the Prince of Wales, who had lived for a similar length of time in the shadow of his mother, Queen Victoria.[3] Sebele opposed every extension of power which might threaten his kingdom but clearly feared the BSAC's threat even more than any other. Bathoen, chief of the BaNgwatese was describe as a veritable Samson and arrived in England dressed in a blue serge suit with a bowler hat.[4] His chiefdom was immediately south of that of Sebele and next to the Molopo River. He was the brother-in-law of Sebele, with whom he shared objections to being taxed as part of the Protectorate. Chief Khama, of the BaNgwato who lived north of the BaKwena, was the third member of the delegation. Better dressed than his two colleagues, it was clear to observers that he had taken care with his appearance in order to fit in with the occasion. A militant convert to Christianity, he had revolted against the heathen beliefs of his father and had gone into exile later reclaiming his throne from his uncle with the help of Sebele. Khama had been tricked into allowing British farmers to occupy part of his land but later was prepared to grant mineral rights which eventually were bought by the BSAC. He had provided warriors to fight alongside Jameson's men in the First Matabele War and was described as a 'loyal ally'. In contrast, however, when Khama believed that the Matabele War was over he had withdrawn

---

1   *Select Committee Report*, Q.6217.
2   The Batswana word for chief is 'Kgosi'
3   N. Parsons, *King Khama, Emperor Joe, and the Great White Queen: Victorian Britain Through Africa* (Bloomington, Indiana: Indiana University Press,1980) p. 37.
4   Parsons. *King Khama*, p. 43.

his men which was rather too soon for the British and Rhodes thought he was a traitor and it is said he enquired how many men it would take to dispossess Khama of his land.[5] Since Jameson had defeated the Matabele, the BSAC set about claiming land which Lobengula, King of the Matabele, had 'owned'; some of which belonged to Khama's people. Khama protested to the Colonial Office and initially gained support from Edward Fairfield, the Assistant Under Secretary, but later Fairfield changed his support to Rhodes. As we have seen, when Rhodes was in conversation with Chamberlain, there was mention that the 'Colossus' believed that every man had his price.

Their three months visit to England was something of a triumph for the three Chiefs. Dressed in the best European attire available in the Cape, they toured Britain and visited many London attractions such as Madame Tussauds. They were feted in many of the places they visited; events which were recorded by a fascinated British Press. Bathoen enjoyed the experience but was not always happy with the crowding in the bigger cities. He is reported to have told a British soldier stationed in Mafeking during its siege, that 'he liked Sheffield better than London, because in Sheffield he could go where he liked but in London, he had to follow the stream of people'.[6] Sebele's militant Christianity proved popular in certain quarters and, assisted by the London Missionary Society, the Chiefs proclaimed their loyalty to the Crown and claimed that the BSAC would not only steal their land but corrupt their people with strong drink. Consequently, they became favourites of many temperance societies. Their visit to Leicester was particularly well received. The Belvoir Street Baptist Chapel was packed to hear what they had to say about the BSAC and other speakers made it clear that the Government should listen to public opinion on this matter. Rhodes popularity began to wane, and he was mocked as 'the Pooh Bah of Africa'.[7] The Chiefs had an audience with the Queen, whom they called 'Mrs Little Old Lady', at Windsor Castle. Victoria's address to the chiefs, Reid believes, must have been approved by Chamberlain.[8] She told them she was 'glad to see [them], and to know that they love[d her] rule'.[9]

In discussion with the Colonial Office, the Chiefs made it clear that they were reasonably content with the transfer but strongly preferred the idea that it was the Imperial Government and its officials who would administer the land and with whom they would have to deal. Chamberlain, who was about to go on holiday to Spain, urged the Chiefs and the BSAC to get together in his absence in order to resolve their differences. He also told them that a strip of land upon which to place the railway line would be given to Rhodes. These discussions, in which Rutherfoord Harris took part, failed to reach agreement. Chamberlain then created a land 'reserve' for the Chiefs and allocated the strip to the BSAC. Chamberlain's decision was to only allow the Company a slice of land on which to build the railway line and not give it Bechuanaland. Rhodes, who firmly believed in the superiority of the white race and in particular the British race, was furious. He was humiliated by being beaten by Africans. He also had little respect for those Britons who had supported the delegation whom he abused in very racist terms.[10] The Chiefs may only have gained 'half a loaf' but Parsons believed that it was their delegation which had influenced Chamberlain's decision not to hand over the whole of Bechuanaland to Rhodes.[11]

---

5   Parsons. *King Khama*, p. 49.
6   Parsons, *King Khama*, p. 248.
7   'Pooh Bah', a character in Gilbert and Sullivan's comic opera *The Mikado*, held a large number of offices and was full of his own self-importance. See P Brendon, *Independent*, 23 March 1999.
8   C. V. Reid, *Royal Tourists, Colonial Subjects and the making of a British World, 1860–1911* (Manchester: Manchester University Press, 2016) p. 6.
9   Parsons, *King Khama*, pp. 227-28.
10   His language was extremely racist and it would be inappropriate to quote the words he used.
11   Neil Parsons, '"No Longer Rare Birds in London": Zulu, Ndebele, Gaza, and Swazi Envoys to England, 1882-1894 ' in Gretchen Gerzina (ed.), *Black Victorians/Black Victoriana* (New Brunswick, New Jersey: Rutgers University Press, 2003), pp. 110–44.

Chamberlain, in his evidence to the committee, confirmed had realised that the railway strip would need policing but there was no suspicion in his mind that this would lead to the Raid. Chamberlain maintained that Rutherfoord Harris, during an interview, had attempted to entice him into a plot and offered to tell the him secret information through 'a guarded allusion'. The Colonial Secretary claimed to have immediately stopped him, arguing that he was a Minister of the Crown and could only hear information which he could officially use. Hercules Robinson was Chamberlain's eyes and ears in the Colony and he would tell him what he needed to know. Chamberlain, however, confirmed that Rutherfoord Harris had mentioned unrest in Johannesburg and hinted that there was a necessity for police to be based near the border. Finally, Chamberlain, in the strongest terms, denied any knowledge of the plot or that he had the slightest suspicion that there might be a hostile Raid. Meade, Fairfield and Lord Selbourne, the Under Secretary, were equally in the dark.

Van de Poel, after researching Sir Graham Bower's papers, felt that Chamberlain's position was one of official ignorance but unofficial knowledge. She believed that he encouraged the Jameson Raid as being the best solution to the South African problem[12] and suggested that Bower, out of loyalty, was persuaded to say he had not told Chamberlain about Jameson's intentions and to claim that only he knew of the intended Raid.[13] In his account of the affair Bower, however, made it clear that this admission of his failure to tell Chamberlain was made out of loyalty to the Chief rather than being the truth.[14] Bower's loyalty, however, was not to be rewarded. A similar sacrifice by publicly admitting failure to tell Chamberlain was demanded of Edward Fairfield, Bower's counterpart at the Colonial Office. Fairfield was not so keen to be as loyal but died shortly after being told what was expected of him, which was to defend Chamberlain. This conveniently enabled the Colonial Secretary to safely deny knowledge of the Jameson Raid whilst paying eloquent tribute to Fairfield '… who had misunderstood his orders being so unusually deaf.'

Bower's memoirs suggest that it had always been Chamberlain's intention to use Fairfield as a scapegoat and he (Bower) had received a letter from a very distressed Fairfield which claimed that he was being instructed to confirm that Chamberlain knew nothing of the Raid. He also asked Bower to burn their correspondence, but whether this was to protect Chamberlain or himself is not clear.[15]

Labouchère almost spoiled the Colonial Secretary's hauteur by getting him to confirm that he had seen some of the telegrams sent between Rhodes and Rutherfoord Harris in June 1896. No other member of the Inquiry asked the Colonial Secretary questions and it might be thought that their silence spoke loudly.

Rutherfoord Harris was recalled and he revealed how telegrams had been handled at the BSAC. Personal telegrams would go directly to Rhodes and telegrams sent to the BSAC in the Cape would be translated by Rutherfoord Harris' personal clerk and then given to Rhodes. Rutherfoord Harris had not seen the telegrams since he resigned and believed they had been destroyed after Bobby White's code book had been found by the Boers. Further probing elicited that it was actually he who had ordered that they be destroyed. Rutherfoord Harris had handed the personal telegrams to Rhodes during their journey to England and had not seen most of them since. Harcourt relentlessly pursued the whereabouts of the 'missing' telegrams. Did they still exist? Did Hawksley have them? Had they been shown to the War Office? Rutherfoord Harris' answers were somewhat vague, and he did not seem sure of anything.

He did, however, confirm that he knew that Rhodes sympathised with the *Uitlanders* in Johannesburg and would send them arms if it had been requested. Indeed, Rutherfoord Harris had been instrumental in obtaining some weapons under the guise of arming a volunteer force in Matabeleland. Under certain

---

12   Van der Poel, *The Jameson Raid*, p. 27.

13   Van der Poel, *The Jameson Raid*, p. 47.

14   D.M. Schreuder,& J. Butler (eds.) *Sir Graham Bower's Secret History of the Jameson Raid and the South African Crisis, 1895-1902* (Cape of Good Hope: Van Riebeek Society, 2002).

15   Schreuder & Butler, *Bower's Secret History*, p. 329.

circumstances, and at Rhodes' direction, a portion of the weapons were sent to Johannesburg. Rutherfoord Harris, who had been absent from the Cape, claimed that he did not hear of the *Letter of Invitation* until the week before the launch of the Raid. He pleaded ignorance about Heaney's attempts to stop the Raid but had simply provided him with a train to get to Mafeking without knowing the reason for Heany's mission. Rutherfoord Harris' testimony proved to be one of ignorance of the facts, and suggested he was only obeying orders and he had acted unknowingly, in good faith. This, of course, might have been far from the truth but an example of further loyalty to Rhodes.

The second day of Rutherfoord Harris' evidence began with a clarification of the BSAC's code book which Hawksley had supplied to the Committee at their request. It was established that there was a 'double code'. Rutherfoord Harris made it clear that his knowledge of the application of the code was vague as it was carried out by his secretary. Rutherfoord Harris was unsure of the quantities of ammunition which had been ordered in his name and the types of weapons which had been bought and he frequently claimed to have forgotten details contained in the telegrams. The Committee, having had enough of hearing about some of the telegrams second hand, adjourned Rutherfoord Harris' interrogation until they could obtain copies of the telegrams to examine themselves.

Lionel Phillips was called and there was a polite exchange between the Committee Chair and Arthur Cohen QC, Phillips' barrister, during which Jackson apologised for the short notice the Committee had given Phillips to appear before it and promised to take account of his unpreparedness. In order to save time Jackson decided that, rather than allowing Cohen to read Phillips' statement, Cohen was allowed just asked him questions about it. Cohen agreed to do so which meant that he, as Phillip's barrister was, initially, allowed to lead the Commission's questioning.[16] Beginning by establishing Phillips '*bona fides*' as a person of some influence in Johannesburg, Cohen reminded his client that in 1894 he had clearly stated that he did not wish to mix business with politics. However, in spite of this assertion, Phillips did feel that people in Johannesburg were justly concerned by the ZAR's attitude towards the *Uitlanders* and its lack of sound government. It was Loch's visit to the ZAR which had opened Phillips' eyes as to the real feelings of the *Uitlanders* and, having spent two and a half years using constitutional means to change the ZAR's attitude, he believed that an armed revolution was the only way to bring about change. He acknowledged that such an action would result in Johannesburg being besieged and it was therefore necessary to stockpile arms in preparation for this. Jameson was on the border in order to facilitate this revolt but he was, on no account, to enter without the express permission of the Reformers. Phillips believed that, when the uprising did take place, Robinson would come to Johannesburg in order to intervene between the Reformers and Kruger and this would limit any bloodshed. However, aware of Jameson's impetuosity, Philips had personally telegraphed him not to move. The Reformers had no intention of interfering with the independence of the ZAR but simply wanted improved treatment. The proof of this was centred on the issue of under which flag the uprising would take place. The need to clarify this point was, according to Phillips, one of the reasons why both the revolt and Jameson's intervention should be postponed. Johannesburg Race Week was a second reason for postponing since it would bring as many as 5,000 extra people into the town who would have to be accommodated if there was a siege. Surprisingly, Phillips mentioned there were three reasons why the Reformers felt the revolution should be postponed, but he could not recall the third.

The third reason might have been that the bulk of ammunition and the Maxims provided by Rutherfoord Harris did not reach Johannesburg until the 31 December by which time Jameson had already begun his Raid. To admit to the impending delivery of the arms might further incriminate the Reformers but it had no purpose as they had not actually risen against the ZAR but needed them to defend their town. Clearly the Reformers had very cold feet and after forming the Reform Committee and electing Phillips as its Chair, they issued a statement which clearly demonstrated that they did not want to challenge the authority of the

---

16   *Select Committee Report*, Q.56787-7155.

ZAR but they realised that Jameson's actions would mean that it was likely that Johannesburg would be besieged. They urged its citizens to cooperate with the defence of the town against such a possibility. Such was the strength of support from the town's people; the Reform Committee received 20,000 requests for the 2,500 rifles it actually had.

Phillips, now under questioning by the Committee, went on to confirm the visits of the ZAR representatives who had offered an 'olive branch' by suggesting that Kruger was willing to acquiesce to the Reformers' demands. At the official meeting with Judges Kotzé, Ameshoff and General Kock, Philips had indicated that although they had not wanted Jameson to cross the border, they were as one with his intentions in assisting them to improve their conditions. Clearly when the Raid failed this admission played into the hands of the ZAR, as did the decision to provide Kotzé with a complete list of the Reformers which later enabled the ZAR to charge each of these individuals with treason.

The Commission having continuously heard about the numerous telegrams which were vital for them to evaluate who said or knew what and when, had become frustrated by the fact that only some of these documents were available They finally called John Dennison Pender, the Managing Director of the Eastern Telegraph Company, which had previously provided them with some of the telegrams.[17] He arrived before them with telegrams which had not been previously presented. Amongst these there were the original telegrams which had been sent from England, but the Telegraph Company only had what it described as 'service copies' of those which had been sent from abroad; made during the course of their transmission It was the usual practice of the Telegraph Company, Pender told the Committee, to destroy both originals and copies of telegrams after a certain period which meant that only those of either type from 1 November 1895 were still retained.[18] Fletcher Moulton QC, Pender's barrister, informed the Committee that he had been instructed by Hawksley, acting on behalf of Rhodes, not to provide the Committee with these retained telegrams. The Eastern Telegraph Company intended to follow these instructions unless ordered to do so by a legal authority but the Telegraph Company was at least prepared to inform the Committee of Hawksley's (Rhodes') attempt to withhold this evidence. It had since been ordered to produce the telegrams by the Committee but Pender was uncertain if it had the authority to do this. The Company would like to know why Hawksley objected to them handing over these telegrams. It seems that Hawksley had also written a similar letter to the Telegraph Company on Rutherfoord Harris' behalf thus protecting his communication with Rhodes.

Hawksley, sensing danger, tried another attempt to protect his clients from what the telegrams might reveal. He argued that the BSAC had already agreed to surrender any telegram which it had sent or received. It was the production of 'private' telegrams from and to individuals such as Rhodes and Rutherfoord Harris which they had refused to hand over. Pender was naturally familiar with the Telegraph Convention and his own Company's terms and conditions, both of which stated that telegrams should not be revealed to third parties.[19] If the Committee wanted him to do so, he argued, they must make a specific Order, but they should first consider whether this was a dangerous precedent to set.[20] No ones' communications would be confidential in future.

Somewhat challenged, Jackson ordered the room to be cleared whilst Committee could discuss this objection. When it returned, the Attorney General gave his legal opinion that, since the Committee of Inquiry had a similar status to a court of law, and courts of law were able to demand evidence such as letters and telegrams which were normally confidential, then the Telegraph Company's objection should be overruled.

---

17   Not to be confused with his father, John Pender, an entrepreneur who founded over 30 telegraph companies.

18   *Select Committee Report,* Q.7158.

19   John Dennison Pender Managing Director of the Eastern Telegraph Company was to threaten Marconi's attempts to establish transatlantic wireless communication failing to see it as a threat to cable communications. His Board compounded this failure by deciding to invest in Marconi's company in 1901. *Select Committee Report,* Q.7158.

20   *Select Committee Report,* Q.7158.

Jackson, in an attempt to ease the Company's conscience made it clear that the Committee would only use telegrams which pertained to their brief and not discuss any of a genuinely private nature. Conscience cleared and legally justified, Dennison Pender handed over 46 telegrams, five of which, surprisingly given Pender's evidence, were dated prior to 1 November 1896.[21]

Phillips was recalled and Labouchère launched into a detailed examination of the issue of the dynamite monopoly and the true cost of this essential product. This probing had gone on for some time when Jackson interrupted to observe that he didn't know where Labouchère's line of questioning was going. It was clearly off the track of getting to the bottom of the Raid. Labouchère explained that Phillips wanted to show the Committee that the monopoly placed on this vitally important product to the mining industry in the ZAR had created extremely high prices and such practices were at the heart of the discontent amongst the *Uitlanders*.

In an attempt to spring a trap, Labouchère, then asked Phillips if he knew that a Mr Beit had received shares in The Dynamite Company which didn't actually make the explosive but only imported and packed it. Phillips strongly denied the allegations that Alfred Beit's brother Werner's company had made large profits in this way from the dynamite monopoly. Labouchère was suggesting that, since Beit and Rhodes were hand in glove, they were making high profits from the monopoly as did the ZAR Government. Continuing this line of questioning, Labouchère queried the effects which these monopolies had on Phillips' commercial interests. In an oblique way, Labouchère was trying to suggest that at least Phillip's objections to the conditions under which the *Uitlanders'* lived and worked were really based on commercial disadvantages to his business interests rather than having political objectives. The Attorney General cautioned Labouchère that he was again straying off the point but Labouchère explained that Phillip's grievances were similar to those of the current Opposition in Parliament and which were about excessive taxation. In making this comparison Labouchère had missed a key difference between Britons and the *Uitlanders;* since the latter were paying enormous taxes to the ZAR but had no representation or voice as to how these taxes were spent.[22]

It was during this part of the questioning that the name of Flora Shaw was first raised in the Inquiry. She was mentioned in a letter, allegedly written by Phillips and published in a Dutch Transvaal newspaper. The letter was addressed to one of the Beit Brothers and reminded the recipient that they must make sure that Flora Shaw '…got her share'.[23] Phillips denied all knowledge of the letter and Labouchère's trap was only half sprung since he was unable to produce a copy of the newspaper at this crucial moment. Phillips eventually seemed to have vaguely remembered the letter but said that its subject was not part of the Committee's brief. How he knew this without clear knowledge of its contents is interesting.

Following Labouchère's argument, other members of the Committee reminded Philips that though it was true that the ZAR was making huge profits from monopolies, the Randlords were also becoming very rich. They asked if their objection to high taxes was simply so they might make even higher profits? Phillips took the opportunity to reinforce his argument that those paying these high taxes were not receiving much benefit from the ZAR for them by citing the provision of education in the ZAR. English children had to be fluent in Dutch, the medium of instruction, before they could access education in ZAR funded schools. Phillips had donated some money to create 'English' schools since the standard of Dutch required was so high as to be almost impossible for the children to achieve.[24] He argued that English was the language of the whole country, an exaggeration which was explained by his secondary claim that it was the language of commerce and teaching foreign (*Uitlander)* children Dutch to the standard required was an impossibility.

---

21   C.M. Woodhouse, 'The Missing Telegrams and the Jameson Raid,' Part One, *History Today*, 1 June 1962, p. 398.
22   *Select Committee Report,* Q.7281.
23   *Select Committee Report,* Q.7302.
24   *Select Committee Report,* Q.7413.

Phillips was then drawn into discussing the Reformers' plan to seize the fort at Pretoria but Chamberlain quickly diverted the questioning back by asking him to repeat his evidence about the education of *Uitlander* children being impossible. Chamberlain questioned the amount of profits which the Randlords made and compared these with the cost of educating non-Boer children. Chamberlain mollified Phillips' obvious discomfort by this interjection, which had obviously touched a raw point, by asking him whether the ZAR's promise to redress the *Uitlanders'* grievances had been kept. Phillips confirmed they had not.

The next five witnesses were the Duke of Abercorn, President of the BSAC, the Duke of Fife, Lord Gifford VC, Sir Horace Farquhar and George Cawston; all Directors of the BSAC. Their evidence had a similar ring. They were aware of the purchase of arms for the Rhodesia Horse which was necessary to meet the Companies increased responsibilities. There was, however, no connection, they claimed, between these purchases and the subsequent events at Pitsani. Abercorn confirmed that Rhodes was the real power behind the BSAC and, by giving him such dominance, the Board of Directors had abdicated both power and, more importantly, immediate responsibility.[25] Rhodes would do many things and inform the Board afterwards by telegram or letter rather than seeking permission. Although these actions were discussed, the Board usually accepted Rhodes opinions and Abercorn doubted whether the Board was ever critical of them. Labouchère established that the first real criticism of Rhodes was on 2 January 1896 when the Board discussed the Raid. Abercorn proved something of a weak source of information about this meeting since as he had not been present during the first part of the proceedings, and was unaware as to whether James Rochfort Maguire, Rhodes 'alternate' on the Board, had spoken or what he might have said on Rhodes' behalf. No Director knew any more than any other but there was a lot of discussion as to whether Rhodes and Maguire should resign after the publication of the telegrams from Bobby White's dispatch case. Rhodes did resign but then changed his mind but, eventually, the Board demanded his resignation. Abercorn was also a forgetful witness and was taken through his testimony by leading questions and reminders by his interrogators but he could contribute nothing to what the Committee already knew.

Labouchère took the opportunity to go off track again, much to the Attorney General's and Bigham's frustration, by questioning the Duke as to what shares he had in the BSAC and how he had come by them. Labouchère explained the reason for his questions was to establish whether the Raid was really to boost the BSAC's share price. Bigham objected to this line of questioning and the room was cleared again whilst a ruling on its admissibility was made. When the Committee reconvened, Jackson asked the Duke whether he had bought or sold any shares in the last six months of 1895. He had not and said it would have been strange if he had done so, even though the share prices had fallen, had it become public knowledge that he, the Chair of the Company, was selling shares this would have made the share price fall even further. One might suggest that this was not the real point of Labouchère's question, which was seeking to determine whether a successful Raid would have boosted BSAC shares and whether this was one of Rhodes' motives for approving its planning. Sydney Buxton, who was to become second Governor General of South Africa, wishing to further expose the BSAC Board's ineffectiveness, asked Abercorn why they waited to be told by Chamberlain's to dismiss Jameson as Administrator of Bechuanaland rather than acting on their own initiative? It must be remembered that Jameson embarked on the Raid on 29 December and Chamberlain's letter of instruction was dated 31 December. The Boards' agreement was confirmed in a letter to Chamberlain on the 2 January: a gap of 5 days. Is it unlikely however, that a Board of Directors so ineffective with Abercorn, as its figurative head, and unused to having any authority could have responded more quickly to the disturbing events of the Raid? A rapid response would be even more implausible if they were ignorant of the plot and did not immediately realise its implications for the Company. Chamberlain's letter arrived before the Board Members had time to respond to these events, and Rhodes' absence left the Board leaderless and needing to be told what to do.

---

25   *Select Committee Report*, Q.7534.

John Ellis, Member of Parliament for Rushcliffe in Nottinghamshire, may have been trying to implicate Chamberlain by suggesting that Abercorn, the Duke of Fife, and Lord Grey were the official Directors appointed to the Board by the Colonial Office under the BSAC's Charter, so Chamberlain was indirectly responsible for their actions. Abercorn's vague answer to this suggestion was interrupted by Chamberlain denying there were any such official directors.

The Duke claimed that he was unaware that Rhodes was 'in it' when the Board heard about Jameson's incursion.[26] He seemed to have remained in ignorance for at least the first six months of 1896 and he claimed that, when Rhodes attended the Board earlier in 1896, he did not tell them of his involvement in the Raid. However, Ellis pressed the Duke further who was forced to admit that Rhodes had said something about it but he couldn't remember exactly what it was. Again, under Ellis' pressure, Abercorn was forced to admit that he understood that Rhodes was responsible but, such was Rhodes sway over the Board members, they did not ask for his resignation but sought advice from Chamberlain again as to what they should do. However, neither the Board nor Abercorn thought it appropriate to tell Chamberlain that Rhodes had left the impression that he was involved in some way with the Raid.

Abercorn was a very poor witness. The question which arises is why this was so? Was he trying to absolve himself and his co-directors from blame by covering for them through his own ignorance? Or was he and the Board in such thrall to Rhodes that they were mere rubber stamps to the Colossus? Even the Duke's interrogators were surprised that a man who was the Chair and a life director of the BSAC should have been apparently so ignorant and forgetful in such an important matter.

The Duke of Fife was a more certain witness answering 'No' to every question regarding his or the Board's knowledge of the Raid, the deployment of the Company's police at Pitsani, or involvement with the Reformers. He had, however, sold some shares in the last 6 months of 1895 but he argued that this was in no way connected with the Raid which he deplored.[27]

Fife was not present at the meeting when Abercorn claimed that Rhodes had confessed his involvement but heard about it later. The Board had not communicated with Chamberlain because they knew that Rhodes had a meeting with the Colonial Secretary the day after the Board meeting; further evidence that Rhodes was not only controlling the Board but was also its mouthpiece. The Duke accused Rhodes of lying as he had not told the Board of his involvement but Ellis reminded Fife that he had not been present at the crucial meeting. In response, the Duke went on to assert that Rhodes, for whom he had great respect, did not make his involvement in the Raid and its preparations clear to the Board. When questioned as to why the Board did not repudiate Jameson immediately after they had received Chamberlain's letter, Fife responded that they did not wish to act precipitately. Again, Fife painted a picture of a Board which was either very ineffective or taken by surprise by events having been completely outwitted by Rhodes.

Labouchère wanted to press the question of Fife selling shares and there was a spat between him and the Chair, who eventually prevented him from asking the question. Jackson's point was that Fife had already answered the question about shares but Labouchère explained he wanted to probe Fife's motive for the sale. The Attorney General, more subtlety asked Fife whether the sale of shares had anything to do with the disturbances in South Africa or whether he had known that Rhodes had financed the Reformers in Johannesburg. The Duke's answer to both questions was a decisive 'No'.

Lord Gifford, the third Board member called, unequivocally denied knowledge of the Raid, its preparations or that Rhodes and Jameson had ever communicated to him their intentions. Gifford was a military man, had earned his VC for bravery in the Third Ashanti War in 1874 and had experience as a Colonial Administrator. He admitted to his part in equipping the Rhodesia Horse with arms and ammunition, but this had nothing to do with the subsequent Raid. Gifford seems to have understood the procedure of

26   *Select Committee Report*, Q.7635.
27   *Select Committee Report,* Q.7607.

the Boardroom rather better than his Chair for, having discussed with Jameson, Rhodes and Willoughby the number of arms and ammunition which was needed, he only authorised their requisition after he had informed the Board about this discussion. The requisition was for roughly 1,500 Lee Speed rifles and a million rounds of ammunition. The Committee, with limited military knowledge, thought this was an excessive amount, but Gifford explained that it was decided to make sure that the Rhodesia Horse was equipped as if they were a British regiment at home. In addition, nine Maxims were also ordered but there was nothing exceptional or sinister about this requisition. Gifford confirmed that he had not known that some of these arms were diverted to Johannesburg. He had no knowledge that Rhodes was financing the Reformers and it was only after the Raid that he became suspicious. However, like Abercorn and Fife, he had not thought it necessary to personally investigate this matter with Rhodes.

The Committee also called John Jones, the Assistant Secretary of BSAC, who had decoded the much-discussed telegrams for their inquiry. For Jones to be asked to appear as a witness was a strange request since he was an employee of the Company and might have tweaked the telegrams to its advantage. The Committee was obviously aware of this fact for it made Jones swear that, to the best of his ability, his renditions were accurate. He provide translations of three telegrams which were relevant to the Committee's remit. Jackson was fulsome in praising Jones for his great assistance in providing the decoded telegrams but noted that some telegrams were still missing, and these were to haunt Rhodes and Jameson for the rest of their lives.

Jones was followed by Charles Leonard, the Chair of the National Union and leading *Uitlander*. Leonard had avoided arrest, he rather weakly claimed, in order to appear before the Inquiry. He most strongly denied that the *Letter of Invitation* was intended to give Jameson *carte blanche* to act when he wished without further consultation with the Reformers. He was anxious to put his side of events, especially concerning his visit to Rhodes on 28 December 1895. Whilst the Committee realised the importance of this testimony, it was aware that the clock was running down on their investigations and it was anxious to keep Leonard's evidence as short as possible. Leonard was determined to make his points, however, and read a shortened version of his manifesto setting out the things which the Union wanted reformed. Newcomers to the ZAR were keen to take part in the political life of the country which is why the franchise was such a crucial issue. Some Boers were favourable to this view, but, in Leonard's opinion, it was Kruger who was the source and fount of opposition to anything English. Leonard argued that the *Uitlanders'* revolt had honourable motives and was not brought about for financial reasons. It was true that the mine owners and entrepreneurs' money had financed the movement but their desire to increase their profits was not its cause. This was something of an attempt to clear men such as Rhodes and Beit from the accusation of trying to overthrow the government of the ZAR in order to increase their wealth. Similarly Leonard reported his conversation with Rhodes in Cape Town when the latter assured the former that his intention was to reform the ZAR not make it a British Colony.[28] The controversy of the British flag he argued had resulted from a loose comment by Rutherfoord Harris.[29] One suspects that Leonard was either mistaken in his assumption of Rhodes' arch-imperialist intentions or fooled by events.

Leonard accused Jameson of exploiting the *Letter of Invitation* for his own purposes and it was never meant to be used as an excuse to justify the Raid. However, he did not go so far as to repudiate Jameson, and in his evidence did not clearly say why this was so. He attempted to justify his escape from the fate of his Reform Committee colleagues; he had been ill as the result of the strain of events and then realised that he was the only Reformer not to be in jail so it was his duty to come to England and put their case. John Ellis questioned whether Leonard had the authority to do this as he was no longer a representative of the Reformers. He had not gone back to Johannesburg and his reports of the events there were hearsay. However, Leonard agreed

---

28   *Select Committee Report*, Q.7936.
29   *Select Committee Report*, Q.7957.

that in order to gain the franchise the *Uitlanders* would have to be prepared to give up their British citizenship, but the vote was more important.

Labouchère had heard enough and launched into a barrage of questions in an attempt to discredit Leonard's assertion that the majority of Englishmen in the ZAR would be prepared to renounce their British citizenship. Leonard was forced to agree and also to admit he was a wealthy man paying comparatively little tax to the ZAR. Labouchère also tried, with less success, to get Leonard to admit that the Second *Volksraad* set up by Kruger in an attempt to satisfy the *Uitlanders'* demands for representation, really had some powers but though Phillips agreed that it had powers to debate issues, nothing would come of its recommendations without the assent of the First *Volksraad* which Kruger controlled. In developing this line of questioning Labouchère was attempting to establish that Rhodes and the Rand Lords were really interested in the wealth which the Transvaal could provide and that the best way to achieve this was through a British federation.

The Inquiry, having obtained the telegrams, recalled the unfortunate Rutherfoord Harris. Using the telegrams as a series of prompts they asked Rutherfoord Harris what was meant when they mentioned 'Dr Jameson's plan' and whether this was in accordance with the British Government's policy of federation. Rutherfoord Harris explained that the 'Jameson Plan' meant having a British force on the border of the ZAR which was ready to intervene should there be a revolution in Johannesburg. He also confirmed that, at the time of sending the telegram during the Drifts Crisis, he understood that this was in accordance with British policy and Chamberlain was considering 'a more active intervention' in South Africa' of which Rhodes disapproved. Rutherfoord Harris did not know that Chamberlain was acting in concert with the Cape Cabinet.[30]

The Committee attempted to get Rutherfoord Harris to throw further light on the telegrams but in doing so further clouded their meaning. For example, in Telegram No. 3 there was a reference to Willoughby, which Rutherfoord Harris explained was the Reverend William Charles Willoughby not the Colonel of that name.[31] Similarly, with regards to Telegram No. 6, which included the name of Lord Grey, Rutherfoord Harris was asked about who was being referred to by the phrase the 'best man' to deal with Chamberlain. Rutherfoord Harris explained it meant Rochfort Maguire. He added that this was not a reflection on Earl Grey's ability but referred to the fact that he was often away from the capital whilst Maguire was resident in London. These two examples illustrate the difficulty understanding telegraphese, especially when they were written in code.

Telegram No. 7, mentioned that Rutherfoord Harris had a frank conversation with Edward Fairfield of the Colonial Office. The former said that he would not say anything derogatory about Fairfield who should have answered for himself. Although Fairfield's version would probably not have differed significantly from his own Rutherfoord Harris hoped, as Fairfield had died, he would not be asked to give his version of their conversation. Cleary this was a question of 'dead men tell no tales.' In the end having been further hardpressed, Rutherfoord Harris admitted he had spoken frankly to Fairfield as to the likely events.

Chamberlain was anxious to defend his late junior official and, also perhaps himself, by reading a private letter from Fairfield dated 4 November 1895 which cleared up the decoding of the telegram and suggested that the Colonial Office should spend more time and effort in attempting to address the *Uitlanders'* grievances which otherwise might lead to a greater disaster than it intervening in the Drift Crisis which was merely a local commercial squabble. Chamberlain was quick, however, to distance himself from Fairfield's opinion and put his own interpretation on the tenor of the letter.[32] This was an easy stratagem

---

30   *Select Committee Report,* Q.8196-8198.
31   The Revd, Charles Willoughby of the London Missionary Society had been responsible for introducing the three Bechuanaland chiefs into London society in 1895. He had also supplied Labouchère's *Truth,* with anti-BSAC material.
32   *Select Committee Report.* Q.8579.

for Chamberlain to employ since Fairfield was unable to give evidence in person and offer his own inter-pretation of its meaning. Fairfield's letter could have proved that the Colonial Office at least had prior knowledge of the Raid and the agreement to absorbing the Bechuanaland Police into the BSAC's force was done in preparation for an incursion.

Rutherfoord Harris' interrogation continued and the meaning of a number of telegrams was sought and given. In doing so the names of a number of those involved were clarified and the part they have played in the preparation for the Raid. These names included Robert Meade, Fairfield, Goold Adams, The Boundary Commissioner in Bechuanaland, and Flora Shaw, the South African correspondent for *The Times*. It would seem that this process of dissecting the telegrams, in an attempt to identify to whom or to what they referred, led the Committee further and further away from its brief. However, with the mention of the code word 'Flora', they had struck gold. It referred to Flora Shaw, who seems to have had some influence over the plot for in Telegram No. 32 she had suggested the appropriate day for the uprising in Johannesburg would be Dingaan's Day, the 16 December. The irony of this suggestion would not have escaped by anyone familiar with the ZAR's history. As Rutherfoord Harris answered more questions it became clear that Flora Shaw had played an important part in the plot and it was agreed that she should be called to appear before the Commission in a few days' time.

Throughout his evidence Rutherfoord Harris was prone to use the pronoun 'we' and was frequently ques-tioned as to whether he meant 'I' or 'we' and if the latter, who the 'we' were to whom he referred. The answer seemed to change from question to question and one is left with the impression that Rutherfoord Harris was often attempting to divert the Committee's focus from himself onto others. He also seemed to have had some difficulty with maintaining confidentiality and had often showed letters and other documents, in part or in whole, to various officials who were, at least technically, not part of the BSAC's staff. He was caught out when questioned by Harcourt about Telegram No.6 which stated clearly that Rhodes told Flora Shaw to persuaded Chamberlain to support *The Times'* views. Rutherfoord Harris said that if Rhodes were to indicate the course he wanted, *The Times* to adopt with regards to the Transvaal, Flora would act.[33] Rutherfoord Harris attempted to distinguish between Flora Shaw the person and her as *The Times* South Africa Correspondent. There is no doubt that Shaw was a formidable character in her own right but it seems somewhat obvious that *The Times* newspaper, which was perhaps the most influential broadsheet in Britain, was involved in the plot through her connection with it. When asked whether Miss Shaw knew about the Jameson Plan, Rutherfoord Harris initially said 'No' but when challenged he said he had not told her about it but, changing his mind again, said he had discussed it with her when he was in England. Harcourt, having digested the fact that Rutherfoord Harris had told a journalist about the Plan, pointed out to him that he had failed to tell the directors of the BSAC. Rutherfoord Harris replied that he had told her because he knew Flora Shaw very well, better even than he knew Beit or Rochfort Maguire; certainly better than the Dukes of Abercorn and Fife, which made her an obvious confidant. Rutherfoord Harris had clearly missed Harcourt's point which was he had spoken to the 'Press' but not his employers about the plan; something of a dereliction of duty.

It has been previously mentioned that the decision of under which flag any revolt would take place had been an important issue. Rutherfoord Harris' evidence differed from the version of Leonard and Phillips, who had said that the uprising would take place under the ZAR flag. Rutherfoord Harris clearly indicated that the one thing Rhodes would insist on was that the uprising should be under the British flag. He also took an unusual stand when being asked whether Chamberlain correctly remembered that he had not actually been allowed to make the 'guarded allusion' about the possibility of an uprising during their conversation. Rutherfoord Harris agreed that this was true although his memory of the conversation differed somewhat. One questions whether Rutherfoord Harris was following Rhodes' instructions not to implicate Chamberlain or whether his own memory was genuinely at fault. Lapses of memory seemed to bedevil many of the witnesses when

---

33   *Select Committee Report*, Q.8300.

they came before the Committee and many were allowed to get away with this excuse.

Rutherfoord Harris was also savaged by Labouchère, who was not satisfied with the BSAC Secretary's attempts to shy away from the conversation with Fairfield because of the latter's death. He forced Rutherfoord Harris to admit that he felt that Fairfield's account of their interview was somewhat less than all-embracing and Hawksley, Rhodes solicitor who had been present, could vouch for this. However, in a final compliment to Fairfield, Rutherfoord Harris initially, very firmly, declared that Fairfield was in total ignorance of the Jameson Raid or of its preparations. Asked again by Harcourt about Fairfield's knowledge, Rutherfoord Harris replied that he had told Fairfield that one of the reasons why Rhodes needed troops on the border was to use them if they were required in event of an uprising in Johannesburg. If this was correct then one could suggest that Fairfield had at least knowledge about the preparations for the Jameson Raid, oblique though this may have been.

Three days after concluding his evidence, Rutherfoord Harris appeared before the Committee again at his own request. He wanted to correct the record as shown in the Minutes of his last appearance. He had not, shown any telegrams to Chamberlain and had not told Earl Grey about the Raid. He also denied any knowledge of Wolff

Henry Du Pré Labouchère, MP for Northamptonshire and bête noir of both Rhodes and Chamberlain. (*The Illustrated American*, 1896)

arranging for supply depots to be set up on Jameson's route. His reappearance gave Labouchère a second opportunity to try to implicate Chamberlain. When asked to explain Telegram No. 6 as to what Flora Shaw was meant to do when she met Chamberlain, Rutherfoord Harris became defensive and tried to explain why the message was vague; this was caused by an attempt to save extra words which cost 7/6 each. Labouchère was incredulous that such economies were necessary if it meant that the message was unclear.

Labouchère recounted that a group of investors who, knowing the Raid could bring about a fall in the price of BSAC shares, chose to sell them and hoped to buy them back at a much lower price; a practice known as 'stock-jobbery'. Labouchère alleged that Rutherfoord Harris, perhaps anticipating this type of scenario, had sold 10,000 shares; there being no honour amongst thieves.[34] Rutherfoord Harris was indignant and asked the Chair to force Labouchère to provide evidence for this accusation. Labouchère said he would have to produce the name of certain stockbrokers who were not part of the Inquiry and so used the now famous confidentiality defence. Rutherfoord Harris continued to assert his innocence and felt that his interrogation was turning into a trial. He challenged Labouchère, whom he claimed had, in the previous week and whilst a member of the Committee, written a letter which appeared in the French newspaper, *Gaulois*, accusing Rutherfoord Harris alongside other investors of profiteering from the Raid by exaggerating the grievances of the *Uitlanders* in order to make a killing on the stock market.

Labouchère had overstepped the mark and the Room was cleared. When the spectators were readmitted, the Chair admonished Labouchère for writing the letter which had been published whilst he was a member of the Committee which was investigating the events concerned. Robert Cecil, who was Rutherfoord Harris'

---

34   *Select Committee Report,* Q.8672.

counsel and was much later to serve in Lloyd George's First World War Government, requested permission to put a question. The Chair was reluctant to allow him to do so as he probably feared that things would get worse. Cecil would not be cowed, however, and argued that, as Rutherfoord Harris' reputation was at stake, it was unfair for him to be questioned by someone who was so very hostile and biased against him. Labouchère joined in what was now becoming an unseemly argument and the Chair cleared the Room again. When Rutherfoord Harris and the others returned the Chair reassured him about the Committee's attitude to Labouchère's reprehensible behaviour but, demonstrating his weak control, allowed Labouchère to continue his questioning as to whether Hawksley had been present when Rutherfoord Harris spoke to Fairfield about the border issue. Rutherfoord Harris confirmed he was but was reluctant to name the others who were present. Were they Beit and Maguire, asked Labouchère? Rutherfoord Harris confirmed this at first, but then changed his testimony to the effect that they were not actually present. However, he had told them of his interview with Fairfield, and that they had already known about the need for troops on the border from some other source which Rutherfoord Harris would not or could not name. Chamberlain, keen to ensure that no one in his Ministry could be accused of knowing about the 'Jameson Plan', reminded Rutherfoord Harris that Fairfield was very deaf and wondered if he had heard what Rutherfoord Harris was trying to tell him especially if it was somewhat vague. If Fairfield had not heard about the plan, how could he tell Chamberlain?

Labouchère continued to pursue his own agenda and requested that the next witness be Hawksley who should be ordered to produce the telegrams which he had shared with Chamberlain but had not been included in the Committee's files. Reluctantly, perhaps because the telegrams might implicate Chamberlain, the Chair agreed. Later Labouchère apologised in writing to Rutherfoord Harris, who, clearly rattled, left the country and the Committee was unable to recall him at the end of their Inquiry.

15

An Inconclusive Conclusion

The Committee members remained vexed because they had not been able see all the telegrams which had been sent to and from London and Cape Town. Rhodes, during his appearance before the Committee, had refused to show them, saying he regarded them as confidential. Hawksley had also refused to hand them over since his client had instructed him not to do so. He had been asked to contact Rhodes again in order to obtain his permission and Rhodes again refused. The Committee had to be content with questioning whether Rhodes had agreed to hand them over to the Colonial Office; which he had. Hawksley had visited the Colonial Office and spoke to Fairfield about the telegrams which in some way justified Rhodes' actions in refusing to provide them since, as Hawksley claimed, the Colonial Office had already seen them. The telegrams had originated in England and Fairfield had consequently written to Hawksley after their meeting and, in order to show that Fairfield's understanding of the situation was clear, Hawksley read from Fairfield's letter. It detailed that Fairfield had discussed the telegrams with Meade and they both agreed that they should inform Chamberlain of the telegrams' existence. On hearing about them, Chamberlain was concerned about their contents and who had seen them. Fairfield did not remember saying anything about a pending insurrection and '…would greatly care about it if it became public'.[1] A somewhat roundabout way of saying he would not like it if it was suggested that he knew about a pending uprising in Johannesburg. This does not seem an emphatic denial that the uprising was not discussed; perhaps it was his deafness again. Fairfield ended his letter by suggesting that Hawksley came to see him with the telegrams. Hawksley's letter of reply to Fairfield should have been reassuring; it indicated that Chamberlain knew what Hawksley knew but there was absolutely no intention to make these confidential messages public. The question of who knew what was further complicated when Hawksley admitted that the Colonial Office had received the telegrams in June 1896 and had returned them with additional notes actually written on them. Clearly Fairfield's letter demonstrated that the Colonial Office and Chamberlain were already aware of the telegrams' contents. There are at least two theories why these telegrams were not released by Rhodes. First, the telegrams implicated Chamberlain in some way and Rhodes was upholding his promise not to expose him. Or, alternatively, the telegrams did not implicate Chamberlain or the Colonial Office which would disprove Rhodes' claim that Chamberlain knew all about the plan. The frustration of the Committee was obvious, and its members debated amongst themselves, with input from Counsel, as to whether to order Hawksley to hand over the telegrams as evidence.[2]

Whilst deliberating what action they would take over the telegrams, the Committee decided to interview Flora Shaw. Miss Shaw, who had clearly been following the Commission's proceedings in detail, was easily able to refute the claim, made in one of the telegrams, that Rutherfoord Harris had 'sent' her to Chamberlain. This was not true, she argued, as she did not work for Rutherfoord Harris. She also explained

---

1   *Select Report*, Q.8752.
2   *Select Committee Report*, Q.6758-8809.

that the telegram which suggested that she was 'solid' in support of the views of Rutherfoord Harris and Rhodes was poorly punctuated which changed its meaning. She was forced, however, to admit that she did suggest the 16 December was the appropriate date for an uprising but argued this was in idle conversation. This is a questionable response. Why should her suggestion have been thought significant enough to include in a telegram if it was only a passing comment? Why should she mention a date at all if she didn't think that the rising was likely? She had been given the BSAC code book but claimed to have had only used it to communicate with Rhodes. 'Unfortunately,' she replied, that she was unable to give the Committee copies of her telegrams and couldn't remember them word for word but would provide the 'gist'; a case of uncooperative cooperation.

Her first telegram to Rhodes in December 1895 she said, asked for the date of the Johannesburg uprising for journalistic reasons. He replied that he thought it would be in the beginning of the new year. Her response to this information, she remembered, did include the phrase 'delay was dangerous 'but she had received no reply to this comment.[3] Towards the end of December, in light of the Venezuelan dispute making things more complicated, she cabled that 'it should be at once'. One wonders whether this was the vested interest of journalist Flora Shaw coming to the fore since the uprising would be relegated to the middle pages of *The Times,* if a bigger story such as one involving Venezuela occurred; a story which would not carry her by-line. She also told the Committee that, in her mind there was a 'now or never' element to the timing of the rising. She couldn't remember if she had a reply from Rhodes but, if she did, it was formal and indicated that the uprising didn't just depend on him. A strange remark if she really couldn't remember if it existed.

When questioned by Harcourt, she agreed that Rutherfoord Harris had told her about the 'Jameson Plan' and she was a regular visitor to the Colonial Office for 'journalistic' purposes. Demonstrating that she had a command of her audience rather than the Committee controlling her, she indicated that she felt that the Committee was confusing the 'Jameson Plan' with Jameson's Raid. She wished to make sure they understood the difference between the two. Leading the Committee somewhat by the nose, Flora Shaw claimed that the likelihood of an uprising in Johannesburg was known to her and by the previous government since 1892. In 1895 she had noticed that there was a gathering of BSAC troops on the border of Bechuanaland and had conjectured that there was a link between the two stories. During a meeting with Rutherfoord Harris in September 1895, she asked him directly if there was a connection between an uprising and the assembly of troops and he admitted that there was, and then explained the Jameson Plan which consisted of seven steps:

- The *Uitlanders* would revolt in order to have their grievances redressed;
- they would be supported by a large proportion of the Dutch population;
- the existing government would be deposed;
- the *Uitlanders* would set up a provisional government;
- they would then place themselves in the hands of the Imperial Government by requesting that the High Commissioner come to Johannesburg in order to mediate;
- although no resistance was expected, it would be impossible to pre-warn the High Commissioner in order he could have troops at the ready;
- Jameson would have the responsibility of having such a force in readiness for a call from the High Commissioner'.[4]

The Inquiry was keen to discover how much of this plan was communicated to the Colonial Office. Miss Shaw was equally anxious that they understood that the information which was sent to London was very different from what had actually occurred in South Africa. On 30 December 1895 she had seen a telegram

---

3   *Select Committee Report*, Q.8844.
4   *Select Committee Report*, Q.8875.

in Beit's office which stated that Jameson had disregarded instructions and crossed the border with 400 men.[5] In the tradition of journalists she claimed this was a scoop but felt that she must immediately inform the Colonial Office in the person of Sir Robert Meade; Chamberlain being at his home for the Christmas holidays. Meade sent a message to Chamberlain and within a couple of hours the Colonial Office received official confirmation of the Raid from its own sources. This, she claimed was the only occasion she had given information to the Colonial Office but she had not mentioned anything she had heard earlier in the year. She had known of the likelihood of an uprising in Johannesburg but did not know at the time that Rhodes was encouraging the *Uitlanders* to revolt. She was aware that arms were being sent to Johannesburg but did not know that Rutherfoord Harris was sending them.

There followed a series of questions and answers which is best described as 'verbal fencing'. Sir William Harcourt tried to establish how much Flora Shaw really knew and she was careful to keep her answers as vague as possible without directly lying to him. A good example of this exchanged is Harcourt's questions about the *Letter of Invitation* which Rutherfoord Harris had cabled to Flora Shaw on 31 December.[6] Harcourt assumed, and Flora Shaw agreed, that the reason for Rutherfoord Harris sending a copy of the letter was for it to appear in *The Times*. When asked if she believed the letter's contents, she admitted she did but when asked if she agreed with the Poet Laureate's description of the Raid's purpose being to rescue 'the girls of the Golden Reef' she would not commit herself, and it is not clear whether this was a literacy criticism on Flora Shaw's part or an denial of the Raid's purpose. Flora Shaw had believed in good faith that the letter was correct and this was the reason for Jameson's actions but it also seemed to imply that there might have been other reasons for the Raid. Pressed further, she said that the 'women and children issue' could be the only reason why Jameson would deviate from the previously described plan; to ride towards Johannesburg without the uprising having started. Harcourt then queried the article in *The Times* which criticised Chamberlain for attempting to stop the Raid. Flora Shaw replied that she should not tell the Committee about what happened in *The Times'* office. She didn't know what the Committee would feel about not her answering but thought she ought not to. Harcourt didn't press her for an answer. This was yet another example of the 'confidentiality defence' used by many of the witnesses and demonstrates a continuing confusion as to the Committee's status as being equivalent to that of a Court of Law.

When Edward Blake, the Irish National Federation MP for South Longford, Ireland, asked her directly whether she knew that Rhodes was engineering the uprising she confirmed that Rhodes 'knew' of it, was being informed as to what was happening but was evasive in saying he actually agreed with it.[7] Previously, when asked about her telegram which said she thought that it should happen quickly she felt she needed to qualify the event to which she had referred which was the uprising and not Jameson's incursion.

Labouchère scored a small hit when he was able to get Flora Shaw, known as 'Telemones' in the telegrams, to admit in a roundabout way that the Colonial Office would probably have liked the events in Johannesburg to happen quickly and that any veiled reference to the Colonial Office really meant Chamberlain.[8] She expressed surprise, somewhat self-deprecatorily, that her 'off the cuff' comment about the incursion occurring on 16 December had been taken seriously enough to include it in a telegram. Chamberlain was quick to establish that, although Flora Shaw may have alluded to the Colonial Office being happy if the uprising occurred in her telegrams, that he had never said this to her directly. She agreed; she was only expressing a personal opinion. This may sound a little hollow as she had mentioned earlier in her evidence, that she had been visiting the Colonial Office for seven years as a journalist and it is obvious that she had numerous

5   *Select Committee Report*, Q 8878.
6   *Select Committee Report*, Q.8894-8903.
7   The Canadian-born Dominick Edward Blake had been leader of the Liberal Party in Canada and the second premiere of Ontario. He had entered the British Parliament in 1892.
8   *Select Committee Report*, Q.8196.

interviews with officials concerning happenings and policy in South Africa. Ironically, the Chair thanked her for the clear way in which she had given her evidence. Perhaps his chivalry got the better of him.

According to Moberley Bell, Managing Director of *the Times*, Flora had been instructed to take any blame which might be attributed to his newspaper in order to protect it and its editor, George Buckle. She was to make it clear that she only guessed at, rather than knew about, the conspirators' intentions. Buckle instructed her to take the blame for the telegrams and to claim they no longer existed although there were drafts in *The Times'* offices in Printing House Square.[9]

There has been some speculation as to the use of the *Letter of Invitation* by *The Times*. The Boers had discovered the letter after the Battle of Doornkop on 2 January 1896. Yet, as the *South African-Telegraph* noted when the English newspapers arrived in Cape Town by sea later that month, how could *The Times* Correspondent telegraph a copy of the letter have telegraphed a copy of the letter from Cape Town to London the day before it had been found? The *Telegraph* suggested that this was because *The Times'* office must have had a copy for some time and was waiting to use it when the time came.[10] The answer, as has been shown, that it wasn't a *Times* correspondent but Rutherfoord Harris who had forwarded the letter and had changed Jameson's dating to 28 December.

Rhodes, who was well aware of the power of the press, having learned of Jameson's impetuosity informed Frederick Hamilton, Editor of the *Johannesburg Star*, and Charles Leonard that that they were 24 hours in front of public opinion and they must go round to all the newspapers and get them to prepare the 'mind of the public.'[11] The men's visits successfully persuaded the most influential newspapers in Cape Town such as *the Cape Times* and *The Cape Argus* that Jameson had gone into the Transvaal to save unarmed women and children. Rhodes' strategy did not completely work as *The Diamond Fields Advertiser*, which was not approached by Rhodes' emissaries and *The South African Telegraph*, which was always critical of Rhodes, condemned Jameson out of hand.[12]

Flora was later to be recalled and became, in fact, the Committee's final witness. The telegrams to which she had referred to were now in their possession. They had been decoded and Flora Shaw agreed that the translation was reasonably accurate. Two of the telegrams had escaped her memory; a fact for which she apologised, which she said had been caused by the pressure of work. She set out the order in which the missing telegrams had been received. Jackson then led her through each of the telegrams and Miss Shaw seemed extremely cooperative but without given much away. By checking her household accounts, she found that she had sent a fourth short message of which the Committee were entirely unaware. She offered this snippet of information as an indication of her desire to be precise and tell the truth but, again she couldn't remember the details nor obtain a copy of the actual telegram, but its essence was that 'Chamberlain was extremely angry'.[13] Using the excuse that the telegrams were never intended for public examination, the fact that she was working very hard and in a hurry, the code she was using and the telegrams were very short since she was paying for them herself. She argued that they did not mean what they apparently seemed to mean and each of them needed explanation in order that they made sense to the uninformed. In advancing this argument, Flora Shaw again showed her control of the Committee by almost directing them as to what questions they should ask and this gave her the opportunity to give answers she had previously prepared. Her comments on how much Chamberlain knew were interesting. She claimed that his protestations of ignorance were a double

---

9   E.M Bell. Flora *Shaw* (London: Constable, 1947), pp.186-88. In *The History of the Times* Vol. 3, there are reproductions of the telegrams in Bell's handwriting. *The Times' Office, The History of the Times. Vol. 3: The Twentieth Century Test 1884-1912* (London: MacMillan, 1947), pp. 210, 244, 246.

10   *South African-Telegraph*, Occasional Notes, 25 January 1896.

11   Colvin, *Life of Jameson*, Vol. 2. p. 121.

12   Gerald, Shaw, 'The Letters of Edmund Garrett to his Cousin 1896-1898', Unpublished M.A Thesis, University of Cape Town, 1983.

13   *Select Committee Report*, Q.9624.

bluff and he actually knew a great deal.[14] This revelation, however, was tempered by her determination to persuade the Committee to distinguish between the 'Jameson Plan' about which Chamberlain was aware and the actual Raid about which he was not.

In a further attempt to obtain Rhodes' telegrams, Hawksley was recalled and finally heard the judgement that the Committee's authority was those of a Court of Law and it was thus entitled to demand the telegrams in spite of Rhodes' instruction to Hawksley to withhold them. Hawksley questioned the Attorney Generals' ruling and still refused to hand them over. A threat was made to report this fact to the House of Commons but Hawksley stuck to his guns and refused to give them up. This seems a strange exchange since he had earlier handed over copies of the telegrams to the Colonial Office and its officials must have been aware of their contents. Surely, they could have been asked to bring the copies which they would undoubtedly have made. In fact, Hawksley was not 'reported' to the House which was a further example of the Inquiry's weakness.[15] As Lady Longford noted this was a farcical situation since the Attorney General already knew of the telegram's contents.[16]

Alfred Beit, the German financier and director of the BSAC, during his appearance before the Committee, agreed that he had always advised the *Uitlanders* to bring about reform through constitutional means but had changed his mind when he realised that, under the Kruger regime, constitutional means would fail to bring about an improvement in *Uitlander* fortunes. It was therefore necessary, Beit argued, to have a force on the border in order to ensure that a rebellion was successful and as short lived as possible. Beit, however, denied that he thought that having such a force in place would precipitate a rebellion. It was to support an uprising not to start one. He claimed he had no knowledge about the Raid until it had occurred.

The Committee again pursued their theory that those involved with the BSAC had made a profit by selling shares before the price collapsed when the news of the Raid hit the stock market. When questioned, Beit confirmed he had not done so and, furthermore, he took the opportunity to put his grievances against Labouchère's allegations that the Raid was part of a plan to make a killing on the stock market which, as he had already been forced to acknowledge, had not been based on any evidence. Beit pointed out that there had been other allegations in Labouchère's own publication, *The Truth,* which, in a number of articles, had suggested that Rhodes and Beit had been responsible for planning the Raid and implied that Beit was one of the men who broke the market as a result. Beit required the Committee to call upon Labouchère to either substantiate his claims or withdraw them for good. Harcourt brushed aside this request and continued to question Beit as to when he first knew about the *Uitlanders'* grievances and to further to elucidate his knowledge of the connection between Jameson's force on the border and the uprising. Beit suggested that Jameson's force was actually at the border in order to prevent an uprising!

This came as a surprise to Harcourt as no other witness had made a similar suggestion. It was confirmed that it was Beit who had told Phillips and Leonard that it would be a good thing if Jameson assembled in the border but when pressed, however, the financier had to agree that he hadn't actually mentioned to them that such a force was there to prevent an uprising. An incredulous Harcourt pressed him further and peeled back the layers of confusion which covered Beit's true involvement in the Raid. Eventually Beit admitted that he, or more properly, his companies, had contributed between £175,000 and £200,000 towards the uprising.[17] Harcourt was surprised that such sums appeared not to mean much to the multi-millionaire and then pursued the idea that being taken over by the BSAC might not improve the financial position of the miners in Johannesburg; a suggestion which Beit denied. Harcourt was clearly trying to establish whether Beit's

---

14   *Select Committee Report*, Q.9674.
15   *Hansard*, Vol. 51 cc 1093-182 House of Commons Debate 26 July 1897. Since he was denying the authority of the Select Committee he would presumably be accused of 'Contempt of Parliament'.
16   Longford, *Jameson's Raid*, p. 283.
17   Between £22.25 million and £22.5 million in modern values.

motive in supporting an uprising was really to improve the *Uitlanders'* situation or to increase the profits of his companies and the BSAC.

Beit was not a good witness and although it was clear that he knew about the 'Jameson Plan', he did not know about the Raid and only heard about it after the event nor did he communicate his knowledge to the directors of the BSAC. He was led, especially by Labouchère, down the labyrinthine path of profit making in the gold mining business and the Chair was not strong enough to keep Labouchère's questioning to the point. Chamberlain defended Beit to some extent against these accusations but one is left with the impression that Beit was not fully aware of what was going on and was, to some extent, Rhodes' stooge.

The final new witness was Rochfort Maguire, Rhodes' 'alternate' on the Board of the BSAC, who admitted that he was aware of what was happening in Johannesburg and that Rhodes was involved but, surprisingly, he claimed to have had no communication with him during the period in question. Rochfort Maguire also claimed to know nothing about the 'Jameson Plan' but had discussed the Johannesburg situation with Alfred Beit and Rutherfoord Harris. Harcourt was keen to get to the bottom of how and when Rhodes communicated with his proxy, but Rochfort Maguire claimed that he had not received any communications from Rhodes during December 1895 which, as Harcourt said, was the critical month.[18] Maguire had no information other than that which Flora Shaw possessed and this led him to believe that the uprising in Johannesburg would take place at the end of December. Such responses make one question Rochfort Maguire's ignorance and how he was aware of the contents of Flora Shaw's telegrams if he had not seen or discussed them.

Rochfort Maguire proved to be yet another very vague witness and, in spite of Harcourt's attempts to get to the truth of what he knew and to whom he had conveyed this knowledge, Rhodes' proxy displayed convenient lapses of memory and a failure to answer difficult questions. One concludes that either he was in almost total ignorance of what Rhodes was planning either at Pitsani or in Johannesburg, or he knew more that Harcourt could get him to reveal. The first conclusion seems strange if he was Rhodes' genuine proxy but Rhodes had demonstrated his tendency to do things his own way and to leave the Board of the BSAC in the dark. The second conclusion would seem to fit in with the responses of other witnesses who were keen to protect themselves and the BSAC from censure. It is, of course, probable that in Rochfort Maguire's case that both conclusions apply to some degree. All those connected with the BSAC were keen to protect the Charter and this was a reason from sparing Chamberlain from censure.

Labouchère was able to demonstrate Maguire's naiveté with regards to the decision to show the Colonial Office the telegrams. The 'alternate' could think of no reason why they were shown to the Colonial Office other than they might have requested them. He knew of no benefit to the BSAC which might result. He seems to have been unaware that they might implicate either Chamberlain or any officer of the Colonial Office and was thinking only in terms of the BSAC.

Believing Rochfort Maguire to be the last witness, Chamberlain requested that he be allowed to return to the witness chair. In fact, as we have seen, Flora Shaw was to follow him. He presumably wanted his to be the last evidence the Committee heard. Chamberlain wished to clarify Rutherfoord Harris' suggestion that he had made a 'guarded allusion' by which he had told Chamberlain about the uprising; an allegation which Rutherfoord Harris had later partly withdrawn.[19] This allusion or hint suggested that Rutherfoord Harris had told Chamberlain about the reason for having a force on the borders of Bechuanaland. It also implied that Chamberlain was at least partially in the know about the 'Jameson Plan'. However, Chamberlain could not remember the actual words which were said during the meeting; an excuse also used by Rutherfoord Harris. As to Rutherfoord Harris' conversation with Fairfield, witnessed by Hawksley, during which Rutherfoord Harris claimed to have told Fairfield that the troops were on the border in case an uprising took place, Chamberlain assumed that either the words were not spoken in that way, were misunderstood, or not heard

---

18   *Select Committee Report*, Q.9361.
19   *Select Committee Report*, Q.6354–6366.

by the deaf Colonial Official at whom, Chamberlain claimed, one had to shout very loudly in order to make sure that Fairfield understood. The Colonial Secretary found it impossible to believe that, if the conversation took place in the manner described by Rutherfoord Harris, the honourable and trustworthy Fairfield would not have failed to report it to his Colonial Secretary. It has already been explained that Fairfield was dead and could not give his account of the meeting. Chamberlain went on to point out that Fairfield thought that Hawksley knew nothing about the planned incursion, but he was mistaken. Labouchère could not miss an opportunity to implicate Chamberlain and asked him directly whether he had asked Hawksley for the telegrams because he thought they might contain compromising material and could be used to persuade the 'Authorities' not to punish Willoughby and his officers. Chamberlain claimed he did not know if this was the intention of his Department. Not exactly a denial.

Lord Selborne, the Colonial Under Secretary, appeared before the Committee to clarify the question of Rutherfoord Harris' evidence. Whilst confirming that the Colonial Office knew nothing about the 'Jameson Plan', he was convinced that, although Rutherfoord Harris thought he had communicated some information about it, the representatives of the Colonial Office had '...quite failed to understand its meaning'.[20] However, Edward Blake dug a little deeper and reminded Selborne of the meeting when Rutherfoord Harris had tried to speak to Chamberlain on a confidential matter at which Selborne had been present. Blake's question was how far had Harris got in his attempt to air the confidential matter before Chamberlain had cut him short? Selborne said that Rutherfoord Harris' preceding conversation was about the situation in Johannesburg and Selborne assumed that this was going to be the topic of the confidential information which Rutherfoord Harris intended to give Chamberlain. Not really an answer to Blake's question.

The Committee had almost ended its laborious process and had only two more sessions before it had to complete its deliberations. It decided to finish by allowing the counsel for the witnesses to sum up their clients' evidence if they so wished. Pope, who was appearing on behalf of Rhodes hit the nail on the head when he pointed out that the Committee had spent many hours and examined many witnesses but had got no further than the Cape Committee except for obtaining a few telegrams which shed little extra light on the affair. It is unsurprising the Committee's work was described as 'the lying in state at Westminster' and 'a hushing up in public.'[21] W.T. Stead believed that, in spite of their intelligence, the Committee members were guilty of not seeing evidence 'when it lay straight before their noses.'[22]

The Committee had met from 5 February until 2 July 1897 and its evidence came to 535 pages which recorded 9,862 questions and responses and yet its Report was published on 13 July; the need to debate its findings before Parliament's summer recess was very pressing and the lack of time was also a reason why no further action was taken against Hawksley.

Much of the Majority Report was written very quickly by Harcourt and since the Committee's methods of working and the evidence of all its witnesses has already been examined is perhaps unnecessary to further scrutinise the Report in detail. It condemned Rhodes; after all he had confessed that he was responsible for planning the uprising and a possible incursion. The Raid and the plans which made it possible were deserving of absolute and unqualified condemnation.[23] The Report agreed that Jameson had 'gone in' without Rhodes' permission but such an action, if not its timing, had always been part of the plan. Rhodes had deceived the High Commissioner, hidden his intentions from the Cape Parliament, misled the Board members of the BSAC and led his subordinates to believe he was acting with the approval of the Colonial Office.

Beit and Maguire also knew of the plans but the Report stated that there was no evidence Sir Hercules Robinson had been told of Rhodes' intentions and the Committee concluded that there had been a plot

---

20   *Select Committee Report*, Q.9596.
21   Arnold Morley quoted in Longford. *Jameson's Raid*, p. 299.
22   Stead, *Joseph Chamberlain Conspirator or Statesman?*, p. 86.
23   *Select Committee Report*, p. 16.

The South African Committee. (*Vanity Fair*, 1897)

to keep such information from him. In this respect, Sir Graham Bower was guilty of a grave dereliction of duty and Sir Frank Newton was similarly culpable. The Committee determined that Chamberlain and the officials at the Colonial Office were in ignorance of the plan and its development. The Report also had much to say about the genuine grievances of the *Uitlanders* which, although they did not justify Rhodes' and Jameson's actions, had been unsuccessfully addressed by constitutional means.

As to the second part of its brief, inquiring into lands administered by the BSAC, the Committee had insufficient time to pursue. The Charter was saved! The belligerent Labouchère was not happy with these official conclusions and felt it necessary to produce a Minority Report of his own. He observed that some of the witnesses before the Committee had been reluctant to tell all they knew and there were many examples when they actually refused to answer questions. The important telegrams had not been produced, Hawksley had not been reported to Parliament, nor was Willoughby's letter to the War Office produced. The Committee could not therefore pretend to have full knowledge and understanding of the Jameson Plan or the Raid. Whilst Labouchère acknowledged that the *Uitlanders* had justifiable grievances, he felt there was no evidence that the majority were prepared to abandon their nationality in order to obtain their rights.

Labouchère continued with a scathing attack on the Rand Lords' claim that they were overtaxed since they made huge profits and could well afford to pay them. Similarly, professional men such as Charles Leonard had a good income and paid little tax in return. Individual miners paid only indirect taxation. In spite of the denials of witnesses, Labouchère could not accept that stock-jobbing, the practice of manipulation of share prices, had not been one of the motives for the Raid. The Directors of the BSAC had not filled their roles appropriately and Chamberlain should not have cut Rutherfoord Harris short when the Doctor attempted to take him into his confidence. Labouchère, however, agreed with his colleagues that the Imperial Government were completely innocent in complicity with the Plan or the Raid.

Harcourt sent his draft of the Report to Chamberlain promising that the Colonial Secretary, who had been racked with anxiety throughout the Inquiry, would find it 'satisfactory'.[24] Most of the witnesses had played the game and not implicated Chamberlain either by denying his knowledge and involvement or through giving vague and unclear answers when Chamberlain's knowledge was questioned. Only Bower had deviated from this practice because of his sense of honour and the mistaken belief that he would be protected by his Chief.

Parliament was interested to know whether the Government intended to take any action with regard to the Report. On 16 July this question was raised in the House by the Liberal anti-imperialist MP Sir Wilfrid Lawson. The reply raised some eyebrows when Lawson was told that the Government was considering the future control of the BSAC territories which, as we have seen had not been discussed by the Inquiry; which meant that the First Lord of the Treasury, Arthur Balfour's, answer was somewhat evasive since the matter was only being 'considered'. When asked whether any prosecutions would result from the Report's conclusions, Balfour was equally uninformative by replying he was not aware that there would be.

During a Motion to allocated additional funding to the Colonial Office, on 19 July 1897, H.O. Arnold-Forster, a Liberal Unionist, described the Inquiry as a conflict between wealth and interest on the one side and the national interest on the other.[25] The incursion had confirmed Arnold-Foster's belief that, to entrust the control of such large swathes of land to a small knot of men whose objective was to make money, was a mistake. He went on to criticise Rhodes as one who had made big promises but had delivered little, certainly not enough to forgive his part in the conspiracy. The composition of the Committee of Inquiry had been subject to partisanship and Arnold-Forster described its Report as a '…very inadequate and unsatisfying document.' He was particularly critical of the use of the *Letter of Invitation*, the publication of which was which he described as a '…gross abuse of the best sentiments of men's hearts.' Why had the Inquiry been curtailed? Arnold-Forster made the most of his opportunity to raise the issue but his arguments were rebutted by Balfour, Chamberlain and Harcourt.

---

24   Garvin, *The Life of Joseph Chamberlain*, Vol. III, p. 119 and Longford, *Jameson's Raid*, p. 298.
25   *Hansard*, House of Commons, Debate 19 July 1897, Vol. 51, columns 479-506.

16

The Government Wins the Day

Shortly before the debate on the Committee's report, Arthur Balfour, Chancellor of the Exchequer clarified with the Speaker as to whether the motion concerning the Select Committee was to be tabled as one complete paragraph as currently on the Order Paper or as two paragraphs; one which criticised the Committee for the inconclusiveness of its Report and one which identified its failure to censure Rhodes and report Hawksley to the House for failing to produce the telegrams when he had been requested to do so. The Speaker consider the matter and ruled that the Motion would be one paragraph as originally set out on the Order Paper. This decision to include both parts of the censure would have significant consequences when the Members of Parliament came to vote.

The debate was opened in the House of Commons on 26 July 1897 by the Liberal MP for Burnley, Phillip Stanhope, who moved the Motion that 'The House regretted the conduct and inconclusive Report of the Select Committee, and especially its failure to recommend action against Rhodes and to order Hawksley to report to the Bar of the House and be ordered to produce the telegrams.'[1] However, Stanhope went on to praise Chamberlain's prompt, effective and courageous action which had prevented the outbreak of war with the ZAR when he heard the news of the Jameson Raid. After Kruger had handed over Jameson and his officers for trial, Chamberlain had promised a searching inquiry which was mentioned in the Queen's Speech. In the debate which followed there was considerable opposition to the BSAC and the need for its Charter to be revised or even rescinded. There was little mention of the Raid and it seemed that Chamberlain was to be left with a free hand to deal with the BSAC. The Inquiry had failed to get to grips with the question of the Charter or the question of stock-jobbing with the excuse there was not enough time left in the Parliamentary session to do so. Rhodes, argued Stanhope, was supposed to be a patriot but questioned if it was usual for patriots to make millions at their country's expense. Whatever Rhodes' services to Britain had been in the past, the Government should show its disapproval of his involvement in the uprising and he should have had his status of Privy Councillor withdrawn and be prosecuted. Alfred Beit, whom it was claimed was also a patriot, was a German patriot, and should also have been prosecuted. Was the reason for the failure to do so because of his wealth and popularity in society so he was not the type of individual to be prosecuted? Why had Hawksley, continued Stanhope, not been dragged before the Bar of the House. Both the Committee and the Government had hesitated to do this and, by not doing so, brought into question the authority of Parliament. The fact that the Colonial Secretary was aware of the telegrams and knew of their contents but had remained silent suggested that he was keener to protect himself and his Department from criticism than take action against the guilty. When, Labouchère, during the Inquiry, had supposed that Chamberlain would be glad to see the telegrams being presented, the Colonial Secretary's reply of indifference was outstanding; an indifference which was not shared by the general public. At this point Chamberlain

---

1   *Hansard*, House of Commons Debate, 26 July 1897, Vol. 51, columns 1093-182897.

is recorded as shouting that he never said that the telegrams were in circulation or they were incriminating and Stanhope change his wording to 'might' be incriminating.

In order to vindicate the national honour and the good name of Englishmen throughout the world argued Stanhope, it was the Government's duty to expose the truth and then punish offenders no matter how high their station. It was also the Government's duty to address the grievances which had arisen because of the maladministration in South Africa and make certain that such poor practice did not reoccur in the future. Stanhope wound up his censure of the procedure of the Committee by repeating his criticism of its failure to order Hawksley to the Bar of the House in order that he should be made to produce the telegrams. Only recently a much less significant case had been dealt with in this way. Stanhope was referring to the case of John Kirkwood, a money lender, who was summoned before the House to the cries of 'Where is Hawksley?' He had been examined by a Select Committee of the House and refused to answer its questions using the 'confidentiality' defence. Kirkwood was interrogated by Mr Speaker (William Court Gully) who gave his excuses short shrift. In spite of protests Kirkwood was ordered to answer the questions put to him and to appear again before the Select Committee on Money-Hauling.[2]

The Motion was formally seconded, but no one from the Government or Opposition Front Benches immediately rose to speak in defence of the Committee. This was too much for Labouchère who, addressing the House, said that he had expected Chamberlain or Harcourt to immediately join in the debate and described what he claimed was a 'conspiracy of silence'. The Committee had found Rhodes guilty of treachery towards all those involved. Rather than making a clean breast of his crimes, Rhodes had refused to answer many questions and evaded answering many others. He had refused to allow Hawksley permission to hand over the telegrams. Balfour's reason for not prosecuting Rhodes was based on his patriotism but Beit, who was a German citizen, was also not proceeded against. Even Rhodes himself had agreed that his motives included those of finance and commerce. He had violated his oath as a Privy Councillor, and this privilege should be withdrawn. Labouchère argued that the imprisonment of Rhodes' subordinates (which implied Jameson and his officers) was particularly unfair since no punishment had been imposed on their superiors. Although Chamberlain had been party to setting up the Select Committee and also participating in its investigations, it was clear, continued Labouchère, that the Committee had not really investigated the connection between Chamberlain and Rhodes with regard to the planning of the Raid. Specific charges had been made against the Colonial Secretary by Rutherfoord Harris, Hawksley, and Rhodes himself. Labouchère then cited examples of how Committee members had tried to thwart its investigative abilities through technicalities and he continued to attack Chamberlain because he believed that the Colonial Secretary was fully aware of the telegrams and the incident when Rutherfoord Harris had tried to allude to the likely uprising and the 'Jameson Plan'.

Why was Hawksley or even Rhodes not ordered to appear before the Bar of the House for refusing to provide the telegrams, asked Labouchère, especially when the Attorney General had already seen them? It would be have been the correct action since the Committee's procedures were being brought into question, Labouchère proposed that the members of the Committee withdraw from the House or, at the very least, did not vote on the Motion which criticised their conduct since this would bring about a fairer indication of the House's opinion on this matter. The failure to bring the evaders such as Rhodes to the Bar of the House belittled the House of Commons as the High Court of Justice of the land and, concluded Labouchère, it would be better if it never appointed another Select Committee to do such work again.

Michael Hicks Beach, Chancellor of the Exchequer, in reply to Labouchère's tirade, reminded the House that it was the MP for Northampton's usual practise to oppose his own Party's leaders. Hick Beach agreed that it was possible that the membership of the Committee was not as good as it could have been. He wished he had not been a member, but its tasks had been made even more difficult because of Labouchère's

---

2   *Hansard*, House of Commons Debate, 16 July 1897, vol. 51 cc312-7.

behaviour as a Committee member. The Committee had reported its findings, but any member of the House could order it to continue its investigations. Stanhope's introductory speech to the Motion had turned into an attack on the BSAC, Cecil Rhodes, and even the Colonial Secretary; all of which were not included in the text of the Motion. The Report, as it stood, was not inconclusive since it dealt thoroughly with the uprising and the Raid. The Committee had explained that it lacked the time to deal with the administration of the lands under the BSAC. The Committee members had spent considerable energy and time and had conducted the Committee's proceedings in the best way they knew how. To pass a Motion of Censure would be poor reward for all their efforts. Hicks Beach expressed disappointment that the Motion did not at least acknowledge these efforts.

The Committee had not reported Hawksley to the Commons since the person refusing to hand over the telegrams was Rhodes. The Chancellor reminded Labouchère that he had indicated that he did not believe that Chamberlain was implicated in the plot, so why was Labouchère keen to have the telegrams produced?

The Committee's brief was twofold, to investigate the circumstances of the Raid and to examine the administration of the BSAC. A Report was produced which did come to conclusions which could be disputed by any of the MPs. The fact that time had run out to examine the effectiveness of the BSAC's administration of the lands under its Charter was not the fault of the Committee. The Commons could re-appoint the same Committee or appoint another one to complete the brief, but Hicks Beach was clear that he hoped this would not happen. Labouchère was not blameless if the Report was thought to be inconclusive, for although he had produced his Minority Report and stated that Rhodes deserved severe punishment, he did not say what this should be. Hicks Beach introduced some humour at this point by saying that in his opinion sitting for thirty-five days on the Committee with Labouchère as a member was what he would term severe punishment.

It was for the Government, said Hicks Beach, to decide what action should be taken against Rhodes such as removing him from the Privy Council but also to consider his services to the Empire. The Chancellor reiterated that it would have been inappropriate to report Hawksley since he was following Rhodes' instruction to provide the telegrams. It was necessary for the House to identify the right man to call to its Bar. Rhodes, who was in South Africa, could have been summoned but, even if he was willing to appear, the delay would have prevented the Committee to complete its work in the current session of the Parliament. As to the rumours of Chamberlain's involvement they were like gigantic bubbles which burst when they reached their optimum size. Hicks Beach, perhaps taking a risk, asked the House whether any present believed that Chamberlain was implicated in the events. This question was answered by silence and even Labouchère, when directly challenged, agreed that he had not made such a suggestion. Hicks Beach reminded him that he had stated, in his Minority Report, that he did not believe that Rutherfoord Harris had conveyed the information to Chamberlain that the purpose of the railway strip was to provide a springboard for troops to invade the Transvaal in the event of an uprising in Johannesburg. Why therefore, was it necessary to produce the telegrams?

Hicks Beach continued to defend the conduct of the Committee at great length; pointing out that there had been many questions asked and answers given. Even Rhodes had stated that he was sure that he did not believe that Chamberlain, either directly or indirectly, knew about the 'Jameson Plan'.[3]

Willoughby's letter to the War Office had clearly stated that it was his belief that the Raid had been sanctioned by the Imperial Authorities and Jameson had told him so. Jameson, in his evidence, had denied telling anyone and it transpired that Willoughby's letter had actually been written by Bouchier Hawksley and signed by Willoughby without properly reading it. One wonders if this was an acceptable excuse for Willoughby's

---

3 This may have been because Rhodes was keen to ensure that no blame was attached to Chamberlain and would be in accordance with his instructions to Hawksley not to implicate the Colonial Office in any way rather than as statement of fact.

part in this false claim or a convenient one since he must have been aware of both Rhodes and Jameson's wish to implicate the Colonial Office. The accounts of the officers involved in the Raid are unclear and it seems that some believed it was an authorised action and others did not or were unsure. Perhaps they were all convinced by Jameson's argument that if they succeeded no one would question who had actually authorised the incursion. One might think this was a big 'if'.

Hicks Beach continued his forensic examination of the allegations against Chamberlain's involvement by referring to Flora Shaw's telegrams which seemed to express Chamberlain's desire for quick action. The Committee had exposed the fallacy which surrounded these allegations. It has already been pointed out, however, that Flora Shaw's evidence was carefully staged and she almost conducted her own examination. One might suggest that Hicks Beach was exaggerating the effectiveness of the Committee's conduct and, since he had been a member, this is not surprising. In his conclusion, Hicks Beach argued that it would be impossible to dissuaded those who determinedly believed that Chamberlain was implicated in some way. Foreigners would always believe that Britain was perfidious in dealing with foreign countries. However, for the sake of peace in South Africa, and to enable Boer and Briton to live together, it was essential that 'this enquiry into the Raid should come to an end'.[4]

Sir William Harcourt was next to enter the fray and pointed out that it was unusual for a member of a Select Committee to support a Motion of Censure against that Committee as Labouchère was attempting to do. He also questioned the suggestion that the Committee, of which he was also a member, had been inconclusive. Harcourt argued, using Labouchère's earlier definition, meant that, in this case, 'inconclusive', referred things which had been omitted from the Committee's Report. Such an accusation could be levelled at both Stanhope and Labouchère They had suggested that inquiry into the way in which the BSAC administered its territories had been purposefully ignored but they did not mention the conclusions the Committee had reached regarding the culpability for the Raid. The Committee had not ignored the question of the BSAC. Some witnesses, who had come from South Africa, had been questioned about this administration but this was for future reference.[5] The complexities of examining the circumstances of the Raid were considerable and the Committee had only limited time at its disposal. Its members were conscious that not examining the BSAC's competence in administering its territories might be seen as inconvenient given the events in South Africa but they had unanimously agreed to concentrate, for the moment, on the circumstances of the Raid.[6] Challenging Stanhope's assertions, Harcourt said that if the Burnley MP would recommend to the House that the Committee be reappointed in the next Parliamentary Session, he would have his support. Nothing in the Report precluded that possibility; but this was for the House to decide.

Harcourt continued by strongly arguing that the Report was far from inconclusive in the areas in which the Committee had concentrated. It had condemned the Board of the BSAC for abdicating their responsibilities and had recommended that the Company should be reformed. The Committee had reported on the activities of Rhodes and criticised his conduct. The Report condemned Bower and Newton and found they had been guilty of a dereliction of their duty. Sir Hercules Robinson, now Lord Rosmead, it concluded that was ignorant of Rhodes' plan and how much the Colonial Office actually knew. The Committee had done its best to understand why, how, and when the events under consideration had taken place. If the Report had made recommendations as to how Rhodes should have been punished the Committee would have gone beyond its brief. Even Stanhope, Harcourt pointed out, had not made any recommendations in his Motion of Censure. Such a Resolution supported by Stanhope, had appeared on the Order Paper but this had been withdrawn. Clearly, Stanhope was himself inconclusive.

---

4   *Hansard*, House of Commons Debate, 26 July 1897, Vol. 51, columns 117-118.
5   Harcourt was probably referring to the two Boers who had been questioned by the Committee and had been full of praise for the BSAC's expertise when compare with the colonial administration.
6   He was not challenged on this point by Labouchère.

Harcourt, after an exchange with Labouchère on the latter's failure to make recommendations as to how Rhodes should be punished, a sign of Labouchère's own inconclusion, suggested that the real bone of contention was the Committee's failure to discipline Hawksley. This, Harcourt said, was because such an action would cause a delay which could not be permitted to happen given the limited time available. The importance of concluding the Report was more important than Hawksley's appearing at the Bar. The need to complete the investigation into the circumstances of the Raid within the current Parliamentary Session had both national and international significance. It was also important to allow sufficient time in that Session for the Report to be debated by the House of Commons. The 'Rhodes' group' could have delayed the Report until the next Parliamentary Session by creating obstacles in the way of the Committee but its members had prevented this from happening.

Harcourt continued his discourse by examining and defending Chamberlain's alleged part in the 'Jameson Plan'. Rutherfoord Harris had claimed that he had hinted at the likely events. But Chamberlain had denied this had happened and Harcourt believed the Colonial Secretary's account. As to Fairfield's knowledge, Harcourt quoted Rutherfoord Harris' own words that Fairfield 'was absolutely innocent of the Raid and any preparations leading to it.'[7] If Fairfield did not know then Chamberlain could not have known.

Flora Shaw had stated that she did not communicate her knowledge about a potential Raid and only provided the Colonial Office with this information after it had occurred. She denied saying anything to Rutherfoord Harris which might have been construed as the opinions of the Colonial Office.[8] Chamberlain's ' spur of the moment' actions on hearing about the Raid, suggested Harcourt, were not those of a man who had previously known about the Raid. Perhaps Harcourt was choosing to forget that the Colonial Secretary had offered his resignation. Labouchère, mocked Harcourt, had said that he did not believe the allegations against Chamberlain and the Colonial Office but only that some people might wrongly believe them. To agree with the Motion under debate would mean that the House of Commons distrusted its Members and believed that the Committee was driven by a sinister motive. To set aside the Committee's conclusions, which were necessary for peace in South Africa and for the vindication of Britain's honour, would be folly.

Leonard Courtney, MP for Bodmin, Cornwall, said he was glad to have heard the speeches from the Committee members but wondered why they had been so slow in responding to Stanhope's introductory speech. Courtney was pleased these speeches had been made and acknowledged the strength of Harcourt's arguments to vote against the Motion. However, he believed that Harcourt had missed the point. Neither the honour of the Committee nor that of the Colonial Secretary were in doubt. Courtney 'acquitted' Chamberlain of having any knowledge of, or complicity in, Jameson and Rhode's intentions or plans with regard to South Africa. It was not the honour of the Committee which was in question but its wisdom. Courtney criticised Parliamentary Committees in general as being too emmeshed in Party Politics. The Committee did not have time to examine the issue of the BSAC's administration but Courtney felt that they should have recommended their reappointment to do so as was the usual practice. Perhaps this suggested that the argument for the need for haste was used as an excuse.

The selection of membership of such Committees often involved the decision by the Party Whips not to recommend anyone who would cause their Party difficulty. This had sometimes led to the Commons itself refusing to sanction Committee memberships which were too clearly biased. Ironically in the circumstances, Courtney believed that the House should consider adopting the method used by the Cape of Good Hope Parliament where membership of Investigating Committees was decided by the Speaker.

The membership of this Committee was particularly questionable. Rather than completing its work by thoroughly investigating Rhodes' activities, it had felt able, as had the Cape Committee, to acquit everyone in the Colonial Service except for Rhodes and 'some wretched underling' whose name Courtney could

---

7   *Committee of Inquiry*, q.1132.
8   It must be remembered that Flora Shaw appeared to be more in control of the Committee than it was of her.

not remember.[9] Neither Rhodes nor Rutherfoord Harris had appeared before the Cape Committee so its findings were imperfect. The Parliamentary Committee had been able to discover additional information after the Cape Committee had produced its Report. Rhodes had deceived the High Commissioner, he had deceived the Cape Assembly, of which he was prime minister, and he had deceived the Board of Directors of the BSAC. He had even deceived the Reformers and these deceptions had continued until he had been told by Schreiner that Jameson had begun the incursion and Rhodes had become distraught. This discomfort did not last long and on the following day he telegraphed Flora Shaw and told her to speak to Chamberlain as well as remonstrating with the High Commissioner for repudiating the Raiders. In spite of this, claimed Courtney, Sir William Harcourt, had praised Rhodes' honour.

Harcourt rose quickly to point out that Courtney had misheard him. The missing telegrams, which the Committee had not obtained, had passed between Rhodes and Rutherfoord Harris. They had both given evidence which was more important than the telegrams. This defence by Harcourt was clearly questionable since Rhodes and Rutherfoord Harris were able to give their own versions of the contents of the telegrams and the Committee was not able to compare these with the telegrams themselves. Although, argued Courtney, Rhodes had violated every aspect of political ethics, and Bower and Newton had been castigated, Rhodes's position on the Privy Council had not been removed because of his '…name and fame in South Africa'.[10] If Britain really wished to promote the good feeling of the Boers, removing Rhodes's name from the list of the Privy Council would achieve this objective..

Though the Committee's defence was that they did not pursue the missing telegrams because of lack of time, it could have signposted that they were important and recommended that they should be investigated at a later date. When the Motion is voted upon, declared Courtney, the response will be made on Party lines which in future some may have cause to regret.

George Wyndham, MP for Dover and a Member of the Committee, reasoned that Courtney failed to see that the Motion did not attack the Committee's honour. As the Committee had not reported Hawksley, they demonstrated that they had not drawn inferences as to the telegram's contents nor made accusations based upon their unknown themes. Flora Shaw's telegram to Rutherfoord Harris, which mentioned that the Colonial Secretary wanted 'it' to be done quickly, referred to the insurrection and not the incursion and it was founded on a passing remark about the need for the Reformers to get on with the revolt if they were going to have one. The Committee had found no evidence that the telegrams had been shown to anyone in South Africa or that the Colonial Office was involved. Wyndham concluded that it was for South Africans to compare the effects of the Raid with the past services which Rhodes had done for their country.

Many in the House had heard enough and were heard to call out 'Divide' indicating they wanted to vote on the Motion. However, Thomas Gibson Bowles, the MP for Lyme Regis, still wanted to know why the telegrams had not been produced even though the Committee had demanded their production on two occasions. Could not the House order their production since it would be better if they were examined now in order to demonstrate the probity of those concerned, rather than some time in the future? He did not believe that they contained anything to Chamberlain's detriment but they could possibly incriminate people whom the Colonial Secretary would like to shield.

Charles Prestwich Scott, Liberal MP for Leigh in Lancashire, felt that there were many in the House who would wish to vote for the Motion but had heard that their Leader, Harcourt, had said to do so would cast a slur on his honour and that of the other Committee members. This was an unenviable position in which to be put but it might be resolved it they placed their country above their party. Scott used the example of Sir Graham Bower to demonstrate that the Committee had failed to pursue issues to a final conclusion. Scott did not doubt that Bower knew about the intention to carry out the Raid. Nor was it in doubt that he

9   Sir Graham Bower was the 'wretched underling', who's name Courtney failed to remember.
10   *Committee of Inquiry*, Q.1134.

concealed this knowledge from his superiors. Bower had reached a high position as Secretary to the High Commissioner, a position which he had held for twelve years and was bound by honour and duty to tell the High Commissioner, Sir Hercules Robinson, what he knew. Why, therefore, did Bower remain silent? The answer, suggested Scott, was that Bower believed, or had reason to believe, that Robinson already knew about the proposed Raid but did not want it to be officially brought to his attention. Frank Newton was in a similar, if less important position, but his reason for not telling his superiors was less convincing as he was too junior to know their inner intentions. Would those officers who took part in the Raid risk their commissions and undertake such a scandalous enterprise if they had not believed that there was 'a power behind them' which would protect them from the consequences? Even Rhodes, who was the author of the whole enterprise, but was not a fool, would be unlikely to risk everything if he did not believe that he had backing from the authorities at home. Why else would he have sent the telegram to Flora Shaw immediately the Raid had begun instructing her to go the Colonial Secretary whom Rhodes consider to be a friend and susceptible to Flora Shaw's influence? Such conjecture was bound to raise the suspicion of foreign leaders and the foreign public.

It had been the Committee's responsibility to pursue these suspicions to the bitter end in order to discover the truth. British public trust was in decline and the House of Commons had a duty to demonstrate that it agreed with such diligence and it should not agree to the suppression of evidence which might possibly implicate the Colonial Office. The House could demand the production of the telegrams and Scott was sure that they could have been produced after a little persuasion. Unless this occurred, there would always be a slur on Chamberlain and the Colonial Office, which would also be transferred onto the Government and the nation as a whole.

At this point the House adjourned, it had been sitting for some hours, but when the Speaker returned, Augustine Birrell, MP for West Fife, moved an Amendment which encompassed most of the objections to the limited nature of Stanhope's original Motion. This Amendment regretted not only the Committee's inconclusive actions and its Report but also its failure to recommend specific steps regarding Rhodes and reporting Hawksley for noncompliance with its request to produce the telegrams. The House was entitled to see them even though others had already done so. The rumours which were circulating would never have begun if the Committee had ordered their production by reporting Hawksley.

George Harwood, MP for Bolton, seconded the Amendment. He believed there was no evidence that the Report was inconclusive. To condemn the Committee for a secondary mistake would be an error. To vote for the original Motion would, Harwood claimed, be to condemn the Committee without sufficient evidence. The House had acted strongly in the case of Kirkwood and must not be seen to be less robust when dealing with those of high status in society.

An anxious Balfour rose to put a Point of Order. He reminded the House that the Speaker had already ruled that the original one paragraph Motion should be put and not offered as two separate paragraphs. He argued that to adopt the proposed Amendment would prevent the House voting on the original Censure Motion which would mean that it did not have an opportunity to record its opinion as to the performance of the Committee. Sir William Harcourt could not agree with Balfour's view since he argued that the Amendment did not prevent the House from voting on the original Motion

The debate then became something of a free for all and the telegrams, their possible contents and how Hawksley should be dealt with became issues which were tossed from one Honourable Member to another. One, Colonel Edward Saunderson, MP for Armagh, and Leader of the Irish Union Alliance, even proposed that the people in Johannesburg should erect a statue to Jameson since, because of his Raid, they had been able to arm themselves without any interference. The Speaker cut him short.

The debate continued at length with Harcourt, Hicks Beech, and Campbell-Bannerman continuing to attempt to defend the Committee's actions. Rhodes must have been gratified in having prevented any evidence which might have incriminated Chamberlain from being presented to the Committee for when the Colonial Secretary in summing up the debate, told the House that the Government did not intend to abolish the Charter and, what was more, Rhodes would not be prosecuted nor removed from the list of Privy Councillors since Rhodes had done nothing to affect his position as a man of honour. Although another MP attempted to follow Chamberlain, the Colonial Secretary had timed his final lengthy speech in order to silence criticism well and the House had heard enough and they voted on the Amendment which was dismissed.

Before the final division on Stanhope's original Motion, Albert Spicer, MP for Monmouth Borough, told the House that Chamberlain's speech had changed his attitude. Not only had Chamberlain stood by the Committee and the Report but he had also practically set out what the Government was going to do; which was very little. Rhodes was condemned by the Committee, but this did not affect his character and he would not be deprived of his status as a Privy Councillor and this meant that the country's honour was at a low ebb. He, for one, would vote against the Government and support the Motion. Spicer proved to be in the minority, however, for when the votes were counted Stanhope's Motion was defeated by 304 votes to 77.

Chamberlain's implied defence of Rhodes and the Charter came as a surprise to many. Labouchère using *The Truth* as his vehicle, claimed that there was a Radical MP in the Commons who had the missing telegrams and other damning documents on hand ready to produce if given a sign by Hawksley, who was observing the debate from the Strangers' Gallery, if Chamberlain reneged on his secret deal with Rhodes to protect the Charter. Hawksley's did not come forward to deny this claim but also did not leave any evidence as to its veracity. If he had been prepared to signal the MP to reveal the documents, Hawksley would have gone against Rhodes' instructions not to implicate Chamberlain, which Hawksley had consistently refused to do even when threatened with jail. This suggests that Labouchère's claim was untrue and was yet another one of his swipes against the establishment. There were many other reasons to criticise Labouchère's attitudes since he was an extreme anti-feminist and virulent anti-Semite. Queen Victoria said that she would have never allowed such horrid men to enter the Government.[11]

---

11   A. Ponsonby (ed.), *Henry Ponsonby. His Life from his Letters* (London: MacMillan & Co., 1943), p. 215.

17

Missing Telegrams

It is almost impossible to examine the circumstances of the 'Jameson Plan' and the Jameson Raid without some comment about the 'Missing Telegrams' which had figured so significantly in both the Inquiry and in the subsequent Parliamentary debate. Equally, one must also acknowledge that a final answer as to what they contained and their real significance on subsequent events is no longer possible to discover. Some were accidently or deliberately destroyed, and others may still be buried in files which will never see the light of day.

Evaluating the importance of the telegrams which the Cape Committee and the Select Committee actually did see is also fraught with difficulty. The Select Committee took a disproportionate time in obtaining and considering some of the telegrams and were not helped by Rhodes' refusal to hand them over, nor Hawksley being prepared to risk imprisonment by following his client's instructions not produce them. Hawksley did provide the cypher book which was used in encoding and decoding the telegrams but the Committee had to rely on a BSAC employee to translate them. Chamberlain, whose Department had seen and copied the telegrams, could have helped the Committee by producing them. One speculates why he chose not to do so. The Telegraph Company provided 46 of the 54 known telegrams but it routinely destroyed copies, in this case those prior to 1 November 1895, which 'explained why eight of the 54 were missing.' However, two of these were dated before the crucial date and the reason why they were not destroyed by the Telegraph Company is hard to explain other than through human error. It has already been mentioned that Rhodes even claimed that Jackson, the Select Committee's Chair, had edited the telegrams which had been available. Even Chamberlain's copies have disappeared.

It is those eight missing telegrams which pose the now insoluble mystery as to how much Chamberlain knew about the 'Jameson Plan' and the Raid. A further complication is raised by the fact that the telegrams were in code. Christopher Woodhouse has suggested that this meant that there were four versions of each telegram.[1] The first was the original message in free hand as written by its author. The second version was the telegram when in code and the third the decoded version of the message given to its intended recipient. The fourth version was the decoded message as given to the Select Committee. The possibility of differences between versions two to four is obvious and these were made more likely because the code book did not include every word which the sender wished to use; such words were inserted *en clair*, such as the use of 'Flora'. Different clerks produced version two and three and four, each of whom possessed different skills and abilities.

Only one telegram is known to exist in its original form; that written in London by Rutherford Harris on 2 August 1895, transmitted on 3 August and received by Rhodes on 5 August. It followed Rutherford Harris' meeting with Chamberlain to discuss the Bechuanaland Protectorate which Rhodes wanted to annex and, to which idea, Chamberlain objected. Rutherford Harris' argument was that a strip of the Protectorate

---

1   Christopher M. Woodhouse, The Missing Telegrams and the Jameson Raid, Part Two, *History Today*, 1 July 1962, pp. 506-14.

needed to be given to the BSAC on which it could build a railway. Jameson's troops would be needed to protect the railway line. How frank this discussion with Chamberlain and his officials was has already been examined. Perhaps the August 2 telegram is the nearest version of what actually occurred. In the *en clare* version Rutherfoord Harris stated that he 'guardedly' told Chamberlain the reason why the BSAC needed a presence and a base in the Protectorate and Chamberlain 'heartily agreed with C.J. Rhodes' policy'.[2] However, Garvin, Rhodes' biographer, in reproducing the telegram, omitted a section which stated that Chamberlain would not change his mind regarding his refusal to grant the BSAC the whole Protectorate. There is a note written by Chamberlain which states that the Telegram was a substantially accurate reflection of the meeting at which the Directors attempted, but failed, to persuade him to change his mind about transferring the administration of the Protectorate to the BASC. By chance the original version of this telegram was sent as a letter by Herbert Canning, who was the London Secretary of the BSAC, to Rhodes. There are some verbal differences between the version seen by Chamberlain and that included in Canning's letter. It appears that Chamberlain had seen the whole version of the telegram and not the incomplete version used by Garvin. Canning's letter confirmed that Chamberlain had completely denounced the original request for the transfer of Bechuanaland by Rutherfoord Harris and was annoyed that the BSAC had not yet begun to construct the railway line which Jameson's men were supposed to guard. It still remains a puzzle why Chamberlain did not allow the Select Committee access to this and other telegrams in his possession since, by not doing so, he provided further grist to the rumour mail as evidenced during the House of Commons debate on the Committee's work.

On 5 January 1900, *L'Indépendance Belge*, a Brussels newspaper, published a series of letters which have become known as the *Hawksley Dossier*. They had been stolen from Hawksley's office, but the newspaper claimed that they had received them from someone involved in the Raid. W.T. Stead published the letters in his book, *Joseph Chamberlain Conspirator or Statesman?* which he claimed were proof of Chamberlain being, at least, aware of the plot.[3] The Dossier consisted of sixteen letters and telegrams including six to and from Fairfield and two from Chamberlain's sister-in-law. There was also one to Earl Grey, who had been with Rutherfoord Harris during his meeting with Chamberlain and Fairfield.[4]

Grey proved to be a genuine *eminence grise* and a mysterious player in the Jameson-Rhodes drama. He was a director of the BSAC, a friend of Chamberlain, a supporter of Rhodes' style of imperialism, and party to the negotiations to transfer Bechuanaland to the Company. In spite of his involvement, Grey was not called before the Select Committee as he was in Bechuanaland; an important witness who was conveniently not asked to give evidence.

How significant is Hawksley's Dossier in throwing light on the importance of the telegrams? They clearly show that Hawksley and Fairfield were in correspondence about the telegrams in question but these letters were not given to the Select Committee by the Colonial Office. They also reveal that the Colonial Office and the Rhodes' faction were in conversation about the composition of the Select Committee and the preservation of the Charter. Fairfield may have been very deaf, but he could certainly read Hawksley's letters.

In his analysis of the Dossier, Stead believed they revealed three conspiracies. The first conspiracy was the 'Jameson Plan' which was known to Chamberlain and the Colonial Office, Lord Grey, Rochfort Maguire, Bouchier Hawksley and Flora Shaw. One would also add that Fairfield also knew as was shown in Chapter 4 which showed that Chamberlain had absorbed information which Fairfield had provided about the plan and possibly the likely Raid. The fly in the ointment which delayed the plan's execution, according to Stead, was

---

2   Garvin, *The Life of Joseph Chamberlain*, Vol III, p. 110.
3   Stead, *Joseph Chamberlain, Conspirator or Statesman?*
4   The telegrams can be found in the Appendix of Stead's *Joseph Chamberlain, Conspirator or Statesman?*, pp. 89-99. See Appendix VII for a sample of some of the most telling Telegrams.

Chamberlain's condition that any uprising should be undertaken under the British Flag which, has already been shown, was a step too far for many of the Reformers.

The second conspiracy was to cover up the first conspiracy through the perjury and the silence of witnesses. Stead claims that just as Rhodes was the architect of the first conspiracy, Chamberlain was the main mover of the second conspiracy. Chamberlain, together with Grey and Wyndham, was able to dupe members of the Select Committee into not demanding the telegrams and not demanding that witnesses answer their questions in a straightforward manner. This was made doubly extraordinary since, after signing the Report which had condemned Rhodes, Chamberlain had then argued in the Parliamentary debate that the 'Colossus' had not committed any dishonourable act which should result in him being struck off the list of Privy Councillors.[5]

Stead acknowledged that the first two conspiracies were things of the past but a third conspiracy still existed when he published his book. This was the conspiracy of silence. The *L'Indépendance Belge*'s publication of the Dossier had caused an outcry concerning the events of the Raid and Chamberlain's involvement in it. This had resulted in a Committee of No Enquiry.[6] To Stead, who was later an opponent of the Second Boer War, the idea that Chamberlain and the Colonial Office were not involved in the 'Jameson Plan' and the Raid was the 'Lie of Lies' which resulted in the Boer War.

Bower, in a similar vein, claimed that the Colonial Office officials took steps to 'cover up their trail'. He suggested that the secret documents referring to the Raid were removed from the Colonial Office and stored in Chamberlain's home and Garvin discovered a number of important documents concerning the Raid amongst Chamberlain's private papers. Research in the 1940s into the Colonial Office files for the period revealed that much of the material concerning the Raid was accessible in various parliamentary papers but otherwise the rest was 'disappointingly meagre.'[7] Rhodes' secretaries were asked to hand over any relevant papers concerning the plan and the Raid but Bower made sure that his papers could not be scrutinised.

On balance it would seem that the Colonial Office had knowledge and understanding of the 'Jameson Plan' and Rhodes' schemes to reduce the ZAR to a British protectorate. As with Matabeleland, it was a scheme to increase the Empire on the cheap. Bower admitted knowing this and was to pay the price. Fairfield knew but died before he could tell, and his deafness became an excuse for the Colonial Office's and Chamberlain's ignorance. Rhodes was determined to sacrifice himself in order to preserve the Charter and Chamberlain, in the end, protected him from total disgrace. Rhodes obviously was involved in the Plan but it was Jameson who acted precipitately. Dr Jim acted without Rhodes' authority but Rhodes' failed to give him a direct order to call off the Raid once it had begun. Probably, they both shared the view that if the Raid had succeeded the Imperial Authorities would be grateful and recriminations would be muted. Afterall Rhodes and Jameson would have expanded the Empire on the cheap and Britain would have gained a very valuable territory. It took an expensive and drawn out war to achieve what the Raid might have achieved at little cost.

The question which has challenged both Chamberlain's contemporaries and historians for almost 125 years is did the Colonial Secretary know about the 'Jameson Plan' and if so, how much did he know? There were those such as Stead, who believed that he knew about the plan. Rutherfoord Harris' 'guarded allusion' was referred to both at the Inquiry and in the Parliamentary Debate. It seems clear that Rutherfoord Harris believed that he had told Chamberlain enough for him to know that something was in the offing. Chamberlain's claim that he cut Rutherfoord off in mid telling may have been correct but no one could or would confirm how far Harris had got with his allusion before this happened. Unlike some of his subordinates such as Bower who had accepted information in confidence, Chamberlain claimed to have told

5   Stead, *Joseph Chamberlain, Conspirator or Statesman?*, p. 100.
6   Stead, *Joseph Chamberlain, Conspirator or Statesman?*, p. 101.
7   Henry R. Winkler, 'Joseph Chamberlain And The Jameson Raid', *American Historical Review*, Vol. 54, July 1949) p. 842 footnote.

Rutherfoord Harris that he did not wish to hear anything which he could not use officially. Others in this drama were ready and willing to do so and this was to cost them their reputation and position. Flora Shaw was a frequent visitor to the Colonial Office and although she claimed these visits were for journalistic purposes, it is also clear that she carried messages from Rhodes and was a confidant of Rutherfoord Harris. In many ways, such as her manipulation of the Committee, she appears to have been extremely formidable and assertive and almost certainly discussed the *Uitlanders* and the ZAR with Colonial Office Officials.

One of Chamberlain's first reactions on hearing that the Raid had begun was both to offer his resignation and to demand the BSAC telegrams. Was this the act of a guilty minister whose plots had gone wrong? Or did he do so because that part of Africa was part of his ministerial responsibility and to have been ignorant of such a momentous and potentially dangerous event would be seen as gross negligence by both his Government and the Opposition? Did all his officials keep things to themselves and not inform the Master? It seems certain that Bower and Newton were prepared to say they had not passed on their knowledge but suffered for their silence. If their claim that they did not tell Chamberlain in order to protect him was true then they were, particularly in Bower's case, hard done by. Bower made it clear that he believed that Chamberlain knew enough not to have been surprised when events unfolded.

Chamberlain's position as member of the Committee of Inquiry is significant enough but his appearance as witness is doubly suggestive. Not only was he one of the judges of the facts but he was also able to officially introduce his own perspective, one might suggest, explanation for the events. He certainly benefited from Rhodes' instruction to Hawksley not to implicate the Colonial Office or its officials. The Committee itself also came in for much criticism for not reporting Hawksley to the House. They could have done so as this was a familiar practice but they chose to allow him to retain what could be vital evidence which might have cleared Chamberlain of complicity but also might have revealed his knowledge

Chamberlain's contribution to the Commons Debate on the select Committee Report in 1897 also raises questions. In the face of considerable criticism that Rhodes was allowed to escape from the consequences of the Raid, Chamberlain defended the 'Colossus'' honour, reconfirmed the Charter and refused to remove Rhodes' name from the list of Privy Councillors. The incompetence of the Board of Directors of the BSAC was made very clear as was their domination by Rhodes. Yet the BSAC was not prevented from continuing to exploit and administer huge swathes of South Africa and it was not long before Rhodes re-joined the Board.

One is led to believe that Chamberlain did know about the plan to support the *Uitlanders*, and also, at the very least, the real reason why Jameson and his force were assembled at Pitsani. His 'Hurry Up' telegram is perhaps the strongest proof of this knowledge. The timing of the uprising in Johannesburg was crucial as this would give an acceptable reason for armed intervention. The number of British Army officers amongst the Raiders also suggests that it was an incursion likely to take place. Against this suggestion of Chamberlains' knowledge of Rhodes' intentions was Chamberlain's instructions to reduce the numbers of men who would be at Jameson's disposal. It seems certain that Chamberlain like, Rhodes, did not know that Jameson would launch his Raid on 29 December 1895 but, unlike Rhodes, he was prepared to cover his tracks and did not allowed his reputation to be damaged by protecting his subordinates which suggests a certain ruthlessness. The unfortunate Fairfield's deafness may have been genuine but it provided Chamberlain with an excuse for his ignorance since, it was argued that Fairfield would have told what he knew.

Rhodes' involvement in the plan is very clear. Harcourt, the Leader of the Opposition in the Commons' Session of 8 May 1896 criticised the idea that Charter Companies were ways to extend the Empire without Britain having the responsibility for their administration.[8] He claimed that this was untrue since power always came with responsibility. He suggested that Rhodes' involvement in the Raid was not motivated by greed but by his desire to extend the empire. One suspects that this is not entirely the case for when the conquered Matabeleland proved not to be an adequate source of gold, Rhodes and Jameson went to look

---

8   *Hansard*, House of Commons Debate, 8 May 1896, Vol. 40, columns 893-940.

elsewhere and as we have seen, their eyes became fixed on the Transvaal. Rhodes was part of the plan's inception, provided the finance and made sure that his Board of Directors were kept in the dark. His brother, Frank, was one of the prime movers of the expected uprising and was in frequent contact with *Groote Schuur*. He had employed Rutherfoord Harris and Flora Shaw as his go-betweens with Imperial Officials. He also authorised the preparations for an armed incursion. He knew that timing was everything, an appreciation which Jameson, in the end, lacked. His influence and an 'unwritten' agreement with Chamberlain did save the Charter but the Plan was a cause of the Second Boer War.

18

Finale

The Kaiser was not the only one to support Kruger in his hour of triumph. Many European countries with interests in Africa were full of his praises. Even Chamberlain was forced to thank Oom Paul for the magnanimity he had shown to the Raiders whom he could have executed. Rubbing salt into the wounds, however, Kruger demanded compensation for the cost of repelling the Raid and not satisfied with demanding £677,938 3s 3d for the material damage the Raiders had caused, he also demanded a million pounds for the moral and intellectual damage the Raid had caused to the Boer Republic. Chamberlain, it seems, faced another confusing telegram since he was unclear whether the million pounds was the total claim or an addition to the claim for damages. In the event, the money was never paid as relations with Britain and the ZAR deteriorated into war.

Chamberlain had survived, both personally and politically, the threat which the Raid had posed to his reputation and career but he was still concerned with the plight of the *Uitlanders* and made the error of publishing a dispatch concerning his views to Robinson before Kruger had been informed of its contents.[1] In order to improve their situation, he had proposed that the Rand become a self-governing municipality, as Kruger had previously suggested, with a modicum of self-government and have powers to make local laws which could be overruled by the *Volksraad*. Everything was up for negotiation, suggested Chamberlain, except the right of Britain to control the Transvaal's foreign relations which were enshrined in Article IV of the London Convention. Kruger's ambition, however, was to ensure that the ZAR was able to establish its own relationships with countries which were less than sympathetic to Britain. Kruger rejected Chamberlain's proposals out of hand since he believed they would interfere with the ZAR's right to control its own affairs. Neither did he offer any suggestions as to how the *Uitlanders'* conditions might be improved. Chamberlain, in a long speech in the Commons on 8 May 1896 in which he discussed the events of the Jameson Raid and the important telegrams, argued that a war with the ZAR would be a very serious, long, and costly event and to go to war with Kruger for the purpose of forcing internal reform would be an immoral and unwise act.[2]

Kruger realised that the ZAR's relations with Britain were deteriorating and made an alliance for mutual support with the neighbouring Orange Free State in 1897. That same year saw Alfred Milner, who believed that negotiating with Kruger would be a backward step, take over Robinson's place as High Commissioner. The Transvaal needed a more progressive government which supported capitalism and was sympathetic to Britain, Milner argued. It was with mixed feelings that Milner saw Kruger elected for the fourth time in May 1898 which increased Oom Paul's determination to keep the *Uitlanders* in the political desert whilst continuing to exploit them with heavy taxation. Thomas Pakenham believes Milner operated according to

---

1   *London Gazette*, 7 February 1896, p. 712.
2   *Hansard*, House of Commons Debate, 8 May 1896, Vol. 40, columns 893-940.

his own agenda and was determined there should be war.[3] He quotes Milner's statement, "The present policy of compromise in South Africa…offered no chance of restoring Britain's power.[4]

As relations with Britain continue to worsen, Kruger set about arming his little Republic. He realised that rifles would not be enough to defend it and, as Chamberlain claimed, in a letter to Salisbury in April 1897, the ZAR built up a stock of weapons of all kinds which were enough for a European army.[5] Britain also needed to improve its military presence in order to defend the Cape Colony against a possible attack. Modest reinforcements were sent to Natal together with a naval squadron to Delagoa Bay. Kruger realised the implication of this potential threat and retreated from a direct confrontation with Britain by repealing the Aliens Immigration Bill and moderated his harassment of the British press in the Rand. However, Kruger's intransigence to protect his Republic from foreign domination and Milner's belief that this could only be changed through a direct confrontation between Britain and the ZAR, made such a collision almost certain in spite of Chamberlain's desire to avoid such a crisis as long as possible.

The situation was further aggravated when a British *Uitlander* was shot by a Transvaal ZARP. The ZARP was acquitted of murder and consequently the *Uitlanders* petitioned the Queen to help secure their franchise. Persuaded by Milner's belligerent attitude, Chamberlain informed Kruger that Britain could not ignore the *Uitlanders'* grievances any longer. Schreiner, Rhodes' successor as Prime Minister of Cape Colony, proposed that Kruger and Milner should meet to resolve their differences. The meeting took place at the Bloemfontein Conference on 13 May 1899 during which Kruger offered to reduce the franchise qualification from fourteen years residency to seven. Milner demanded that it should be reduced to five years in spite of Chamberlain's more conciliatory advice. The Conference ended on 5 June and President Steyn of the Orange Free State, minded of his Republic's alliance with the ZAR, immediately ordered arms and ammunition from Germany. Milner advised Britain to send 10,000 troops to South Africa.

That July the Volksraad attempted to calm the tension by actually reducing the franchise qualification to seven years as Kruger had offered at Bloemfontein and also suggested other proposals in an attempt to satisfy the *Uitlanders* grievances. In return, Chamberlain suggested that a joint inquiry should be set up to examine the new proposals but, at the same time, gained Parliament's approval to use force if Kruger remained obdurate. Oom Paul, whilst continuing to obtain arms, did offer concessions but they were encompassed by conditions which were unacceptable to Britain. War became inevitable and began on 11 October 1899.

As Jan Smuts subsequently observed:

> The Jameson Raid was the real declaration of war in the Great Anglo-Boer War Conflict. And that is so in spite of the four years truce that followed…[during which the] aggressors consolidated their alliance…the defenders, on the other hand, silently and grimly prepared for the inevitable …[6]

3   Thomas Packenham, *The Scramble for Africa* (London; Abacus, 1992), p. 29.
4   Packenham, *The Scramble for Africa*, p. 30.
5   Garvin. *The Life of Joseph Chamberlain, Vol III*, pp. 140-41.
6   Jan Smuts 1906, quoted in A. Thomas, *Rhodes: The Race for Africa* (London: BBC Books, 1996), p. 337.

19

The Cast

The Jameson Raid was almost a complete disaster for Cecil Rhodes. He may have put up a bravura performance before the Select Committee, but he had accepted responsibility for the Raid and its consequences. For this admission he had been roundly condemned and it had caused some of his closest friends to be imprisoned. The BSAC's administration of Rhodesia and Bechuanaland was placed under increased Imperial scrutiny. Relations between the British Government and *Uitlanders* on the one hand and the Boers on the other were worsened by the Raid and deteriorated into the Second Anglo Boer War. The Charter was saved and, perhaps surprisingly, Rhodes was once again made a BSAC director and was joined on the Board by Jameson, when the Duke of Fife and Lord Farquhar resigned in 1898. The rest of Rhodes' life was a mere shadow of his earlier achievements. He was not entirely finished, however, as his determination to increase the railways from Cairo to the Cape remained a driving force and he persuaded the BSAC to launch a new issue of shares worth five million pounds in order to fund this project. The proposition was moved by the Duke of Abercorn. Clearly the BSAC Board had not lost their faith in the 'Colossus' who claimed that the railway would give them ' all of Africa'.

Rhodes had a habit of choosing unreliable companions throughout his life and tolerating their exploitative behaviour. The strangest and most damaging of these companions was Princess Catherine Radziwill, who claimed that she and Rhodes were engaged, and that they were having an affair in spite of many believing that Rhodes was a homosexual. Rhodes refused her proposal of marriage and she then accused him of loan fraud. She was only silenced through the courts when she was sentenced to two years imprisonment by the Supreme Court of Cape Colony for having forged bills amounting to £6,000. After Rhodes' death she published *Cecil Rhodes: Man and Empire Maker*.

In the Second Boer War, Rhodes was in Kimberley during its siege and, although he had strained relations with Colonel Kekewich, the garrison commander, Rhodes' Company assisted the towns defence by building fortifications and providing water for its population. Such was his influence that he persuaded the Government to divert troops to relieve Kimberley when the real military priorities were to attack Bloemfontein and Pretoria.

Constantly dogged by ill-health, Rhodes died aged 48, on 26 March 1902 at his seaside cottage at Muizenberg in Cape Colony. His will, which has been discussed in an earlier chapter, left much of his fortune to his private secretary Neville Pickering whose death actually superseded that of Rhodes. It also established the 'Rhodes Scholarships' which were probably the world's first international study programme. It enabled scholars from territories which were or had been under British rule and, interestingly, from Germany, to study at Oxford. Scholarships are now administered by the Rhodes Trust and have attracted many distinguished Americans to study there. The statue of Rhodes on the façade of Oriel College, Oxford, has caused considerable controversy because of his imperialist and racist views and has sparked the call that 'Rhodes Must Fall'. Even over a hundred years after his death, the 'Colossus' can still cause strong disagreement.

During the Second Matabele War, in which he took an uncharacteristically active part, and which may have endeared him to the Government which protected him after the Inquiry, he came across a spot in the

Matopos Hills which he named World's View. It was here he decided he would be buried. On his death, the Cape Government arranged for his body to be transported by rail from the Cape to Rhodesia, with the funeral train stopping at every station to allow mourners to pay their respects and he was finally laid to rest at World's View.

Dr Jim was not ruined by the Raid and remained friends with Rhodes until the latter's death at which he was present. After the Second Boer War, Jameson became leader of the Progressive Party in the Cape Legislature and in 1904, its Prime Minister. In 1907 he was made a Privy Councillor and became a baronet in 1911; finally returning to England in 1912. He died full of honours, on Monday, 26 November 1917, at his home in Great Cumberland Place, Hyde Park. His body was laid in a vault at Kensal Green Cemetery on 29 November 1917, where it

Rhodes funeral at St Adderley, Cape Town on 3 April 1902. (G.F. Williams, *Diamond Mines of South Africa, Vol. II*, New York: B.F. Buck & Company, 1906)

remained until the end of the First World War. Jameson's memorial service on 5 December was attended by many distinguished mourners including the King and Queen, the Prime Minister, David Lloyd George, General Smuts, and soldiers from the Rhodesia Regiment. The event was of such significance as to be recorded by Pathé News. After the First World War Jameson's body was carried to Rhodesia and laid beside his friend at World's View.[1]

Joseph Chamberlain reluctantly had his war with the Boers. After Black Week's rocky start, the war eventually went Britain's way and the Transvaal was formally annexed on 3 September 1900. Feeling confident, the Government called an election which became known as 'Joe's Election' since Salisbury was ill, and Balfour chose to play a subordinate role.[2] Winning the war played a large part in Chamberlain's campaign, his popularity soared, and the Unionists won a large majority in the House. Salisbury's illness and pressure from the Queen forced him to give up managing foreign affairs and, although Lansdowne was appointed Foreign Secretary in his place, the more experienced Chamberlain began to negotiate Britain's foreign relationships with Germany and France, though not altogether successfully.

Concentration camps, which were employed by Britain to subdue the Boer guerrillas, were extremely poor and became a subject of national outrage. Chamberlain ensured that the conditions improved and the worst camps were closed. The war was officially won on 31 May 1902 with the Treaty of Vereeniging and both the ZAR and the Orange Free State were absorbed into the British Empire.

It is beyond the scope of this book to describe the rest of Chamberlains political career which was to cover many areas including Education and tariff reform. He collapsed from a stroke on 13 July 1906 shortly after his seventieth birthday and many of his faculties were severely affected; he couldn't see well, couldn't write with his right hand, and could barely walk. Although he never recovered his health, he was returned

---

1   Colvin, *Life of Jameson*, Vol. II, p. 320.
2   It was also known as 'the Khaki Election' because of the influence on public sentiment with regard to the Boer War.

unopposed to Parliament in the General Elections of 1910. In 1914 he decided to retire and died just before his seventy-eighth birthday.

Asquith, the then Prime Minister, in his tribute, described Chamberlain's personality as:

> [V]ivid, masterful, resolute, tenacious, there were no blurred or nebulous outlines, there were no relaxed fibres, there were no moods of doubt and hesitation, there were no pauses of lethargy or fear.[3]

This does not sound like a man who would be in ignorance of events in the Colonies, for which he was responsible, which were of such significance as the Raid.

Kruger, realising the war would end in defeat, left the ZAR for Mozambique on 11 September 1900. He hoped to escape on the steamer *Hertzog* of the German East African Line but, because of British insistence, the Portuguese authorities intervened. When Kruger's train arrived at Lourenço Marques, he was placed under house arrest where he remained until 21 October when a Dutch warship, *The Gelderland*, sent by Queen Wilhelmina of the Netherlands, arrived to take him to Marseille where he was welcomed with great acclaim. He was equally welcomed in Cologne, but the Kaiser refused to receive him and Queen Wilhelmina, because of the neutral status of the Netherlands, could offer him no additional material support.

For the next three years Kruger wandered around Europe whilst the Boers were eventually defeated, and his Republic became part of the British Empire again. He refused to return home, since this would require him to become a British citizen. He spent his last days in the village of Clarens, overlooking Lake Geneva, and died of pneumonia on 14 July 1904. To admirers, Kruger was a shrewd, perceptive, interpreter of people, affairs and law, who faithfully protected a disparaged people and became a forlorn popular idol.[4] To his critics he was 'an anachronistic throwback', a determined, stubborn, untrustworthy protector of a prejudiced ideal and a persecutor of native Africans. The truth is probably somewhere in between, but he was an important player in Boer history and one of the most extraordinary South Africans in the early years of the Republic.[5] In an act of magnanimity, Milner gave permission for Oom Paulus's body to be returned to his beloved land where he was buried in what is now called 'Heroes Acre' in Pretoria. In his last letter to his people he wrote; 'It is true: much that has been built is now destroyed, damaged, levelled. But with unity of purpose and unity of strength that which has been pulled down can be built again.'[6]

Sir John Willoughby returned to South Africa in the company of Jameson at the outbreak of the Second Boer War. They were both in Mafeking during the siege. Later Willoughby served under Major General Archibald Hunter and was Colonel Mahon's Deputy Assistant Adjutant General, for which service he was awarded the DSO and restored to the active list.

Flora Shaw had already come to public attention before her appearance at the Select Committee. She had become *The Times* South African Correspondent and the highest paid woman journalist. In an article in *The Times* in January 1897 she had suggested that the British Protectorate on the Niger River should be given the more accessible name of Nigeria; a name which was adopted and used today. She was, as we have seen, close to Rhodes but there were two others with whom she was associated in the expansion of the British Empire in Africa. The first of these was Sir George Taubman Goldie KCMG FRS, who played a key part in the creation of Nigeria. In many respects, his role was comparable to that of Cecil Rhodes in South Africa, but he lacked Rhodes' desire for public acclaim.

---

3   Herbert Asquith quoted in A. Macintosh, *Joseph Chamberlain: An Honest Biography* (London: Hodder & Stoughton, 1914), p. 358.

4   J. Meintjes, *President Paul Kruger: A Biography* (London: Weidenfeld & Nicolson, 1974), p. 14.

5   Meintjes, *President Paul Kruger*, pp. vii–viii.

6   Meintjes, *President Paul Kruger*, p. 236.

The third man linked to Flora Shaw was Sir Frederick Lugard whom she married in June 1902. Lugard had a chequered career as British soldier serving in Second Anglo-Afghan War, the Sudan Campaign, and the Third Anglo-Burmese War, and was awarded the Distinguished Service Order in 1887. After a short period in England he returned to Africa and became a mercenary for the African Lakes Company leading two expeditions against the Swahili but with limited success.

Lugard then turned his hand to exploring and on the behalf of the Imperial British East Africa Company undertook a number of trips into Uganda. He later occupied a number of Colonial posts including Governor of Hong Kong and Nigeria. He was knighted and thus Flora Shaw became Lady Lugard but in 1918 was created a Dame Commander of the Order of the British Empire in her own right for her work serving on the War Refugees Committee which dealt with the difficulties of Belgian refugees during the First World War. She died of pneumonia on 25 January 1929, aged 76.

Sir Graham Bower was made to pay for his connection with the Raid and died a disappointed man. He had hoped to be made Governor of Gibraltar but never regained his status in the Colonial Office and was given the less prestigious post of Colonial Secretary in Mauritius having been eighteen months without salary.[7] He had allowed himself to become the scapegoat for the Colonial Service and his account gives a partial insight into the happenings at Pretoria over the crucial period.

Frank Newton, the Commissioner at Mafeking, who was also criticised by the Select Committee fared better than Bower. Initially, he was demoted and his pay reduced as a consequence of this criticism. However, through Chamberlain's recommendation, in 1898 he was made Colonial Secretary of British Honduras, now Belize, and in 1901 he became Colonial Secretary of Barbados. On his return to South Africa he was nominated to the Legislative Council of Southern Rhodesia in 1903 and appointed Treasurer. In 1914 he was Acting Administrator of Southern Rhodesia for a short period and in 1923 he was appointed Colonial Secretary of Southern Rhodesia. He stood for election to the Assembly in 1924 for the constituency of Mazoe, a position from which he quickly resigned to become High Commissioner of Southern Rhodesia to the United Kingdom; a post he occupied until 1930. Newton died in 1946.

Sir Hercules Robinson, having been made Lord Rosmead, died of oedema a few months after the Select Committee reported.

Sir Robert Mead could have retired in 1896 but was persuaded by Chamberlain to remain. His health deteriorated as a result of a fall and he was too ill to appear before the Inquiry and died of suppressed gout.

Sir Edward Fairfield died two day before Rutherfoord Harris appeared before the Inquiry. His deafness was used as an excuse as to why he hadn't understood what Harris was trying to say in his 'guarded allusion'. He had been warned that he must take the blame for the Colonial Secretary's ignorance but died before he could do so.

Colonel Francis Rhodes, after his release from prison, joined his brother Cecil in Matabeleland. In 1898 he joined Kitchener's Nile Expedition as a war correspondent but could not resist taking an active part. At the battle of Omdurman he was severely wounded in the right arm. So valuable were his services in the Campaign that he was restored to the Army's active list. Although he continued as a war correspondent he was trapped during the siege of Ladysmith and took part in the Relief of Mafeking. He retired from the Army in 1903 and became Managing Director of African Trans-Continental Telegraph Company until his death in 1905 at *Groote Schuur*, his brother's estate in Cape Colony.

Frederick Rutherfoord Harris, after running from the Committee of Inquiry to South Africa soon returned to England. He was later described as Rhodes' 'Achilles Heel'.[8] *The Times*, which he had persuaded to publish the *Letter of Invitation* as if it were a request from the *Uitlanders* for immediate help, perhaps somewhat

7   Hansard, House of Commons Debate. Vol 79, 19 February 1900.
8   Gerald Shaw (ed.), *The Garrett Papers*(Cape Town: Van Reibeeck Society, 1984), p. 28.

pompously, wrote in September 1920: 'The cloud of this act of deception was heavy over Harris for the rest of his life'.[9]

He returned to Britain and was elected MP for Monmouth Boroughs in 1900. He was unseated after a lawsuit alleging electoral irregularities and was disqualified by the Court from standing again in the constituency for seven years. Somewhat strangely, the judges insisted that no blame should be attach to Harris personally. A local committee subsequently raised almost a thousand pounds as a gift on his behalf.[10] Undaunted, he stood in a by-election and was elected as MP for Dulwich in 1903. After three years he went back to South Africa but returned to Britain and died in Eastbourne at the age of 64 in 1920. Tragically his wife committed suicide shortly afterward his death; it was said out of grief.

John Hays Hammond was one of seven Americans who were arrested for their participation in the events in Johannesburg. Many were influential in the *Uitlander* community and their incarceration became a *cause célèbre* in the American press. Most American newspapers condemned the sentence of death levelled on Hammond even though they criticised the Raid and were not always sympathetic to the *Uitlanders'* clamour for their rights. William N. Stewart, the Republican Senator for Nevada produced a petition addressed to President Kruger which asked him to pardon Hays Hammond because of his previous high character.[11] The petition was signed by all the members of the Senate and many from the House of Representatives. Rowland B Mahaney, the Republican Representative for New York, entered a resolution which asked the Secretary of State, Richard Olney, to take immediate action to protect Hay Hammond's interests and to use his Department to safeguard these interests if possible. During the debate which followed, Republican Ebenezer J. Hill was warmly applauded when he said the it was high time that the American Government protected its own citizens abroad.[12]

The 'Hays Hammond Affair' became entangled with that of Venezuela in shaping American official attitudes to Great Britain. The American Ambassador in London, Thomas Bayard, was instructed to discuss unofficially Hays Hammond with Lord Salisbury and ensure that Hays Hammond and the other arrested Americans was protected by British officials in South Africa. This was regarded as an acted of friendship by America to Britain which had previously been threatened by President Cleveland over its stance on Venezuelan territory. This may have been the case but there was also extensive lobbying by Hays Hammonds friends in the United States for the Cleveland's Government to do something. It is easy to forget that Britain was not the only country working hard to protect the Reformers and that other countries such as the US engaged in extensive lobbying and it was this which convinced Kruger and the Executive that executing the Reformers or keeping them in prison for long periods would damage the ZAR's international standing.[13]

In 1900 Hay Hammond returned to the United States and continued with his career as a mining engineer. He became a professor of mining engineering at Yale and Managing Director of the Guggenheim Exploration Company and is said to have earned 1.2 million in his first year. In 1911 he attended the Coronation of George V as the Special US Ambassador. Friend of five Presidents, Hay Hammond's life and achievements were celebrated in *Time Magazine* in May 1926. Hays Hammond died in 1936 having been honoured by his profession and his nation. His reputation in the 'Land of the Free had perhaps been enhanced by his stand for *Uitlander* rights and his brush with death.'

---

9   *The Times*, 3 September 1920.

10   *The Times,* 12 December 1903.

11   *New York Herald*, 29 April 1896.

12   House of Representatives, John Hays Hammond Resolution, 282. 54th Congress, 1st Session, 28 April 1896, Congressional Records 28, pp. 4128-4529.

13   · For a detailed account of the Hammond Affair, see C. Tesehloane Keto, 'The Aftermath of the Jameson Raid and the Decision Making in Foreign Affairs, 1896', *Transactions of the American Philosophical Society*, Vol. 70, Part 8, 1980.

Appendix I

The Raiders

(Substantive ranks in parenthesis)

Lieut. Colonel Sir John Willoughby, (Major): Royal Horse Guards Commanding

Major Hon. Robert White, (Capt.): Royal Welsh Fusiliers Senior Staff Officer

Major C. Hyde Villiers, (Capt.): Royal Horse Guards Staff Officer

Captain Kenneth Kincaid-Smith, (Lieut.): Royal Artillery Staff Officer

Captain James Kennedy, BSAC. Quartermaster

Captain E. Holden, Derbyshire Yeomanry AQM

Surgeon Captain Farmer, BSAC Medical Officer

Surgeon Captain Seaton Hamilton, late 1st Life Guards Medical Officer

Lieutenant Howard Grenfell: 1st Life Guards Remount Officer.

Lieutenant James Jesser-Coope: BSAC Transport Office

Captain Lindsell: late Royal Scots Fusiliers i/c Scouts

Major John Stracey: Scots Guards

Major Heany: BSAC Officers temporarily

Captain Cyril Foley, 3rd Royal Scots attached to Staff

Lieutenant Harry Holden, late Grenadier Guards

Officers of Mashonaland Mounted Police

Lieut.-Colonel Hon. H. F. White: Grenadier Guards Commanding

Inspector William Bodle: late 6th Dragoons 2nd i/c

A Troop

Inspector Martin Straker, Sub-Inspectors Harry Scott and Rowan Cashel

B Troop

Inspector Lawson Dykes, Sub-Inspectors A. Tomlinson and H. Chawner

C Troop

Inspector William Barry, Sub-Inspectors A. Cazalet and G. Williams

D Troop

Inspector Gordon Drury, Sub-Inspectors W. Murray and H Constable

Artillery

Inspector F. Bowden Sub-Inspector W Spain

Regimental Sergeant-Major Abbott NCOs and men

Totalling   356

Bechuanaland Border Police

Lieut.-Colonel Raleigh Grey, 6th Dragoons.	Commanding
Major Hon. Charles Coventry, 3rd Worcester's	2nd in command

G Troop

Captain A. Gosling,	Sub-Lieutenants A. Hoare and E. Wood

K Troop

Captain C Munro: Seaforth Highlanders	Sub-Lieutenant McQueen
Surgeon-Captain E Garraway	Medical Officer
Veterinary –Lieut. W. Surgeon Lakie.	Veterinary Officer
NCOs and men	
Total 113	

Major Crosse, late of the Dragoon Guards who was convalescing, accompanied the Column in order not to miss the 'fun'.

Casualties

	Total	Officers	Other Ranks
Killed in Action	0	16	16
Severely Wounded	1 (died of wounds)	14	15
Slightly Wounded	3	38	41

Appendix II

The Boers

It is difficult to give an exact description of the Raiders opponents because of the nature of the Boer military arrangements. Every Boer adult male was supposed to respond to the call to form a *Commando* when danger threatened. They were meant to supply their own rifle, ammunition and a horse. This would, in normal circumstances, be no hardship: the majority of the Boers were, as their Afrikaner name suggest, farmers. They relied on a horse for day to day movement and had a rifle readily at hand in case of attacks by wild animals or the indigenous people with whom they were often at odds. They were crack shots as their lives and often their food depended on their skill.

Each *Commando* was attached to a town after which it was named and the town was responsible for Wards which spread around the town. Command was almost a democratic affair and each *Commando* would choose its own *Kommandant* or commander and each Ward would be commanded by a *veldkornet* or field cornet. The field cornet was responsible for collecting his part of the *Commando*, policing the area, collecting taxes and distribution arms. If large enough, a Ward was divided into Corporalships which consisted of roughly 20 *Burghers* more often than not from the same family.

Each *Commandant* was responsible to a General who, theoretically, was responsible for four *Commandos*. The system did produce some very able generals such as General Koos de la Rey and General C. R. de Wet but could also produce inept officers who were chosen for the wrong reasons. The senior Commander was the Commandant General who reported to the President.

The only professional body was the *Staatsartillerie* who were responsible for the Boers heavy weaponry. The commander was the only officer other than the Commandant General appointed by the Government.

The *Commandos* who were responsible for defeating the Raiders were:

Krugersdorp *Commando*	*Commandant* F J. Potgieter approximately 800 men
Marico *Commando*	*Commandant* L. Botha approximately 200 men
Carolina *Commando*	*Commandant* D.J. Joubert approximately 200 men
Potchefstroom *Commando*	*Commandant* P.A. Cronjé approximately 200-300 men
Rustenberg *Commando*	*Commandant* H.P. Malan approximately 200 men

There was also a contingent of the Staatsartillerie under Commandant S. Trichardt towards the ender of the battle.

It is clear to see that as the *Commandos* gradually gathered and followed the Raiders, the latter would soon become out numbered.

The Boers reported their casualties as 4 killed and 5 wounded but this may well be an underestimation.

Appendix III

National Union Charter

The following is an extract from Charles Leonard's National Union manifesto which articulated *Uitlander* demands.[1]

'What do we want?' We want:

1   The establishment of this Republic as a true Republic;
2   A *Grondwet* or Constitution which shall be framed by competent persons selected by representatives of the whole people and framed on lines laid down by them—a Constitution which shall be safeguarded against hasty alteration;
3   An equitable franchise law, and fair representation;
4   Equality of the Dutch and English languages;
5   Responsibility of the Legislature to the heads of the great departments;
6   Removal of religious disabilities;
7   Independence of the courts of justice, with adequate and secured remuneration of the judges;
8   Liberal and comprehensive education;
9   Efficient civil service, with adequate provision for pay and pension;
10   Free trade in South African products.

---

1   N. Hays Hammond, *A Woman's Part in a Revolution*, Chapter 1 and Fitzpatrick *The Transvaal from Within*, pp. 334-35.

Appendix IV

First Subscribers to the Reformers' Relief Fund

H. Eckstein & Co.	10,000
Lionel Phillips	5,000
Consolidated Goldfields	15,000
George Farrar	10,000
Lace & Thompson	5,000
Lingham Timber Syndicate, Ltd.	1,000
Abe Bailey	5,000
S. Neumann & Co.	10,000
Barnet Bros	10,000
Fehr & Du Bois	1,000
H.B. Marshall	2,000
W.D. ("Karri") Davies	1,000
W.H. Adler	1,000
Victor Wolff	250
Johannesburg Hebrew Congregation	100

Appendix V

Kaiser Wilhelm II's Telegram

The Emperor William to President Kruger, January 3rd, 1896
Drafted by Kayser, of the Foreign Office (Colonial Section). (Sent off at 1120 hours)

I express my sincere congratulations that, supported by your people, without appealing for the help of friendly Powers, you have succeeded by your own energetic action against armed bands which invaded your country as disturbers of the peace, and have thus been enabled to restore peace and safeguard the independence of the country against attacks from the outside.

WILHELM I.R.

Appendix VI

Reformers on Trial

Lionel Phillips
Colonel F.W. Rhodes
George Farrar
J.H. Hammond
J.P. Fitzpatrick
S.W. Jameson
G. Richards
J.L. Williams.
G. Sandilands
F. Spencer
R.A. Bettington
J.G. Auret
E. P. Solomon
J.W. Leonard
W.H.S. Bell.
W.E. Hudson
D. F. Gilfillan
C. H. Mullins
E.O. Hutchinson
W. van Hulsteyn
A. Woolls-Sampson
H.C. Hull
A. Brown
C.L. Andersson

M. Langermann
W. Hosken
W. St. John Carr
H.F. Strange
C. Garland
Fred Gray*
A. Mackie Niven
Dr W.T F. Davies
Dr R.P. Mitchell
Dr Hans Saiier
Dr A.P. Hillier
Dr D.P. Duirs
Dr W. Brodie
H.J. King
A. Bailey
Sir Drummond Dunbar
H.E. Becher
F. Moseuthal
H.A. Rogers
C. Butters
Walter D. Davies
H. Bettelheim
F.R. Lingham
A.L. Lawley

Note
* Committed suicide before the Reformers were sentenced.

Appendix VII

Telegrams

On Friday 5 January 1900, *L'Inépendance Belge*, a Brussels newspaper published a selection of telegrams which became known as the 'Hawksley Dossier'. The Belgian newspaper vouched for the authenticity of the telegrams and claimed that it had obtained them from someone involved in the Raid. Bouchier Hawksley, Rhodes solicitor, reproduced sixteen of these telegrams. They feature in an Appendix in Stead's, *Joseph Chamberlain, Conspirator or Statesman? An Examination of the Evidence of his complicity in the Jameson Conspiracy, together with the newly published letters of the Hawksley Dossier*. Stead claims that the telegrams showed that Chamberlain was aware of the work of Rhodes and Chamberlain in the Johannesburg revolt. The latter charged Fairfield to secure the acquittal of Jameson and Rhodes before the Select Committee. Stead argues that the telegrams show that prosecution evidence was doctored and important documents were withheld from the Select Committee.

The *Congressional Serial Set*, which is similar to the British *Hansard*, in a section on the South Africa War dated 21 May 1900,[1] also reprinted these telegrams with comments about the significance of each. It points out that although the Dossier was reproduced by 'the entire Continental press', they were repressed by the British Government which had made no attempt to refute them. The document concluded: 'This silence is so unanimous that we can only treat it as a concerted attempt to suppress awkward but authentic evidence against Mr Chamberlain and his friends.'[2]

Chamberlain admitted in the House of Commons on 1 February 1900 that the correspondence between Hawksley and Fairfield was substantially if not verbally correct and they had been sent under his authority though he might not have seen them at the time. In response to Chamberlain's reply, John Swift MacNiell, MP for South Donegall asked, hinting that Chamberlain had lied, Arthur Balfour what the Government would do if a member of the Cabinet is deliberately charged with personal dishonour and public falsehood. Balfour replied that such an accusation should be treated with contempt.[3]

See below for some of the telegrams reproduced by *L' Indépendance Belge*.

Hawksley to Fairfield 17 July 1896
Hawksley's attempt to influence the Committee's membership

My dear Fairfield:
Is the rumour true that I hear to the effect that the Government have decided upon the appointment of a select committee of the House of Commons to inquire into the circumstances of Dr Jameson ' s action in December last ? If so, I suppose it will be possible for the views of the directors to be to some extent

---

1   *Congressional Serial Set*, Document 386, Senate, 56th Congress, 1 Session, 21 May 1900.
2   *Congressional Serial Set*, Document 386, p. 2.
3   *Hansard*, House of Commons Debate, Vol. 78, 1 February 1900, cc258-60.

considered in appointing some of the members. In this case may I suggest the names of Mr Carson Q C, Mr A Cripps Q C, and Mr George Wyndham? Will it be possible to have an opportunity of discussing with you the terms of the reference to the Select Committee?

Hawksley to Fairfield 15 June 1896
The Telegrams given to the Colonial Office and their confidential nature

My Dear Fairfield
Referring to your letter of the 9th inst., you will remember my letter to you on the 6th inst. Covering the copies of the cablegrams stated. These copies were sent for confidential perusal and return, I do not think that I am at liberty to assent to any use being made of copies until I have had the opportunity of communicating with Rhodes. Shall I cable him?

Hawksley to Earl Grey 20 February 1897
Hawksley's assessment of the Select Committee's work so far

My Dear Grey,
Thank you for your letter of the 9th inst. Which I read with great interest. You, of course, will have heard that the Committee was reappointed and has got to work. I send you official prints of the evidence already taken. Rhodes has done very well. And I think will come out on top. He was nervous the first day, though his evidence was good even then. Yesterday he was simply splendid.

I do not think we are by any means out of the wood, but there does seem an off chance of the plea of public interest being recognised, and the cables of the last half of 1895, or rather the negotiations of that period, not being disclosed. I am bound to say that personally I think the balance of probability is that they will have to come out.

If they do then Mr Chamberlain will have no one but himself to thank.

(Hawksley concluded by informing Grey of the pressure he had been under with regard to the Protectorate for the previous 15 months/two years).

John Bigham to Hawksley, 7 August 1897
A confidential meeting with a witness

Can Mr Charles Leonard come down to the House of Commons tomorrow at five o'clock? The Committee meet (privately) at half past four in Colonel Legg's room and I could see Leonard after the meeting breaks up.[4]

Hawksley to Jackson, Chair of the Select Committee 2 April 1897
Evidence of influencing the Committee as to how to interrogate witnesses

Dear Sir,
I send you a memo, about Sir John Willoughby. Will you put the points in this memo, to him, and also the two first paragraphs in the enclosed print? With regard to the official report it does not seem necessary that this should be read through, but Sir John will mark certain paragraphs and read them. I am giving Mr Nicholson further prints for circulation among the Committee.[5]

---

4   Document 386 states that it was doubtful if Bigham (1st Viscount Mersey) who became a Judge on the Queen's Bench later that year, was employed to interview witnesses in private prior to the case being heard.

5   There is no mention of this print in the Committee Report. Perhaps Hawksley was guilty of undue influence.

Bibliography

Archives

South Africa
National Archives of South Africa (NASA) TAB SP 892, Van Niekerk to Tossel, 27 January 1896
Killie Campbell Africana Library (KCAL), Trimble Collection, F. Rhodes to C. Rhodes, 8 January 1896
Bower Papers, 'Reminiscences', unpublished, South African Public Library Cape Town

United Kingdom
The National Archive (TNA) WO 327485, Buller to Haliburton1 August 1896. Note by Landsdowne
British Library (BL), Lansdowne Mss. 88906/16/9, Lansdowne to Salisbury and Mead to Bower correspondence 19 September 1896

Official Printed Sources

Congressional Serial Set, Document 386, Senate, 56th Congress, 1st Session, 21 May 1900
South African Republic, *Report of the Select Committee on the Jameson Raid into the Territory of South African Republic* (Cape of Good Hope: Parliament House, 1896)
HMSO, Second *Report from the Select Committee on British South Africa* (London: Eyre & Spottiswoode, 1897)
Hansard, Commons Debates, 1893-97
House of Representatives. *John Hays Hammond Resolution,*282. 54th Congress, 1st Session, 28 April 1896
London Gazette, 7 February 1896

Secondary Sources

Ash, Chris, *The If Man: Dr Leander Starr Jameson: the inspiration for Kipling's Masterpiece* (Solihull: Helion & Co. Ltd, 2012).
—— *Matabele: The War of 1893 and the 1896 Rebellions,*(South Africa: 30o South Publishers, 2016)
Aston, P.E. (ed.), *The Raid on the Transvaal by Dr Jameson* (London: Dean, 1897)
Bell, E..M.., *Flora Shaw* (London: Constable, 1947).
Bleksley, A..H., *Johannesburg Gezondheids Comite, Sanitary Department* (Johannesburg: Standard and Diggers New Printing and Publishing Company, 1896)
Breutz, P.L., *History of Botswana* (Ramsgate (RSA): Breutz, 1989)
BSAC, Rhodesia*: South Africa Company 1892* (London: BSAC, 1909)
Buckle, G.E. (ed.), The *Letters of Queen Victoria, Third Series* (London: John Murray, 1931)
Chisholm, Hugh (ed.), 'Alfred Milner, Viscount Milner', *Encyclopaedia Britannica*. 18, 11th ed. (London: CUP 1911)

Clarke, Edward, *The Story of My Life* (London: John Murray, 1918)

Cloete, Stuart, *African Portraits* (London: Collins, 1946)

Colvin, Ian, *The Life of Jameson,* Vol. II (London: Edward Arnold, 1922)

Crisp, R, *The Outlanders: The Story of the Men Who Made Johannesburg* (St. Albans: Granada Publishing, 1974)

Conan Doyle, Arthur, *The Great Boer War* (London: Nelson, 1903)

Dugdale E.T.S., *German Diplomatic Documents,* Vol. II. (London: Harper & Brothers, 1929)

Eybers, George van Welfling, *Select Constitutional Documents Illustrating South African History, 1795-1910* (London: Routledge, 1919)

Farwell Byron, *The Great Boer War* (London: Allen Lane 1977)

—— *The Encyclopaedia of Nineteenth-Century Land Warfare: An Illustrated World View* (New York: W.W. Norton, 2001)

Fisher, John, *Paul Kruger: His Life and Times* (London: Secker & Warburg, 1974)

Fisher, William, Garrett, *The Transvaal and the Boer: A Short History of South African Republic, with a Chapter on the Orange Free State* (London: Chapman & Hall, 1900)

Fitzpatrick, James, Percy, *The Transvaal from Within. A Private Record of Public Affairs* (London: Heinemann, 1900)

Flint, John, E., *Cecil Rhodes* (Boston, Little Brown, 1974)

Garrett Edmund, G. & Edwards F.J., *The Story of an African Crisis* (London: Archibald Constable, 1897)

Garvin, J.L., *The Life of Joseph Chamberlain* (London: MacMillan, 1934)

Gerzina Grethchen (ed.) *Black Victorians/Black Victoriana* (New Brunswick, New Jersey: Rutgers University Press, 2003)

Gibbs, Peter, *A Flag for the Matebele* (London: Frederick Muller, 1955)

—— *The History of the British South African Police,* 1889-1980 Vol. 1 (Salisbury: BSAP, 1972)

Giliomee, Herman, *The Afrikaners: Biography of a People* (London: C. Hurst & Co., 2003)

Halt, Edgar, *The Boer War* (New York: George A. Putnam, 1958)

Hays Hammond, John, *The Truth about the Jameson Raid as Related to Alleyne Ireland* (London: Heinemann, 1900)

Hays Hammond, Natalie, *A Woman's Part in a Revolution* (London: Longmans, Green & Co., 1897)

Hensmen, Howard, *History of Rhodesia* (London: Blackwood 1900)

Kelly, Richard N. & Cantrell, John, *Modern British Statesmen, 1867-1945* (Manchester: MUP, 1967)

King, James. *Dr Jameson's Raid: Its Causes and Consequences* (London: George Routledge & Sons Ltd..1896)

Krout, Mary Hannah, *A Looker on in London* (New York: Dodd, Mead & Co., 1899)

Kruger, Stephanus Johannes Paulus, *The Memoirs of Paul Kruger, Four times President of the South African Republic Told by Himself* (Toronto: G.M. Morang & Co. Ltd, 1902)

Kruger, Rayne, *Good-bye Dolly Gray* (London: Pan Books, 1959)

Kuitenbrouwer, Vincent, *War of Words, Dutch Pro-Boer Propaganda and the South African War 1899-1902* (Amsterdam: Amsterdam University Press, 2012)

Lockhart, John, Gilbert, & Woodhouse Christopher Montague, *Rhodes* (London: Hodder and Stoughton, 1963)

Macintosh, Alexander, *Joseph Chamberlain: An Honest Biography* (London: Hodder & Stoughton, 1914)

Marshal Hole, Hugh, *The Jameson Raid* (London: Philip Allan, 1930)

Martin, Gilbert, *History of the Twentieth Century, 1900-1933, Vol. I* (New York: William Morrow & Co., 1997)

McKnight Nichols, Christopher, *Promise and Peril: America at the Dawn of a Global Age* (Cambridge, Massachusetts: Harvard University Press, 2011)

Meintjes, Johannes, *The Commandant General* (Cape Town: Taflelberg-Uitgewers, 1971)

—— *President Paul Kruger: A Biography* (London: Weidenfeld & Nicolson, 1974)

Meredith, Martin, *Diamonds, Gold, and War: The British, the Boers, and the Making of South* (Cambridge, Massachusetts: Harvard University Press, 2011)

Crewe-Milnes, Robert Offley Ashburton, Marquis of Crewe, *Lord Rosebery* (London: John Murray, 1931)

Millin, Sarah, Gertrude, *Rhodes* (London: Chatto & Windus, 1933)

Nasson, Bill, *The South African War 1899-1902* (London: Arnold, 1999)

Packenham, Thomas, *The Scramble for Africa* (London: Abacus, 1992)

Quigley, Carroll, *Anglo-American Establishment: From Rhodes to Cliveden*, (New York: Books in Focus, 1981)

Ranger, Terence, *Revolt in Southern Rhodesia, 1896-97: A Study in African Resistance* (London: Heinemann, 1967)

Reiz, E.(ed.), *Cambridge History of the British Empire, Vol. III* (London: CUP, 1959)

Rodney, C.M., *Jameson's Ride to Johannesburg,* (Johannesburg: Argus Printing & Publishing Co.,1896)

Rhoodie, D., *Conspirators in Conflict,* (Cape Town: Tafelberg-Uitgewers, 1967)

Rider Haggard, Henry, *The Last Boer War* (London: Keegan Paul, Trench, Trubner, 1899)

Rouillard, Nancy, (ed.), *Matabele Thompson – His Autobiography* (Johannesburg: Central News Agency, 1957)

Roberts, Phillip, *Cecil Rhodes: Flawed Colossus* (London: Hamish Hamilton, 1987)

Shaw, Gerald (ed.)., *The Garrett Papers* (Cape Town: Van Reibeeck Society, 1984)

Schreuder, Deryck & Butler, Jeffrey, *Sir Graham Bower's Secret History of the Jameson Raid and the South Africa Crisis, 1895-1902* (Cape Town: Van Riebeek Society, 2002)

Seymour Fort, George, *Dr Jameson* (London: Hurst and Blackett Ltd, 1908)

Sonntag, C., *My friend Maleboch, Chief of the Blue Mountains* (Pretoria: Sonntag, 1983)

Spender, John, Alfred, *Life, Journalism and Politics,* Vol.1 (London: Cassell & Co. Ltd, 1927)

Stead, William, Thomas, *Joseph Chamberlain, Conspirator or Statesman? An Examination of the Evidence of his Complicity in the Jameson Conspiracy, Together with the Newly Published Letters of the Hawksley Dossier* (London: Review of Reviews, 1900)

Stephens, John, Russell, *The Censorship of English Drama 1824-1901* (London: CUP, 2010)

The Times Office, *The History of the Times, Vol. 3: The Twentieth Century Test 1884-1912* (London: MacMillan, 1947)

Thomas, Antony, *Rhodes* (London: BBC Books, 1966)

Van der Poel, Jean, *The Jameson Raid* (London: OUP, 1951)

Weaver, J.R.H., *Dictionary of National Biography*, Fourth Supplement, 1922-1930 (Oxford: Oxford University Press, 1937)

Whyte, Frederic, *Life of W.T. Stead*, Vol. II (London: Johnathan Cape Ltd., 1925)

Williams, Basil, *Cecil Rhodes* (New York: Henry Holt & Co, 1921)

Crwys-Williams Jennifer, *South African Despatches, two centuries of the best in South African Journalism* (Johannesburg: Ashanti Publishing, 1989)

Wills A. & Collingridge L.T. (eds.), *The Downfall of Lobengula: The Cause, History and Effect of the Matabele War* (London: Simpkin, Marshall, Hamilton Kent & Co., 1894)

Journals

Anon., *Transactions of the American Philosophical Society*, Vol. 70, Part 8, 1980

Beckett, Ian, 'Daring a Wrong Like This: The War Office and the Jameson Raid, *Soldiers of the Queen*, Issue 161 September (2015)

Blainey, Geoffrey,' Lost Causes of the Jameson Raid', *The Economic History Review*, Vol. 18, Issue 2, August 1965

Friend, D.G, 'Uniforms of the Staatsartillrie: Influences and Developments', *Military History Journal*, Vol. 9, No. 4 The South African Military History Society, December 1993

Galbraith J.S., 'The British South Africa Company and the Jameson Raid', *The Journal of British Studies*, Vol. 10, No. 1, November, 1970

Gauntlett, J., 'James Rose Innes: the making of a Constitutionalist', *Consultus*, Vol. 1, 1988

Hall, D.D., 'The Artillery of the First Anglo-Boer War 1880 – 1881', *Military History Journal*, Vol. 5, No. 2, The South African Military History Society, December 1980

Hyslop, Johnathan, Political Corruption in South Africa; before and after apartheid, *Journal of Southern African Studies*, Vol. 31. Issue 4, 2005

Keto, C. Tesehloane, 'The Aftermath of the Jameson Raid and the Decision Making in Saks, David, 'The Jameson Raid; A Failed Dress rehearsal for the Anglo-Boer War', *Military History Journal*, The South African Military History Society: Vol. 12 No 5, 2003.

Makhura Tlou John, Another Road to the Raid, *Journal of Southern African Studies*, Vol. 21, Number 2, June 1995

Rotberg, Robert Irwin, Did Cecil Rhodes Really Try to Control the World?, *The Journal of Imperial and Commonwealth History*, Vol. 42; Issue 3, June 2014

Wilburn, Kenneth, 'The Drift Crisis, and the Missing Telegrams and the Jameson Raid: A Centennial Review', *The Journal of Imperial and Commonwealth History*, Vol. 25, No. 2, May 1997

Winkler, Henry R., 'Joseph Chamberlain and The Jameson Raid', *American Historical Review*, Vol. 54, July 1949

Woodhouse, Christophe Montague, 'The Missing Telegrams and the Jameson Raid, Part One', *History Today*, 1 June 1962

—— The Missing Telegrams and the Jameson Raid, Part Two, *History Today*, 1 July 1962

Wurts, John., 'Seen at the Jameson Trial', *Yale Law Journal*, Vol. 6, Issue 1, 1896

Newspapers

Bulawayo Chronicle
Cape Times
Daily Chronicle
L'Indépendance Belge
Melbourne Argos
Morning Advertiser
Punch
Rhodesian Herald
Saturday Review
The Times

Unpublished Theses

Shaw, Gerald, The Letters of Edmund Garrett to his Cousin 1896-1898, Unpublished MA Thesis, University of Cape Town, 1983

Muller, Cornelis Hermanus, Policing the Witswaterand: A History of the South African Police, 1886-1899, Unpublished PhD Thesis, Bloemfontein: University of the Free State, 2016

Pyeatt, Duane Niler, Heligoland and the Making of the Anglo-German Colonial Agreement, Unpublished MA Thesis, Texas Tech University, 1988

Other

Lord Hoffman, Leonard Hubert of Chedworth, 'The Third Keating Lecture', 16th October 2004

Index